THE
COMMUNICATION
GAP

Language can be a bridge—between man and his environment, between man and his fellow man. It can also be a wall, shutting out perceptions, closing off communication.

In recent years, thinkers in every discipline have come to face the problem of language. For there is no more universal need than to have an adequate picture of reality, or be able to transmit one's inner vision to others.

Considering the various approaches that have been made toward the complex questions that language poses, and adding his own notable insights, Professor Max Black has written a study that superbly encompasses the current state of our knowledge in this all-important area. Here is a book about words and language that brilliantly demonstrates in its own lucidity and charm how language should and can be used.

"The uses of language . . . expressed with wit and spirit"—*Saturday Review*

THE BRITANNICA PERSPECTIVES, issued in commemoration of the Encyclopaedia Britannica's 200th anniversary, took five years of planning and research and $1,000,000 to produce. Each book is written by a leading authority in a major field of modern man's endeavor and is a summary of that field's current status and future aims. **THE BRITANNICA PERSPECTIVES** are both essential additions to the Encyclopaedia itself and independent, comprehensive works intended for the scholar and general reader alike.

Other Britannica Perspectives in MENTOR Editions

The Labyrinth
Of Language

Max Black

A MENTOR BOOK

PUBLISHED BY THE NEW AMERICAN LIBRARY,
NEW YORK AND TORONTO

Library of Congress Catalog Card Number: 68-19506

THE LABYRINTH OF LANGUAGE is a *Britannica Perspective*
prepared to commemorate the 200th anniversary of
Encyclopaedia Britannica.

This is an authorized reprint of a hardcover edition
published by Frederick A. Praeger, Publishers.

MENTOR TRADEMARK REG. U.S. PAT. OFF. AND FOREIGN COUNTRIES
REGISTERED TRADEMARK—MARCA REGISTRADA
HECHO EN CHICAGO, U.S.A.

MENTOR BOOKS are published *in the United States* by
The New American Library, Inc.,
1301 Avenue of the Americas, New York, New York 10019,
in Canada by The New American Library of Canada Limited,
295 King Street East, Toronto 2, Ontario

FIRST PRINTING, JULY, 1969

PRINTED IN THE UNITED STATES OF AMERICA

Preface

IF THE READER has the patience to follow the discussions here presented, he may feel that the term "labyrinth" is well chosen. No topic of fundamental importance is harder to simplify, without doing violence to relevant detail. The reader should be warned, once for all, that competent experts, whether linguists or philosophers, may be outraged at the extent to which I have deliberately ignored subtleties that they might consider essential. I have aimed to present a point of view about controversial issues, rather than a transcript of divergent opinions. And even a distorting mirror may be of some help.

My numerous debts to the rich literature on language and related topics will be obvious from the numerous acknowledgments in the text. I apologize to the many talented writers who have taught me so much, if I have in any way misrepresented their thought.

M. B.

CONTENTS

CHAPTER 1

GENERAL INTRODUCTION

I SHALL OFFER here a preliminary view of some of the questions that will receive detailed discussion later. I also include some mention of topics, such as "information theory" and the psychology of learning to speak, which limitations of space and time will prevent me from developing in the main body of the essay.

Man as Talker

What, if anything, most clearly distinguishes men from all other animals? What makes men truly human?

It would be naïve to expect any simple answer, of the form "Man is *really* such-and-such." Darwin and his heirs have destroyed the theological gap between man as a moral agent and the merely "brute" creation. We look for biological continuities everywhere and find little reason to flatter ourselves upon some fancied moral advantage. It is tempting to regard Man as simply the most cruel, if the most intelligent, of the primates.

Still, men are the only animals to be curious about their own nature or to take pleasure in simple answers to impossible questions. If we still want to play the game of asking, "What is Man?", we can choose from a large number of traditional answers: Man is the tool-using animal (*homo faber*), the social animal (*zoon politikon*), the only animal to feel shame ("the animal with red cheeks"), the sole inventor of gods created in his own image, the only mammal that can laugh at jokes, tell lies, or do arithmetic.

Many such answers subvert a difference of degree into a

9

supposed distinction of essence: "lower" animals have been found to use primitive tools; many live in colonies that are highly organized; others show the stirrings of aesthetic response to their environment. But diplomacy, morality, science, religion, and such other "higher" activities are all inconceivable in the absence of speech. It would be astounding to discover insects or fish, birds or monkeys, able to *talk to one another*.

Of course, jungles and prairies—even the oceans, we now think—are noisy with whistling and shrieking, grunting and squeaking, bird calls, and the radar of bats. The embryonic science of "Animal Communication" is a source of much interesting information that we must glance at in due course. But animal "signals," however interesting as a subject of study, are sharply different from *speech*.

Man is the only animal that can talk (*homo loquens*). More generally, he is the only animal that can use *symbols* (words, pictures, graphs, numbers, etc.). He alone can bridge the gap between one person and another, conveying thoughts, feelings, desires, attitudes, and sharing in the traditions, conventions, the knowledge and the superstition of his culture: the only animal that can truly *understand* and *misunderstand*. On this essential skill depends everything that we call civilization. Without it, imagination, thought—even self-knowledge—are impossible.

No Primitive Languages

The indispensable role of speech in human culture may help to explain the surprising fact that all known societies, however "primitive" in other respects, possess fully developed languages. The African Bushman and the Australian aborigine command a vocabulary and a complex grammar that strain the learning capacity of an expert linguist. Indeed, complexity and elaboration of grammatical structure regularly mark the languages of so-called primitive societies. A high degree of sophistication is needed, it seems, in order to simplify grammar. Human beings have sometimes trodden the earth virtually naked, carrying all their material belongings in one hand, but they have never been *dumb,* in either sense of the word. To be deprived of speech is to lack the indispensable prerequisite for a human community.

The Variety and Unity of Language

As remarkable as the ubiquity of speech is the extraordinary variety of distinct languages.[1] Several thousand different languages are still used by large bodies of men.[2] Far greater must be the number of "dead" languages that have disappeared with the societies that used them.

This rich panorama of diverse linguistic instruments must surely serve some constant human needs and purposes. Yet, at first sight, nothing in language looks invariable. Any sound that the human larynx can produce seems somewhere to have been used as a conventionally significant phonetic element (a "phoneme"[3] in modern terminology); names and things directly nameable vary remarkably from one language to another; and the indispensable organizing principles of grammar seem protean in their concrete manifestations. (It is much too late in the day to treat Latin or the Indo-European languages as universal models.)

This babel of tongues generates urgent practical problems. If a common language provides a universe of shared meanings for its speakers, it also separates them poignantly from the others. Not for nothing did the Greek word "barbarian" arise from the supposedly unintelligent, because unintelligible, babble of lesser breeds. The old principle of "Here's somebody who talks differently: let's throw a stone at him" still operates in national and international affairs. But the urgent practical problems of fostering what may be called "inter-literacy," whether by the wasteful way of bilingualism or by the ineffective propagation of artificial languages ("Esperanto," "Volapük," "Basic English," etc.), depend upon the solution of some basic theoretical problems.

Among the most important of these is the disclosure of the *invariants,* or—some prefer to say—the "universals"[4] of language. It is easy to be overimpressed by the extensive variety of known languages. Consider, for the sake of contrast, the

[1] Roughly speaking, two persons are using different languages if neither can understand the other. The lines between "language," "dialect," and "special jargon" are not sharp. There is a certain degree of idealization in thinking of English, say, as a single language.

[2] It has been claimed that the following languages were being used, at mid-century, by more than 50 million speakers: Chinese (450), English (250), Hindustani (160), Russian (140), Spanish (110), German (100), Japanese (80), French (75), Malay, Bengali (60), Italian, Portuguese (55), Arabic (50) (David Crystal, *Linguistics, Language, and Religion,* Burns & Oates, Ltd., London, 1965, p. 111).

[3] This important notion is discussed later in this work. See p. 33.

[4] See, for instance, the papers assembled in Joseph H. Greenberg, ed., *Universals of Language,* The M.I.T. Press, Cambridge, Mass., 1963. The results of the discussions reported in this volume were somewhat inconclusive.

equally broad variability of known art forms. Here, concrete embodiment in a specific medium, under the control of relevant conventions, determines the very identity of the work of art: it would be pointless to try transposing an Indian *raga* into a score for a piano. But every language can, within broad limits, be translated into any other.[5] Behind the motley and variegated surface of linguistic phenomena, in all their bewildering variety, we may reasonably expect to uncover principles of order, corresponding to the shared purposes of all men. We shall be constantly concerned in this work with the search for such principles: however interested in the variable details of the topics to be discussed, we shall always try to press on to general ideas that will provide a satisfactory *model* of language. Our task, to adopt Wittgenstein's expression, is that of reaching a "perspicuous view" of language.

The Marvel of Language

To insist upon the importance of language may seem like battering at an open door. But there are times when it is necessary not to flinch from the obvious. In the society to which we belong, talking and listening, reading and writing, are so constantly present that familiarity blunts perception of the extraordinary character of such activities. Yet it really is remarkable that arbitrary sounds or marks should be able to convey accurate or misleading information, arouse fear, gratitude, or any other passion, set machines in motion, topple governments, or consign men to the firing squad.[6] How extraordinary it is that revolutions or wars can be started by words! The common sense answer is that it is the *meaning* that counts. But the concept of *meaning* has proved so troublesome that many writers on language have tried to ignore it altogether. For us, however, questions about "The Meaning of Meaning" will be of central concern.

No less wonderful than the communication of meaning, however imperfect, is the acquisition of speech. Learning to speak, which we commonly take so much for granted, is probably the most remarkable intellectual feat the ordinary man accomplishes. (If he could do as well later, our society

[5]Poverty of vocabulary is a surmountable difficulty; lack of fit between the two grammars concerned can be more troublesome. When language is used as an artistic medium, translation becomes correspondingly less satisfactory.

[6]Wonder at this marked disproportion between the insignificance of the verbal means and the importance of the effects evoked is one source of magical views concerning language.

would look very different.) Sophisticated research in phonetics and acoustics, the physiology and neurology of speech, only heightens the marvel. The delicacy and subtlety of control involved in as commonplace an utterance as "Pass the salt, please" present analysis and explanation problems that still baffle experts.

The Primacy of Speech

Writers about language, who are prone to disagree about fundamentals, nowadays agree in thinking that *speech* ought to be the primary object of investigation:

> The linguist distinguishes between *language* and *writing*, whereas the layman tends to confuse the two. The layman's terms "spoken language" and "written language" suggest that speech and writing are merely two different manifestations of something fundamentally the same. Often enough, the layman thinks that writing is somehow more basic than speech. Almost the reverse is true.[7]

It might be objected that speech and writing are "fundamentally the same" in being instruments for *communication*. (Therefore, it seems advisable, in this work, to use "language" in a very broad sense, to cover not only writing and speech, but even certain "paralinguistic" phenomena accompanying or, occasionally, replacing speech: gestures, facial expressions, significant features of context.)

The point of Hockett's insistence upon the primacy of speech, which might be paralleled from a score of equally able theorists,[8] is plain enough. All human beings first learn to speak in simple *tête-à-tête* situations, where all the essential features of communication are already manifested, and many speakers never learn to read or write. A great advance in sophistication is needed in order to communicate with an unseen, or even unknown, partner. Replacing the fleeting sound by the permanent mark, *i.e.*, the invention of writing, is a remarkable achievement that many cultures have failed to produce. Yet for all the importance, in our own society, of the written word, it remains, for the most part, a substitute for speech, with logical and stylistic peculiarities best under-

[7]Charles F. Hockett, *A Course in Modern Linguistics*, The Macmillan Company, New York, 1958, p. 4.
[8]One important source of this emphasis is Ferdinand de Saussure's distinction (1916) between *parole* (individual speech) and *langue* (the normative linguistic system).

stood as efforts to overcome obstacles arising from the hearer's absence. (To the extent that writing is necessarily a monologue, which the hearer cannot interrupt by questions, successful communication becomes harder to achieve.)

A case can be made for going further than Hockett or other professional linguists might wish, by making *individual speech acts* (episodes of verbal interchange) the point of departure. Conversation, direct verbal encounter between visible participants, might be said to be the "begin-all" of our inquiry. But it cannot be the end-all. The most casual and informal communication, when it rises above the level of an exchange of grunts, is molded and controlled by conventions, accepted by both partners, but not invented by them: the *words* employed belong to a given language (sometimes a deviant dialect or *argot*) that the speaker has to accept as a *datum*. (Sometimes he can make changes for a special purpose, but usually there is no time for that—and linguistic revision must be piecemeal at best.) The same applies in even greater measure to word order and other grammatical features. In short, a speaker's freedom to express and to convey *his own* meaning is sharply limited by his use of a social instrument, having a relatively stable and autonomous existence. The most casual face-to-face conversation, which is all informality and immediate influence from one perspective, can also be viewed, from the standpoint of an expert linguist, as illustrating abstract structural principles.

Interplay between the individual and the social aspects of language, between the immediate interests of the conversation-partners and the constraints of the language-system will be of recurring interest in this work.

The Legacy of Scholarship

Scholarly interest in language is very ancient. In the West, the level of sophistication shown in Plato's dialogue, the *Cratylus* (with its still readable discussion of the role of convention in language), implies an even older tradition of speculation about the nature and the origins of language. Able Greek grammarians produced elaborate analyses, based, to be sure, exclusively upon the structure of their own language, regarded as embodying universal principles of reason. The climactic grammars of Dionysius Thrax (2nd century B.C.) and of Apollonius Dyscolus (2nd century A.D.) were used as models by a long line of Roman grammarians, who in turn exerted massive influence well beyond the Middle Ages.[9] The dogmatic and oversimplified grammars still taught in Western schools are often unwittingly modeled on Priscian's analysis of over 1,300 years ago—as if men could think only in the categories of classical Latin.

India has given us Pānini's grammar of Sanskrit, composed some 2,000 years ago, which has been described as "one of the greatest monuments of human intelligence."[10] Chinese works on philology have survived from the period of Confucius.

For all their interest, these impressive beginnings are quite overshadowed by the tremendous explosion of linguistic studies in the 19th century. Such scholars as Franz Bopp, Jacob Grimm, and August Schleicher—to mention only a few of the leaders, mainly Germans—successfully uncovered laws of phonetic change[11] and explored in minute detail the systematic correspondences between the various languages of the Indo-European family. These impressive researches culminated in the daring conception, now solidly established, of the common descent of Sanskrit and most European languages from a single hypothetical prehistoric ancestor ("Primitive Indo-European").

In this way, etymology and comparative linguistics emerged as truly scientific disciplines. A reader who consults any dictionary, such as the great Oxford Dictionary, that is founded "on historical principles" owes a debt to these indefatigable Teutonic philologists and their successors.[12]

The methods elaborated by the German school have since been applied, with outstanding success, to such other language groups as those related to Hungarian and Finnish (the "Finno-Ugrian" family), those mainly spoken in the Pacific islands or on the shores of the Pacific Ocean (the "Malayo-Polynesian" family), and so on. The methods for establishing genetic affiliations between languages have proved to be universally applicable: the over-all history of the evolution of

[9]Details may be found in R. H. Robins, *Ancient and Mediaeval Grammatical Theory in Europe*, G. Bell & Sons, Ltd., London, 1951.

[10]Leonard Bloomfield, *Language*, Holt, Rinehart & Winston, Inc., New York, 1933, p. 11. The chapter containing this remark is a useful summary of the history of linguistic scholarship.

[11]"Grimm's Law," for example, which a hundred people have learned about for one who could state it.

[12]A good impression of the extraordinary degree of expertise that is required for such work may be had from the fine book by A. S. C. Ross, *Etymology*, André Deutsch, Ltd., London, 1958. An hour spent with this book is enough to kill any desire to indulge in "popular etymology."

languages is a task that can, in principle, be solved: it will keep scholars busy indefinitely in the foreseeable future.[13]

Such mainly historical studies ("Diachronic Linguistics," in modern terminology)[14] clearly depend for their accuracy and reliability upon the skill with which a language is described at a given stage in its development (a "still picture" of a changing process taken at a particular instant). This may, indeed, be applied to all historical investigation: there is little point in searching for the origins or antecedents of anything that is ill-defined or imperfectly delineated. Gradual extension of comparative historical linguistics to "exotic" North American or African languages, where descriptive categories derived from European languages could not be stretched to fit, rendered the task of systematic description of linguistic structure at a given time ("Synchronic Linguistics") increasingly urgent.

The great achievement of linguistic research in the first half of the 20th century was the solution of this task.[15] Our present mastery of the structure of language has reached a point at which systematic procedures of analysis are available for the adequate description of any language, however unfamiliar or remote from Indo-European patterns. This exciting efflorescence of general linguistics promises also, in developments still controversial, to transform for the better our common notions about grammar.

Even the most rapid survey of scholarly and scientific research in the general area of language would need, at this point, to mention a variety of studies in phonetics and the perception of speech, in the psychology of learning to talk, and much else. It would also be reprehensible to exclude the wealth of more philosophical inquiries, characteristic of the first half of the 20th century, into the logic, rhetoric, and poetics of discourse, the relations between thought and language, the use and abuse of symbols, etc. Unlike the work in linguistics already noticed, these studies have been controlled by no generally accepted methodology. Since a mere catalogue would be of little value, it seems preferable to begin by

---

[13]Of course, only gross and global changes can be reconstructed (with many gaps, even so): minute variations and innovations in individual habits that must be ultimately responsible escape detection.

[14]The contrast between "diachronic" (literally: two times) and "synchronic" (one time), *i.e.*, roughly between the dynamics and statics of language, goes back to De Saussure. These convenient labels are now well established.

[15]Some of the dominant concepts and methods employed will receive detailed attention in the course of this study.

considering, somewhat more systematically, the possible variety of approaches to the topics that interest us here.

An Embarrassment of Strategies

Until comparatively recently, the prevailing conception of the nature of language was straightforward and simple. It stressed communication of *thought* to the neglect of feeling and attitude, emphasized words rather than speech-acts in context, and assumed a sharp contrast between thought and its symbolic expression. In this view, language, as a mere intermediary between thoughts, might appear relatively unimportant. If specialists have an academic interest in the idiosyncrasies of particular languages, this can hardly concern the layman. "Thought," the "ideas" that lurk somehow behind or within "words," deserves our best attention; but to worry overmuch about words is like being obsessed with money and ignoring wealth.

This conception of language, still powerful after more than 2,000 years, obviously has some truth to it. But it has come to seem progressively more inadequate and in need of replacement by a radically improved perspective. If the root idea of the older view is that thought and language are, in principle at least, wholly independent, the correspondingly basic insight of the newer position is that there can be no fully articulated thought without symbolic embodiment.

Language no longer appears as a tiresome, if necessary, medium of exchange between ideas, but rather as the very stuff of which "ideas" are made. To separate thought from its symbolic manifestation would be as futile as to try separating a mind from its embodiment in a human organism.

"Thought" now appears as only one of the many things transmitted by language: emphasis upon "non-cognitive" aspects of language is characteristic of much modern work. For this, and for other good reasons, there is a strong tendency to restore words to their proper and natural setting in human activity: "Words are part of action and they are equivalents to actions."[16]

This radical shift of perspective tends to make the study of language nearly coextensive with the study of all human behaviour. Thus comprehensively and liberally conceived, the study of language has intimate relations with psychology, sociology, and anthropology—not to mention logic, literary

[16]Bronislaw Malinowski, *Coral Gardens and Their Magic*, George Allen & Unwin Ltd., London, 1935, vol. 2, p. 9.

criticism, and aesthetics. And all these disciplines stand to profit immensely from linguistic advances.

An obvious danger is that no well-defined object of investigation will remain; but the cure for that is, equally obviously, deliberate, if provisional, limitation of interest. Language is like the elephant in the old fable, that felt so different as the blind men happened to touch its tail, its foot, or its trunk. But the deliberate myopia called "specialization" is one secret of scientific method. Given the extraordinary richness and complexity of what we call language, we may deliberately choose to concentrate upon the "synchronic" rather than the "diachronic" aspects; to emphasize the concrete and specific "speech-act" or to highlight the "systematic" aspects of the language institution; to view speech as a specially important type of bodily action—or to search for the abstract resemblances between language and other methods for transmitting "information"; we may be concerned chiefly to report or our hearts may be set upon reform; and so on. (But the elephant is a single beast, for all that.)

In what follows, I shall briefly note, by way of preliminary orientation, some of the modes of approach that have been intensively pursued. (Some, but not all of these, will have important contributions to make to the broadly philosophical purpose of this work.)

SPEECH AS THE PRODUCTION OF SOUND

Thought, communication, culture, society are woven together by language. But the web is, in a way, both fragile and precarious. For its existence depends, in the last resort, on the trained capacity of human beings to produce distinctive sounds immediately recognizable by themselves and others. This complex skill—or rather, this constellation of skills—must be learned afresh by every child. (Other animals, such as chimpanzees, have a suitable vocal apparatus, but are hopelessly unable to perform this fundamental task.)

Spoken sounds are produced in the *vocal tract,* the semi-flexible chamber composed of the upper part of the windpipe and the interior of the mouth. The whole can be regarded as a uniquely versatile wind instrument, with lungs and diaphragm for bellows, the vocal cords inside the Adam's apple (the *larynx*) as the "reeds," and the tongue and lips together[17] making the "stops" and other changes inside the resonance chamber of the mouth. But playing the vocal tract is incom-

---

[17] Also the *velum,* the small flap that can close the nasal entrance. Changes in shape of the upper windpipe are also involved.

parably harder than playing any artificial wind instrument, if only because the performer cannot observe and is seldom consciously aware of what he is doing.[18]

The task of *articulatory phonetics* is in part that of supplying an adequate description of the vocal repertoire—providing a verbal score, one might say, for the vocal tract's performances. Its distinctive vocabulary of *labials* and *dentals, fricatives, liquids,* and the like, typically identifies vocal features in terms of the muscular adjustments ("articulations") needed to produce them.[19] The point of this type of investigation is partly the theoretical one of recording and understanding what occurs in the vocal tract; there are, however, important practical applications, *e.g.,* to the correction of speech disorders. An important outcome of the progress of phonetics has been the creation of a generalized script (the "International Phonetic Alphabet") applicable to any language.[20]

THE PERCEPTION OF SPEECH

Considered as a physical event, each spoken sound exhibits an intricate structure. A pure tone, as produced by a tuning fork, is a periodic train of pulses of compression and rarefaction, proceeding from the source with a characteristic frequency (rate of repetition). Vastly many pure wave motions of this sort combine to produce the complex aerial disturbance heard as the sound, *kink,* say (as if a battery of different tuning forks were vibrating together). Physicists can now analyze the mixed sound into its components and can therefore reproduce it to any desired degree of accuracy.

In responding to recognized *speech,* however, the ear notices only certain relatively abstract features of the sound. On occasion, we perceive readily enough the different ways in which a given word sounds on the lips of different speakers: we *can* easily notice, also, the variations between fast and deliberate enunciation, and so on. Yet, throughout, we normally "hear the same word" and unless we could, communication would be impossible. To hear, one might say, is necessarily to abstract.

[18]The complexity of the operations needed is staggering. Even a crude description of the sequence of movements needed to produce as simple a sound as *kick* occupies an entire page of an elementary textbook. See Morton W. Bloomfield and Leonard Newmark, *A Linguistic Introduction to the History of English,* Alfred A. Knopf, Inc., New York, 1963, pp. 54–55.

[19]"Labial" and "dental" are intended to suggest the lips (partly closed) and the teeth, etc.

[20]See "Phonetics" in *Encyclopædia Britannica* (1968).

By what physical cues do we recognize distinctive *speech* sounds? Good answers would help us to facilitate communication by making the distinctive features stand out more prominently against the contaminating background of "noise." (One practical application is to the adoption and improvement of a standard international language for aircraft pilots.)[21]

The requisite physical analysis of speech sounds can now be performed in a variety of alternative ways: Magnetic tape recordings can be cut, modified, and recombined to produce artificially varied sound, to be tested upon normal hearers; or the sound waves can be made visible by means of oscilloscopes (television screens on which lines of light oscillate); best of all is the *spectrogram,* in which a physical analysis of the wave motion yields a permanent photographic record (streaks, bands, and dots against a neutral background). Simplified, schematized versions of such spectrograms can be played back (by means of a "pattern feed-back") to test hearers' responses. These instruments have already supplied fascinating and surprising information.

Spectrogram analysis might reasonably be expected to reveal something approximating a point-to-point correspondence between recognized sound and correlated physical feature. The true picture, as it is now beginning to emerge, is more complex. Some speech sounds do have identifiable correlates, but of so abstract a structure as to defy simple description.[22] With other speech sounds, the situation is still more complicated, since the relevant physical cues vary greatly according to the immediate context.

How does the ear cope with this surprising variability? How *do* we recognize the "same" speech sound [k] in this changing physical flux? The specialist's best guess, at present, is that we rely, somehow, upon knowing where and how the sound would be produced in our own speech tract. Imagine the process of recognition slowed down: we can imagine the hearer "reading" a sound by asking, first, "Where and how would I produce a sound like this?" and then, *"What* sound would I then be producing?" That the layman would in fact

[21]Another potentially important application would be the creation of a reading machine for the blind. Such a machine might convert a printed text into a stripped-down but still intelligible sequence of sounds.

[22]The presence of the speech sound [k] in a number of spectrograms is shown, roughly speaking, by the common point of origin of certain bands in the diagrams. An analogy might help: a set of persons in an airport might have little in common except their arrival from a common point of departure.

be unable to answer either question merely enhances the mystery.

LEARNING HOW TO TALK

Nobody knows how language came into existence, although many have tried to guess.[23] In the total absence of any but full-blown languages, it is natural to turn to the way in which children learn to talk. If "ontogeny recapitulates phylogeny" (the individual's history retraces the history of the race), some light ought thereby to be shed on the logic and philosophy of language.

It is surprisingly hard to establish the facts: the speech sounds of young children are not easily recorded in phonetic transcription and the grammar they use needs as careful analysis as an exotic language. Most troublesome is the fact that children necessarily learn to talk in a predominantly adult environment: they tend to be partially bilingual, understanding how their elders speak but using their own pidgin. (To talk to a child as *he* talks only provokes laughter.) The variability of the adult linguistic *milieu* makes comparison between different studies precarious: the children observed are, all too often, the offspring of exceptionally articulate observers.

Psychologists are, however, in reasonably close agreement about the broad superficial facts. The scenario, we are told, is roughly the same for all children and may therefore be determined more by common processes of development (such as gradual control of the articulatory muscles) than by environment. (Teachers of young children willingly agree that in the matter of learning to speak, ripeness is nearly all: Young children of the right age pick up a foreign language almost as easily as they catch measles, while their parents plod laboriously behind.)

A baby, already able to cry at birth, is found, some nine months later, to be gurgling, grunting, snorting, and making other indescribable noises. (It seems to be no more than an old wives' tale that mothers or nurses can "understand" such sounds; the context, rather than the phonetic quality of the cry, seems to provide the clue.) Later comes the "babbling" period in which sounds of the most varied kinds (*e.g.,* gutturals, glottal stops, and vowels with umlauts) can be learned.

[23]Some of these theories have been identified by such fanciful names as "the bow-wow theory" and "the ding-dong theory." They cannot be treated as serious historical speculation; their function is at best that of models that try to render intelligible how language *might* have arisen.

A child responds to simple one-word sentences from adults in attendance before he can himself imitate them; by about twelve months of age he has uttered his first word, although it may take another year for him to produce two-word sentences and so to become a primitive grammarian. These early sentences tend to be "telegraphic" simplifications of adult sentences; much the same is true of the infant repertory of sounds. By the end of four years, in normal cases, the fundamentals of speech have been acquired.

How this happens (and very much more that has been omitted from my hasty sketch) is largely, perhaps almost entirely, unknown. Excitingly far-flung generalizations, such as Jean Piaget's insistence upon the early predominance of "egocentric" over "socialized" speech, have not survived careful empirical test.

SPEECH AS THE TRANSMISSION OF MESSAGES

I shift sharply now to the standpoint of a communications engineer, in order to think of speech with the help of ideas developed in the new discipline of "information theory" (or the "mathematical theory of communication").[24]

Abstractly considered, a *message* consists of a string of symbols selected from a fixed alphabet. Thus, allowing for punctuation signs, a telegram in English may be considered as a sequence of marks selected from a stock of some thirty-two items (with repetitions allowed). Each element of the message has to be converted into a distinctive physical signal (*e.g.*, the energy pulses answering to the dot-dash symbols of the Morse code), according to some predetermined convention and techniques. If this *encoded* message is accurately *decoded* by the intended receiver, the purpose of the communication system has been achieved.

A communications engineer seeks to achieve efficiency as well as accuracy: he would like to transmit a faithful replica of the original message with the least possible expenditure of energy—*i.e.*, as quickly and cheaply as possible. His chief enemy is *noise*, here used in the technical sense of unintended and unpredictable extra signals. "Noise" adulterates the intended communication, increases the chance of error when decoding, and reduces efficiency by wasting the expensive communication channel upon unwanted and disruptive inter-

---

[24]See Claude E. Shannon and W. Weaver, *The Mathematical Theory of Communication*, University of Illinois Press, Urbana, 1949. For a summary, see Shannon's article "Information Theory" in *Encyclopædia Britannica* (1968).

ference. (If dirt is matter in the wrong place, "noise" is energy in the wrong place. Noise in communication is like dirt, or like friction, in being ineradicable. It can be reduced, or counteracted, but never altogether eliminated.)

What is achieved by receiving a correct message? One answer might be: reduction of uncertainty. Consider the simplest case, where the receiver is expecting an answer to a certain yes-or-no question that he has already asked. Before receiving the message, he is uncertain whether the answer is Yes or No; afterwards, this uncertainty has been removed. How this is done is essentially irrelevant: it suffices for the sender to make a choice between two symbols ("Yes" or "No," "+" or "—," "A" or "B," etc.) in accordance with some previous understanding. The expert says that the "amount of information" here conveyed is one *bit* (an abbreviation for "binary digit").

Now let us vary the example. If the receiver knew that the answer to his question must be one of four replies, *A, B, C,* or *D* (*e.g.,* "Monday," "Tuesday," "Wednesday," or "Thursday"), all equally probable, his initial uncertainty would have been higher than in the first example. Here, *two* symbols would suffice for expunging the uncertainty: one to tell whether the answer was in the range *(A, B)* or in the range *(C, D)*, another to select the correct and final answer within the identified range. The sender needs to make two choices, according to an agreed-upon convention. He is said to transmit *two* "bits" of "information."

In general, the number of bits conveyed by sending one of *n* equally likely alternatives[25] is $\log_2 n$. Hence, in a telegraphic system using an alphabet, like English, of 32 elements ("letters"), each symbol carries six bits of information (because $2^6 = 32$).

One way to counteract the uncertainty introduced by "noise" is to increase the *redundancy* of the message. A message is said to be "redundant" when it includes more symbols than are needed to carry its information: if the message sent, in our first example, were "Yes yes" it would be more redundant than a plain "yes"; still more redundant would be "Yes, repeat yes and not no!" Redundancy reduces the efficiency of

[25]When the alternatives are not equally likely, the definition of amount of information must be more complex. In awaiting a yes-or-no answer, if I know that the odds are 11 to 1 that the answer will be affirmative, I am almost certain at the outset—my initial uncertainty is close to zero. (A bore who can be counted upon always to say the same thing supplies no "information.") The relevant measure of transmitted information is here a more complex formula, involving two logarithms.

the message, but is a prophylactic against misinterpretation. (The reader may think of devices like "A for apple, B for baker, etc." used to prevent telephonic misunderstanding.) It is hardly surprising that natural languages are found to have a high degree of "redundancy"—of the order of 50 percent.[26]

This elegant theory, of which the above is a mere preliminary sketch, is all too easily misinterpreted in its application to language. Speech is, among other things, a "communication channel," in the sense of the theory of communications; but it is much more. For one thing, "information," in the technical sense explained above, is not information in any ordinary sense. "Information" has nothing to do with any meaning of the message, being defined entirely in terms of the probabilities of occurrence of the component symbols. (In ordinary language, nonsense words would carry high "information," just because they were initially unlikely to occur!) Some attempts have been made to construct a concept of *semantical* information, but these are still in a primitive state.

The reader should also be warned that the basic notions of information theory are essentially statistical: they provide some interesting insight into global features of language, but are inapplicable to particular utterances.

SPEECH AS INTERACTION

All the approaches so far reported are highly abstract. This is no criticism, since scientific method demands generalization, selection, abstraction. But in trying to be scientific, we risk losing sight of our intended topic. Speech requires skilful articulation of sounds and skilful recognition of their status as elements of speech. It can properly be viewed, through the conceptual model of the communications engineer, as transmitted "information" contaminated by "noise." It is all these things and much more. But above all, it is something social. Even monologue is only a variation and an adaptation of dialogue.

Our primary interest, therefore, is in the full-blooded speech act, as a distinctive type of interaction between partners, united by a shared community of understanding. The two aspects—the directly observable utterances and the invisible network of conventions and understandings that make the utterances meaningful—are of equal importance. Faithful analysis of any determinate speech transaction will lead us

[26]Roughly speaking, we could remove half of any written or printed communication and still be understood. The surplus symbolization is a safeguard against carelessness, inattention, and confusion.

back to the unspoken understandings of the speech partners and still further back to the governing usages of their speech community.

The essential elements are plain to be seen in pre-verbal communication. A reaching gesture is *directed toward* a specific receiver, whose attention is solicited by characteristic gestures and facial expressions. If he "understands," it is because he, too, has similar needs and can project himself into the situation of the "reacher." This capacity to "take the role of other" and to respond appropriately remains essential to verbal communication. The receiver's non-verbal understanding of the sender's "situation" and the sender's anticipation of such understanding by his envisaged receiver control the style and the content of all verbal communication.

Stretching for something out of reach in order to enlist another's help is only one of a large variety of non-verbal gestures that are patently significant. We learn, almost without being taught, how to use specific gestures to praise and discourage, to incite or to inhibit. But what smiles, grimaces, and nods can do, words can do infinitely better. One interest of the study of speech interaction is the elaboration of a good classification of the different functions of speech.

Nobody seems to have undertaken a systematic study of speech interactions. Our materials are scattered in works of psychology, anthropology, sociology, literary criticism.

Among the questions that ought to be raised in an ampler context are the following. How are the main types of linguistic interaction usefully classified and on what principles? How is the specific character of the linguistic situation signalled and perceived? By what means, conventional or informal, is the requisite common background of shared understandings established? How is the speaker's "role" recognized? How (and to what degree) does his utterance acquire "authority"? Such questions need to be raised, even if they cannot always be answered.

SPEECH AS EXPRESSION OF MEANING

The interaction approach emphasizes overt action. It is most sure of itself when an utterance like "Please shut the window" elicits something that can be *seen* to have been done. But the request must be understood in order to be followed; and it can be understood, though disregarded. To try to discuss linguistic interaction without reference to understanding and understood meaning would be like discussing food while ignoring hunger.

Meaning is a dirty word for many theorists. Some of them are old-fashioned positivists, with a naïve prejudice against whatever cannot be measured; others think the word too slippery for serious use. Until recently, many professional linguists have prided themselves on being able to ignore "semantical" questions; logicians have found the complexities of meaning refractory to the constraints of formal systems.

Yet meaning cries out for notice. Even if a simple request or command fails to elicit a visible action, its function may be explained, with some show of plausibility, as that of producing a *disposition to respond*. This tactic cannot cope with the innumerable cases, as in the reading of a narrative, where the only response demanded of the hearer is understanding. In this work, we shall be constantly concerned with the meanings of "meaning."

Our interest is not altogether the theoretical one of exploring the conceptual geography of "meaning." Problems of clarifying meaning are constantly with us, too pressing to be evaded. If we find it hard to understand well, the fault is not altogether that of the writer or speaker. Even at its most lucid, discourse is inescapably *linear,* doling out scraps of meaning in a fragile thread. But significant thought is seldom linear: cross references and overlapping relationships must be left for the good reader to tease out by himself. Much, also, *must* be "read between the lines."

The disparity between linear verbal form and non-linear conceptual structure is as true of mathematics as it is of literature. Both—indeed all forms of discourse—need the services of an *art of explication.*

Lawyers, biblical commentators, translators, literary critics, analytical philosophers have created a variety of informal traditions of explication. In the long run we shall need a well-conceived general theory about the varieties of meaning to correlate and systematize these various sub-traditions. Such a theory will need its own technical "dialect" for expressing its own distinctive concepts.

LANGUAGE AS SYSTEM AND INSTITUTION

When the partners in a speech transaction use a well-developed language, their immediate purposes and actions are controlled by shared knowledge of the rules and conventions defining that language. (They are like players at chess, or any other social game, whose immediate interest in "winning" receives its specific form in terms of the established social practice in which they are engaged. The rules of the game define what it is to "win" and confer a conventional significance on the "moves" that the players can make. Similarly the rules of the language institution define what the speaker's words *mean* and how, by convention, they are to be understood, regardless of what their users would like them to mean.)

Investigation reveals a high degree of systematic organization in the linguistic institutions that we call "English" or "Hindi" or the like. Each language divides the continuum of producible sounds into a finite number of contrasting elements.[27] They form a distinctive *phonetic system,* whose structure can be laid bare, with almost no reference to meaning. Superimposed upon this are to be found a *morphemic system,* constituting the available vocabulary of the language; a *grammatical system,* regulating the modification and arrangement of the vocabulary; and a *semantical system,* determining the conventional meanings attached to words and their combinations. (There is also need to recognize a *pragmatic system,* that specifies the implicit assumptions and claims entitled to recognition in standard linguistic situations.)

These interlocking systems exhibit a high degree of order, relatedness, and patterning. They change slowly and remain relatively independent of individual action. All of them are marked by an atomic structure, comparable in some ways to the atomic structure of the physical world.

For such reasons as these, linguistic systems lend themselves admirably to cumulative and organized research. Attention to the systematic features of language has led modern linguistics to its greatest successes. We shall be discussing them in detail in the pages that follow.

Retrospect: The Aims of This Work

The foregoing introductory survey, for all its length, has probably done less than justice to the extraordinary volume of work on speech and language that has been produced in the 20th century. There would be little point in attempting to impose an arbitrary order upon this plethora of materials. The purpose of this work will be at once more modest and more ambitious: to extract, from what is already known and what can plausibly be guessed about language, some productive *concepts* and controversial *issues.* In short, to develop a tentative linguistic perspective, a way of looking at men, their activities, and their relations to each other and to the universe as they perceive it, *sub specie linguae.*

[27]These are the "phonemes," for which see pp. 33–38 below.

CHAPTER 2

LANGUAGE AS A PATTERNED SYSTEM

IN THIS CHAPTER, I deal largely with the outcomes of modern linguistic analysis, which may be regarded as the least controversial findings of the many specialists who have intensively studied speech and language. Some of the more debatable questions arising are left to the third chapter. The order of progression is, roughly, from the units of sounds ("phonemes") to verbal units of meaning ("morphemes") and their modes of association ("grammar").

The Atoms of Language

THE "ACTUAL SOUNDS"

Consider the following, deceptively simple, speech episode: Somebody who has taken his friend for a country walk suddenly says, "Look over there!"; his companion turns, sees a vivid red bird, and exclaims, "I wonder what that is." (End of scenario.)

The exclamation point inserted in my transcription is a feeble way of conveying the tone of voice (linguists would say the "intonation contour") that is supposed to have been used. I need it in order to draw attention, for a while, to the "actual sounds" produced.

By the "actual sound" I mean all that might be reproduced on a perfectly faithful tape recorder, that is to say, the physical event represented as "Look over there!" in its full concrete and specific particularity. A full description of this

28

"actual sound" would include, among other things, its duration, the precise pitch of each tone included, and so on. An acoustic expert might describe and analyze such an event, without any reference to its meaning or to its role in the English language. He would treat it as a "natural event," like the whistling of the wind.

If it is hard to identify the "actual sound," in our intended sense, the reason is that we normally use an expression with quotation marks, such as, "Look over there!" to refer to the *remark* made by a speaker, and not to the specific acoustic event he produced. But the "remark" is an abstraction: two speakers can easily make the *same* remark while it is almost impossible for two speakers to produce indistinguishable "actual sounds." Two distinct "actual sounds" can easily be cases of the same "remark."

It is rather awkward to speak about "actual sounds" or "acoustical events." I shall therefore borrow a fragment of philosophical terminology, and will now call the acoustical event supposedly produced by a speaker a *speech-token*.[1] Each time a person speaks, he produces a speech-token, a physical event consisting of various complex wave motions in the surrounding air. The intended meaning of "speech-token" implies that two speech-tokens can be alike in all respects, without being identical: if they start at different times, or are produced by different speakers, that suffices to make them different events, different "speech-tokens."

The speech-token uttered by our imagined speaker—"Look over there!"—is obviously complex and is recognized by his hearer as such. One way of describing this complexity is close at hand. Our imagined partners in the speech episode, and anybody else who understands English, would unhesitatingly describe the speech-token (let us call it T) as a *grammatical English sentence*. Echoing Macaulay, we might go on to say that "every schoolboy knows" that T is composed of precisely three English words and each of these in turn is composed of a small number of identifiable "sounds." Thus the man in the street knows, or thinks he knows, that the spoken word "Look" is composed of *three* sounds: "1," "oo," and

---

[1] We treat *the* as a single word in the English language; yet in adding up the number of words on a printed page, we usually count each occurrence of *the* separately. Following the practice of Charles Sanders Peirce, who introduced the distinction, philosophers generally distinguish between *token-words* and the corresponding *type-word*. Thus, there is one type-word, *the*, in the language, but perhaps twenty tokens of that type on a single printed page.

"k." And similarly for the other two words. Although somewhat crude, this commonplace analysis is approximately correct. But the underlying assumption, that the analysis into words and sounds reflects some simple physical analysis of the speech-token, is wildly off the mark. Plausible though it may be, it is quite wrong to suppose that what has been supplied is a physical analysis of the speech-token.

THE ATOMIC NATURE OF SPEECH

Let us pursue this mistaken assumption. Anybody unfamiliar with linguistics is liable to suppose that the speech-token consists of a string of consecutive and separate "sounds," each invested with some immediately recognizable quality. This might be called the "string of beads" theory.

Such a conception would indeed fit the case of a tune played on the piano with one finger: here each tone does end before the next begins and the whole "sound" really does break down into a series of consecutive elementary sounds, each easily and precisely describable (middle C, followed by the E above it, etc.). The case of a speech-token is strikingly different: contrary to popular belief, an utterance is not much like a sequence of different coloured beads. Sounds that are, from the standpoint of a physicist, markedly different are at once recognized by an ordinary hearer as instances of the "same" sound "1"; and the presence of other sounds in an utterance modifies the component sounds by changes in stress, voice, pitch, and duration. We project this sophisticated patterning of the heard sound into a supposed physical structure.

In short, recognition of speech-tokens as composed of elementary "sounds" implies a considerable exercise of sophisticated organization and abstraction. It is, really, quite a remarkable accomplishment to be able to "recognize" the sound transcribed "Look" as being "the same" (as we say), whether pronounced in haste or deliberately, in a loud tone of voice or with suppressed excitement, spoken as a child would or as an old lady might. It is equally remarkable that throughout this extensive range of physical variation the sound we transcribe as "look" is always readily distinguished by speakers of English from the sound we write as "rook."

In listening to what we recognize as speech, we systematically classify diverse "speech-tokens" as being the "same" or "different" *for the language in question.*

The qualification, *"for the given language,"* is essential. A speaker of English thinks the difference between "look" and "rook" obvious; but a native speaker of Japanese finds that difference very hard to notice—still harder to treat as relevant. To him it seems of no more importance than, say, an occasional lisp. In English, the difference between "l" and "r" counts, makes a difference to what is said: in Japanese, not. And so in general: the underlying phonological system (as we may call it) varies from one language to another.

THE LANGUAGE AS A PHONOLOGICAL SYSTEM

All perception involves, to some extent, the recognition of sameness and difference and, more strikingly, of sameness *in* difference. We recognize John Doe even in fancy dress; we interpret his shrug as expressing indifference, even though he may never shrug in exactly the same way twice. (We impose a conceptual grid, a "frame of reference," upon experience.)

So far then, the perception of a speech-token as composed of "sounds belonging to the English language" may seem—complexity apart—no more remarkable than, say, the recognition of some other "actual sound" as a tune played on a violin. But musical sounds, gestures, colours—to take three contrasting examples—are perceived as shading into one another imperceptibly. Each belongs to a perceived continuum. The situation is strikingly different in the phonological system associated with a given language. Here the contrasts are perfectly sharp: when somebody is talking correct English he *must* produce "l" or "r" (or some other "sound"): there is no room left for a sound halfway between the two. A small child, or an adult speaker with a cold or a permanent speech impediment, may sound as if he were producing an intermediate sound but the rules of the language require him to *count* as producing either the "l" or the "r."

Furthermore, the total number of such sharp "contrasts" is finite: the English language, from a phonological point of view, is like a game played with a fixed number of unchangeable pieces. (This ceases to be true if we consider the language "diachronically," *i.e.*, over some substantial time span. Then the "pieces" themselves are found to be changing.) This is true of every known language, among the several thousands that have been studied by linguists, though the "pieces" change from one language to another. Considered as a phonological system, every language has atomic structure.

The practical importance of this universal feature in the design of a language may be brought home by contrasting the following two tasks that might confront an archaeologist. (*a*) He finds and wishes to understand a drawing apparently representing some action; (*b*) he finds a fragment of text in some ancient language. The difficulties to be overcome in the two cases are strikingly different.

In case (*a*) the drawing might vary continuously: there is no sure way of deciding whether the agent's expression is intended to be one of pride, anger, or something else; we might say that there is no such thing as a uniquely correct answer to the problem of interpretation. In case (*b*), however, given what we know about the universally "atomic" character of a language, the archaeologist can confidently count upon the text representing a finite sequence of conventional phonological elements. Here there is one and only one correct analysis and if the scholar can "crack" the phonological code, he may hope to know precisely what that analysis is. (The reader should note that he may then still be in the dark as to how the message would have "actually sounded." We know the phonological system of ancient Latin, but we don't know precisely what sounds the Romans produced.) The determinateness of the archaeologist's second task is obviously a consequence of the existence of a finite number of conventions of contrast in the language under study.

Now much the same can be said of the ordinary hearer's task of interpretation in familiar situations. Had the first speaker in our imagined illustration uttered a cry (a "natural expression" of his surprise), his hearer's task of interpretation would have been substantially different from that of understanding "Look over there!" Cries vary in infinite gradations; but an English sentence can begin in only a finite number of sharply opposed ways. In the one case, there is a flux of experience to be interpreted opportunistically, without the benefit of rules; in the other case, a fixed code to be applied.

A similar point may be made by contrasting the difficulties that children have in learning to "read" facial expressions with the difficulties they have in learning to recognize conventional sounds (phonological elements). The acceptance, among members of a given speech-community, of a precise phonological system obviously facilitates learning. It is easier to learn the conventional rules of a game, or any other social practice, than to master the act of interpreting endlessly variable experience. The imposed conventional grid immensely simplifies the tasks of learning and interpretation.

THE NOTION OF A "PHONEME"

Modern linguists are now agreed in recognizing what I have called the "atomic nature" of the abstract phonological elements of a given language. This basic idea becomes crystallized in the technical notion of a phoneme, which may be provisionally defined as a "unit of sound which makes a difference in the meaning of words,"[2] or, more briefly, as a "minimum significant unit of sound." (The Greek syllable *-eme* is freely used by modern linguists in the sense of "unit." Thus a *phon-eme* is a sound-unit, a *morph-eme* is a unit of form, and so on.)

If the reader finds the notion of a phoneme unclear, he may be helped by the following section. It will be useful, for the present, to consider how the linguist employs the notion and, especially, how he identifies the stock of phonemes of a given language.

A search for the phonemes of, say, the English language is essentially an attempt to lay bare the smallest differences in sounds that make a difference to the standard meanings of utterances. We begin for simplicity with words of one syllable, trying to establish certain obvious differences of meaning produced by sound-changes in similar positions. For example, any competent English speaker will recognize that the words of the following set are all different:

> *pill, bill, kill, chill.*

(I choose for simplicity only a few of the possible variations upon the monosyllabic *-ill* pattern.) The linguist, therefore, provisionally tags the sounds *p-, b-, k-,* and *ch-* as "minimal distinctive units." Again, similar contrasts between consonants can be found at the ends of monosyllables, as for instance in the set of words

> *pip, pick, pitch, pin.*

This fact, in its turn, leads to provisional contrasts between *-p, -k, -ch, -n.* In the first of these, it is easy to notice the difference between the phoneme and the "actual sound." For once attention has been drawn to the "actual sounds" produced, a difference can be heard between the initial *p-*sound and the terminal *-p* sound of *pip* (and similarly be-

[2]R. A. Hall, *Linguistics and Your Language,* Doubleday & Company, Inc., Garden City, N.Y., 1960, p. 37.

tween the -*p*- of *spin* and the *p*- of *pin*[3]). However, given
the perceptible phonetic similarity between *p*- of, say, *pit*,
and the -*p* of, say, *lip*, it is convenient to lump both together as alternative instances or manifestations of the same
phoneme, represented as /*p*/.[4] (The different sounds, such as
the voiced and unvoiced *p*, that are thus grouped together
in a single phoneme are technically called allophones [literally,
"other sounds"] of that phoneme.)

Proceeding in this way, we end up with a list of some
twenty-four English consonants (phonemes). In other languages, however, different lists would result. It is a cardinal
principle of modern linguistics never to identify the phonemes
belonging to different languages. The main purpose of the
notion of a phoneme is to classify and group together sounds
having similar functions within one and the same language;
there would be no point in thus grouping and contrasting
the consonants belonging to two different languages such as
English and French.

The consonantal phonemes of English do not stand in any
simple relation to the letters used in spelling: some, like /*b*/,
are normally represented by a single letter; others, like /*k*/,
sometimes by one, sometimes by another (*c, k*); others like
/*č*/ and /*š*/ by pairs of letters (*ch, sh*), and so on.

By using substantially the same procedure of searching for
"minimal contrasts," the linguist proceeds to isolate the set of
English vowel phonemes. For example, the words

bee, bay, by, boy, boo

differ from one another in sounds which may provisionally be
treated as belonging to distinct phonemes. These provisional
classifications, confirmed and corrected by more extensive
examination of larger samples of English words, lead eventually to the identification of some thirteen or fourteen vowels.

Finally, the inventory of consonants and vowels thus constructed needs to be completed by adding a small number of
phonemes of a different sort: phonemes of stress,[5] of *pitch*,
of *terminal contour*, and of *juncture* (or transition).

[3]If the hand is held in front of the mouth while speaking, a puff of air
will be felt in the one case, but not in the other.
[4]Most linguists follow the convention of indicating a phoneme by using
the two diagonal lines shown here.
[5]There is, for instance, a significant difference in stress between *pérmit*
(the noun) and *permít* (the verb). As for pitch, an adequate description
of "English speech melody" (Hockett) has led linguists to recognize four

I have now outlined—in what is, I hope, sufficient detail—the way in which the modern linguist proceeds to discover the finite stock of distinct phonemes that comprise the *phonemic* or *phonological* system of a given language. (The study of the phonemic structure of a language is called *phonemics* or *phonology*. It must be carefully distinguished from *phonetics*, which studies the "actual sounds" themselves.)

THE SYSTEM OF PHONEMES

There is good reason to think of the phonemes of a given language as constituting a *system*. Consider the three English phonemes /l/, /t/, and /e/ (the vowel of *pen*): they could theoretically be arranged in six different combinations, of which just two—/tel/ (cf. *tell*) and /let/ (cf. *let*) are English words. If the reader thinks that the combinations

$$/*tle/ \text{and} /*lte/ °$$

are unpronounceable, he is mistaken: the chances are that in some exotic language they actually occur as words. The felt oddity of these two combinations is due not to some physical impossibility of utterance, but rather to their marked deviation from an English pattern for the combination of phonemes. (/l/, in initial position, must be followed by a vowel; the only consonant that can follow /t/ in this position is /r/.) The syllable /*elt/ might be an English word, but happens not to be: the case is quite different for the two examples that have just been discussed.

Similar results are found in general: there are broad restrictions, characteristic for a given language, that permit only some combinations of phonemes to "sound right," whether or not they constitute actual words or syllables (parts of words). The phonemes of any recognizably correct utterance occur systematically—they are not bunched together higgledy-piggledy. This is true of every known language, although the

---

different "pitch levels." The difference between a sentence spoken assertively and the same sentence spoken questioningly calls for recognition of perhaps three "terminal contours." Finally, the layman might describe the heard difference between *iced ink* and *I stink* as a "different placing of the pause"; the contemporary linguist prefers to speak of different kinds of "juncture" or "transition." For these somewhat technical ideas, the reader may be referred to the book of Hockett cited in this work, or to some equally good introduction to modern linguistics.

°Here, and subsequently, I follow the linguists' convention of using an initial asterisk to indicate sounds or combinations of sounds that do not occur in the language in question.

patterns of combination vary from one language to the next.

There is another and illuminating way of looking at this property of a language. Roughly speaking,[7] we hear the phonemes of a given speech-token (utterance) *in succession*. If there were no restrictions upon the order of occurrence of phonemes, knowledge of a part of the sequence would provide no clues at all to what was in prospect: after /ka . . . / *any* of the vowels and consonants might be expected. In fact, as we have seen, this is not so: we can predict that some combinations will not occur (e.g. /*kaa/) and can even estimate the probabilities of occurrence of the permitted ones. In an extreme case, we can predict with certainty: /karbunk . . / must become /karbunkl/ and nothing else.

Here we have an example of the important and universal linguistic phenomenon of *redundancy* (in the technical sense of that word). Roughly speaking, a language or any part of a language (a sentence, a clause, a word, a syllable) is "redundant" to the degree that it contains more cues than are required for identification. (Thus the terminal /l/ of *carbuncle* is informatively redundant, since we know that no other sound could occur at that position.) Language is over-supplied with information to the hearer.

It is easy to see the value of this. In the absence of "redundancy" every feature of the utterance counts, and loss of a single feature damages the message irreparably. Now the hearer is very often in a position where his "reading" of the intended message is distorted by the presence of irrelevant noise, by indistinctness and carelessness of utterance, or by his own inattention.[8] Redundancy is a partial safeguard against such distortion: if one feature is missed it can often be inferred from the rest of the message. In this way, a moderate amount of redundancy serves the purpose of communication—helps to "get the message across."

We can now summarize the task of the linguist in describing the *phonemic* (or *phonological*) structure of a language: it is to describe the basic stock of phonemes and the rules for their permissible combinations as simply as possible. The *phonemic system* thus obtained can be linked with the "heard sounds" by means of further rules for passing from the phonemic to a phonetic description.

---

[7]Exception must be made for such significant features as pitch, stress, intonation, that have already been mentioned.

[8]Compare the experienced lecturer's practice of saying everything three times over: once to say it, once to explain what he said, and once more to be sure his audience has understood!

DISPUTES ABOUT PHONEMES

Considering the fundamental role of the notion of a phoneme in modern linguistics, there is surprising disagreement about its proper definition. One writer defines it as "a class of sounds so used in a given language that no two members of the class can ever contrast"[9]; another as "a place in the system of sounds which a given language employs."[10] It has also been called "an idea of a sound, quite distinct from any actual sound." Such discrepancies, which could easily be illustrated by many other examples, may have been responsible for the decision of one highly competent expert to regard a phoneme as a "logical fiction"[11] or the defeatist conclusion that it is undefinable.

These disagreements, however, are not symptoms of lack of basic agreement about the correct or desirable *use* of the term "phoneme." Rather they manifest conceptual confusion about the status of an abstract term such as can easily be paralleled from other domains. They have less to do with linguistics than with a general philosophical discomfort induced by necessary recourse to abstractions such as "phonemes." The very same questions could be raised, for instance, about the status of such an abstraction as a nation. It, too, might be variously regarded as a class of persons, a "place" in a system of classification, an "idea" in people's minds, a "logical fiction," and so on.

We need not enter the lists in these ancient jousts between realism, idealism, conceptualism, and their eclectic mixtures. The need for introducing a terminology of "phonemes" seems plain enough; inspection of how languages actually function makes it inescapably plain that speakers and hearers do recognize and respond to a finite number of "identities" and "differences" between "actual sounds." It is to mark such facts in a systematic, simple, and comprehensive way that linguists introduce their phonological terminology. The proof of the undertaking is its success in fulfilling the intentions for which it was initiated. This can hardly be doubted. To ask, thereafter, what a phoneme "*really*" is or how a phoneme ought "properly" to be defined is like asking the correspond-

---

[9]H. A. Gleason, *An Introduction to Descriptive Linguistics*, Holt, Rinehart & Winston, Inc., New York, 1955, p. 24.

[10]William J. Entwistle, *Aspects of Language*, Faber & Faber, Ltd., London, 1953, p. 80.

[11]W. Freeman Twaddell, "On Defining the Phoneme," in Martin Joos, ed., *Readings in Linguistics*, 3rd. ed., American Council of Learned Societies, New York, 1963, p. 68.

ing question about the arrows that mark directions on a map.

A word might perhaps be added on the question of the "mental reality" of the phonemes. Some very distinguished linguists, Sapir among them, have made a point of insisting upon the "inner" or "ideal" sound-system of a language, conceived as part of the mental furniture of the users of the language. Sapir calls it "an immensely important principle in the life of a language."[12] But the question whether the phonological system uncovered by a linguist is somehow present in the consciousness of an unsophisticated native speaker lacks precision. It is like asking whether Euclidean geometry is part of the mental furniture of an ordinary man who has learned no formal geometry. Well, some geometrical relations and truths he undoubtedly recognizes—but only in a fragmentary and unselfconscious way. Since he does not have explicit command of such distinctively geometrical notions as, say, *median* or *parallelogram*, he can only by implausible fiction be said actually to "know" or "possess" geometry. And the same can be said about phonology. In order to use the language successfully, speakers and hearers, as we have seen, must have an intuition, a working knowledge of "significant distinctions and identities." But the man in the street has no explicit mastery of the apparatus of theoretical description. It is the task of the theorist (the phonologist) to construct an explicit system of appropriate concepts by constructing a language in which to talk about the phonological features of used language. When the layman reads phonology and absorbs it, however, he ceases to be an innocent layman. He looks at his own language afresh, through new spectacles.

Units of Meaning

FROM SOUNDS TO WORDS

Analysis of a given language into a stock of phonemes, together with the associated rules for combining them into admissible sequences, is, for a linguist, only the first stage of a more complex task. For one thing, it is obvious that a language contains words, uses a *vocabulary*. But what precisely do we mean when we produce this commonplace? As with so much that seems obviously true about language, we can be reasonably sure that what we say is approximately right, yet

[12]Edward Sapir, *Language*, Harvest Books, Harcourt, Brace & World, Inc., New York, 1955, p. 55.

may find ourselves embarrassed to explain precisely what we mean.

One plausible way of isolating the words in a given utterance is to ask the speaker to repeat what he said very slowly and carefully. He may then be expected to separate the utterance into words. Indeed, anybody speaking in this artificial way will be found to pause in some places but not in others. And even though he may sometimes break the sentence in one way, sometimes in another (*My father—is coming* as contrasted with *My—father—is—coming*), there are some points between phonemes at which a pause will never occur (**coming*). Hence one might think of defining a word as "any segment of a sentence bounded by successive points *at which pausing is possible.*"[13]

However, there is no guarantee that the procedure will work.[14] A speaker required to produce slow-motion speech, as we might call it, will, for instance, sometimes "break" the sentence into *syllables* (cf. the practice of people in slow dictation). And even if the units that emerge are what we might antecedently expect, the question remains of how the speaker—or we ourselves—know *when* to pause. It looks as if there must be some more basic way of distinguishing and separating words from one another.

One might be inclined to think of a simple word as expressing some unitary meaning. The word *windows*, to take that as an example, is regarded as expressing some concept, and hence we suppose that a word is much the same as the smallest verbal unit that can express an independent meaning. This test will serve to distinguish *windows*, which does have a meaning, from **wi*—which has none (in English, of course); but the terminal *-s* of *windows* does have the meaning of "more than one," and the first syllable *wind-* has a meaning, however irrelevant to the word in which it occurs. Again, single words will conceal complexity of meaning. For most speakers *bachelor* may well have the same meaning as the phrase *man who has not married*, but that fact does not

---

[13] Hockett, *Course*, p. 167.

[14] Yet Sapir averred that he found no such difficulty in his work with native speakers of American Indian languages. They "had some difficulty in learning to break up a word into its constituent sounds, but none whatever in determining the words." He adds that such experiences "do more to convince one of the definitely plastic unity of the word than any amount of purely theoretical argument." (*Language*, p. 34, footnote.) This "plastic unity" sounds somewhat mysterious.

reflect upon the unity of the word *bachelor*.[15] The principle of one word, one meaning, will not survive critical examination.

Let us take another tack. It will be remembered that we considered a simple speech episode, in which somebody said "Look over there!" to his companion in the course of a country walk. This, we said, evoked a normal response. Now we can easily imagine a number of other utterances which might also have produced a "normal" response. Among these would be:

> Look here!
> Look there!
> Look over here!
> Look here quickly!
> Look there for a minute!
> Look!
> Stop!
> Stop there!
> Stop there for a minute!
> Listen!
> Listen for a minute!

Let us call this set of utterances *Group I*. We notice that certain part-utterances, such as *Look, there, here, stop,* and *listen*, recur in a number of the utterances. Again, between the two parts *Look* and *here* of *Look here!* the part-utterance *over* can be inserted to produce another "normal" utterance. On the other hand, the sound **Loo-over-k*, obtained by inserting *over* inside the phoneme string *Look*, produces nonsense.[16] We might try saying, provisionally at least, the following two things:

    (1) a "word" is the smallest segment of an utterance that can combine with other such segments to produce an "intelligible" utterance;

    (2) boundaries between words occur where intelligible insertion of new utterance-segments is possible.

The notions of "normal" and "intelligible" utterances, used above, need some classification. This may be achieved by

[15]"Words are not notional units, for, as Noreen remarks, the word *triangle* and the combination *three-sided rectilinear figure* have exactly the same meaning, just as 'Armitage' and 'the old doctor in the grey suit whom we met on the bridge' may designate the same man." (O. Jespersen, *The Philosophy of Grammar*, George Allen & Unwin, Ltd., London, 1924, p. 93.)

[16]There may, to be sure, be radically different kinds of "nonsense," which would need to be discriminated in a fuller discussion. It is as hard to get clear about the meaning of the convenient word "nonsense" as it is about the meaning of its partner, "sense."

contrasting the utterances of Group I with others which would produce "abnormal" responses. Consider, for instance, the following set of utterances, in the same situation (*Group II*):

> Think!
> Think for a minute!
> Answer!
> Answer quickly!
> Scratch over there!
> Scratch!

These utterances have been constructed from members of Group I by replacing *Look* or *Stop* by *Think* or *Answer*. These utterances would not be "normal" in the situation and in a certain sense not even the first of them would be intelligible. *Stop for a minute!* leads our imagined hearer to understand at once why the remark was probably made. He expects, rightly or wrongly, to see something unusual or interesting—which, after all, often happens in a country walk. But if, out of the blue, he heard instead the sentence *think for a minute!* he would not immediately understand the speaker's likely intention, and would be thrown off his stride, and would have to work at concocting some explanation. Indeed the remark would be so unexpected that he might wonder if it has really been made. Thus a natural response might be: *"Did I hear you correctly?"* (which itself, by the way, would be "normal" after something had been said, but not otherwise). On the other hand, the hearer could readily think of other situations in which this, or any, utterance of Group II might have seemed appropriate. He could easily imagine some other situation in which an utterance of Group II would be normal, however abnormal it was in its given setting.

There is therefore a sense in which the hearer does understand what is said and is puzzled *just because* he understands it. It is not like hearing a remark in a foreign language: the puzzle is not so much *what* the speaker said as why he said it. We might call the utterances of Group II *situationally inappropriate*. Utterances situationally inappropriate in one situation are appropriate in another; they can be called *potentially* normal.

Now consider for contrast the following utterances made in the same situation:

> Stop look!
> [with the same intonation as in *Stop there!*]

There here!
Quickly over stop!
Minute a for listen!

These members of *Group III* suffer from some graver disability than "situational inappropriateness." The natural response to each of them would be not "Did I hear that right?" or "Why do you say that?" but, rather, "I can't believe my ears!" or "What on earth are you saying?" Whereas the members of Group II sounded out of place, the members of Group III sound like "gibberish." They might be called *radically* or *essentially* inappropriate; we cannot imagine any situation in which it would make sense to utter them (except in such a special case as the present context, where we need examples of "gibberish"!).

Why is it impossible to imagine a situation appropriate for the production of members of Group III? One might be inclined to answer that there is something about the individual membership of the words in Group III which prevents them from combining. (So that the absurdity of **Stop look!* can be compared to the impossibility of uniting an atom of gold with one of silver.) It seems safer, however, simply to record the fact that segments of utterance are subject to restrictions upon their order and possibility of combination. Thus we must recognize superordinate rules of combination, superimposed upon the basic rules for combination and sequence of phonemes. To learn how to use a language means, among other things, learning these rules of combinations—recognizing, for instance, the members of Groups I and II as "grammatical" and the members of Group III as "ungrammatical." (For the time being we assume that calling an utterance "grammatical" means no more than recognizing it as satisfying the rules for combining utterance segments. A "grammatical" utterance is like a "legal" move in chess. Both conform to the "rules of the game.") Words are (but only very roughly speaking—see the next section) the smallest units which are combinable according to the given language's rules of combination (syntax).

THE NOTION OF A MORPHEME

The methods outlined in the last section for recognizing and isolating those elements of language commonly called "words" parallel somewhat closely the methods previously described for identifying phonemes. In both types of investigation, linguists rely mainly upon exhibiting variations that make a difference to what might be called the "acceptability" of an utterance. Some relatively small variations in a "heard sound" lead us to say that something else has "been said" (*e.g.*, *Champion* is not the same proper name as *Campion*, in English); and similarly, some variations in the more complex sound called a word give us reason to say that another word has been produced (*nurse* and *purse* are different words). But violation of the underlying rules for combination has different effects in the two cases: *"Thang* doesn't sound like English," but "cat dog mouse" (with the intonation characteristic of assertions) "doesn't make sense" or "isn't grammatical."

Another important difference is, of course, that phonemes have no distinctive meanings[17] while many words[18] do. And of course, the phonemes for a given language make up a small and, for all short-term purposes, unchanging collection, while the stock of words, the vocabulary, is vast and unstable in composition.

In some languages, it is hard to isolate words, in any familiar sense—and even in Indo-European languages, like English, it is harder to decide whether a given bit of the language is a word than anybody who has not wrestled with the problem might suppose. Indeed the contemporary linguist is usually comparatively uninterested in words, preferring rather to focus attention upon *morphemes*. These are usually defined in some such way as *"the smallest individually meaningful elements in the utterances of a language."*[19] (But here, as often before, we notice how considerations of meaning obtrude, to the embarrassment of purists who would like to have as little truck as possible with so debatable a notion.)

This conception leads to the recognition of linguistic elements which would usually not be treated as *words* at all. Consider for instance the syllable *-ed* in *treated*, or the terminal *-ish* in *reddish*, or the *-smith* in *blacksmith*. Each of these is indeed an "individually meaningful element" in En-

---

[17]Some writers would make an exception for the so-called sound-imagery supposedly evoked by certain groups of phonemes. There is some plausibility about the view that the combination *fl-* in such words as *flare, flash,* and *flicker* corresponds to some analogy of meaning. But this becomes less plausible when one recalls such words as *fleet, flag,* and *flap.*

[18]It may be doubted whether proper names have "meaning"; and it is hard to attach definite meaning to such linking particles as *of* and *to* (when used to mark the infinitive).

[19]Hockett, *Course,* p. 123.

glish. The proof is that we can know in advance part of the meaning of a word of the form *-ish* or *-ed* or *-smith*. (More explicitly, we know that *-ish* has the force of qualifying what immediately precedes it as "more or less" or "somewhat"; *-ed* signals that the verb to which it clings refers to something in the past; *-smith* has approximately the meaning of "worker in.") Yet nobody would want to call *-ed* a word and it would be implausible to call *blacksmith* a compound of two words.[20] The three examples I here used are what the linguist calls *bound forms, i.e.,* morphemes that cannot occur except when tied to other morphemes.

What we commonly call words are, roughly speaking,[21] *free forms, i.e.,* such as can stand alone, without being attached to other morphemes.

I drew attention, somewhat earlier, to the familiar fact that words cannot be arranged at random, if intelligible or meaningful utterances are to result. This applies equally to morphemes. As in the case of phonemic analysis, the linguist's task, in this branch of his discipline, is not merely to isolate a stock of morphemes, but to discover and to state, in the simplest and most comprehensive way that he can, the rules of association. We are led to explore the structure of phrases, clauses, and sentences. Here we enter the realm of grammar.

Affinities and Combinations

GRAMMATICAL ANALYSIS

A grammarian has three interrelated tasks. The first is that of classifying words by broad function. It is easy to see that some words have analogous powers and liberties of combining into intelligible utterances. For example, in the sentence *I painted the door, I* can be replaced by *You, He, She* (and of course, by many other words); *painted* by *paint* and *will paint,* and again by *washed, polished, opened, closed,* etc.; *the* by *a, one; door* by *floor, ceiling, picture,* etc. Let us say that words which can replace one another in a given sentence without violation of grammaticality[22] are words

---

[20]Intonation provides a clue: contrast *blacksmith* with *black cat.* Also, if *blacksmith* were really a combination of two words, one would expect its meaning to be predictable by somebody who merely knew the meanings of its two elements.

[21]Some linguists regard the articles *a* and *the* as bound forms.

[22]Not always the same as "nonsense." We can sometimes understand a child or a foreigner who is violating grammar—yet we could hardly do so unless *we* knew the correct practice.

having similar roles in that context. It is an important feature of English (and every other known language) that its words can be divided into mutually exclusive classes[23] by the list of similarity of function in a given context. (Thus, in the above example, none of the following: *You, closed, a,* and *window,* can replace one another without making the sentence ungrammatical. They have different linguistic roles.) Still more remarkable is the fact that by and large[24] exclusive similarity of function extends to *all* contexts: words that can replace one another in one context can do so in *all* contexts; and words that cannot replace one another in a single context can never do so.

Words having "similar roles" in the language (*i.e.,* capable of mutual substitution *everywhere*) are said to belong to the same *form-class.* The classification of words (and other linguistic elements) into form-classes is usually called *morphology.* Morphology is the sophisticated modern version of the ancient search for "parts of speech."

A second task of the grammarian is to describe the more or less systematic ways in which words are "modified" by the addition of prefixes and suffixes, or in more subtle ways, with resulting changes in meaning. (This phenomenon was once called "accidence," though that name is now out of fashion.)

For example, the words *ox, ox's, oxen, oxen's* have related meanings, which might be unwrapped as "ox," "of an ox," "more than one ox," and "of more than one ox." Here is a simple case of *inflection.* (If the example seems artificial, that is because good examples are hard to find in a relatively uninflected language such as English. Inflection is of great importance, however, in such other languages as Latin and Hebrew.) Or contrast the case of a verb such as *cover,* with its variants *covers, covered,* and *covering.* (Not that it is easy to say what the function of the *-s* in covers really is; contrast [*I, you, we, they*] *cover* with [*he, she, it*] *covers.*) In such cases of the conjugation of verbs we have, again, more or less systematic modifications of linguistic forms, linked with associated and more or less systematic variations of meaning.[25]

In old-style grammar books, the accidence of a given language is exhibited by tables showing the most frequent types

[23]This is an oversimplification, since nouns can sometimes be used as adjectives—and similarly for other parts of speech.

[24]The tiresome qualification is, alas, necessary. An accurate grammar of any known language proves to be much more complicated than the layman might expect.

[25]The reader may, perhaps, bear to be reminded that only glimpses of a complex subject can be provided here.

of inflectional changes, in the form of so-called paradigms of "regular" nouns, verbs, and other parts of speech. Even the most "regular" languages, however, contain swarms of exceptions to these patterns, which need to be listed and learned separately.

The third of the chief grammatical tasks is that of presenting the "syntax," *i.e.*, stating rules for the admissible (grammatical) combinations of morphemes. This proves to be a somewhat intricate task. In a sentence such as *The cow jumped over the moon,* to take that as a simple example, various modes of structure can be detected. It seems right to the layman to make a main break or cut after *cow,* so that the sentence divides into

The cow / jumped over the moon.

(A speaker might, for instance, find it natural to pause at the point indicated.) Each of the two phrases thus isolated (sometimes called the "immediate constituents") has further structure; the second divides as follows:

jumped / over the moon

and the process can obviously be continued further. The final analysis might be presented as

The cow / / / jumped / / over / the moon.[20]

It is part of the grammarian's task to replace such vague talk about "natural breaks" as I have indulged in above by precise *formal* criteria for the analysis of phrases, clauses, and full sentences.

TWO SIMPLE MODELS OF GRAMMAR

I shall now try to unify the foregoing brief sketch of the grammarian's aims and techniques by describing two simplified communication systems. While neither can be properly called a language in the full sense of the word, each will illustrate most of the essential features of grammatical structure.

First, imagine a stock of variously coloured and variously shaped wooden disks so constructed that some, but not all, can fit together to make a continuous band. Suppose that

[20]Cf. the use of brackets in mathematical symbolism.

each shape is available with a number of different colours. If we think of the individual disks as corresponding to morphemes, a "sentence" in the disk-system might look somewhat as follows:

The shapes of the disks will indicate the grammatical category of the disk-units: there will be just as many "form classes" as there are distinct shapes[27] and all disks of the same shape will belong to the same form class. Correspondingly, the colours of the disks will mark individual differences between members of the same form class (the colour corresponds to the "phonemic shape" of a morpheme). Finally, the rules that determine which disks can combine to form a continuous band will correspond to the syntactical rules of a language in the full sense.

This model differs from a full language, however, in at least the following respects:

1. There is no provision for phonemic structure: the disks are not constructed out of a finite stock of elements.

2. There is no provision for distinguishing a "sentence" from any other admissible combination of "morphemes" (disks).

3. Nothing answers, in this model, to the levels of division of a sentence into immediate constituents, constituents of these constituents, and so on.

4. The "disk system" is regular, in a way strikingly at variance with the irregularity of all natural languages.

5. The grammatical structure of the disk-elements and their compounds is *explicitly shown* (as a sequence of "shapes") in a manner which is only rarely and approximately the case in natural languages. (Sentences do not have their grammatical structure engraved upon their faces.)

In spite of these marked divergences, the model serves to illustrate a striking conclusion that arises from our previous discussion. In order to identify a disk, we need to know *both its colour and its shape;* similarly, in order to recognize and to know how to use a morpheme, we must know both its grammatical category (*i.e.,* the pattern of functional relation-

[27] Circles of different sizes must count as having different "shapes"— and similarly for the other disks.

ships of combinations, exclusion, cooperation, subordination, etc., with relation to other morphemes) and its "individuality" —what distinguishes it from other morphemes having the same grammatical rules. Stress upon the individual contributions made by morphemes leads to the isolation of a *vocabulary;* stress upon what I have called the "functional relationships" leads to the construction of morphology, accidence, and syntax—of *grammar*. Thus, search for a vocabulary goes hand in hand with search for a grammar—and vice versa. Alternatively: we cannot understand a vocabulary without grasping the associated grammar. Words can be understood only in their interrelationships with other words: to know the meaning of a word is, among other things, to know its place in a system (how it contrasts and interacts with other members of that system).

My second model is drawn from the symbolism of simple arithmetic. Here we have conventional marks intended to be drawn and read, rather than to be spoken and heard. Yet here, too, it is easy to recognize a simple grammar, exemplifying the chief features previously emphasized.

The vocabulary of the arithmetical dialect may be taken to consist of the following elementary symbols:

> (*a*) 0, 1, 2, 3, 4, 5, 6, 7, 8, 9
> (*b*) $+, -, \times, /$ [or $\div$, the sign of division]
> (*c*) $=, <, >$
> (*d*) (,), [,], {,}

These clearly belong to different "form classes." We might think of the members of set (*a*) as nouns or quasi-nouns, those of set (*b*) as conjunctions, those of set (*c*) as verbs, and those of set (*d*) as punctuation signs. From the elementary symbols of (*a*) and (*b*) we can form a variety of noun-phrases—complex symbols resembling the members of (*a*) in their syntactical behaviour—such as 203, $7 - 5$, and $4 + 9$. The simplest "sentences" of this dialect (or sub-language) of English will be signs such as $2 = 2$ or $7 > 5$—*i.e.*, will consist of two members of (*a*), separated by a member of (*c*). An example of a more complex sentence might be

$$\{(39 + 5) - 6\}/2 = \{(4 \times 5) - 1\}$$

It is obvious that the listed symbols have a "syntax"—are controlled by rules that determine which combinations of them are counted as "grammatical" (or, as logicians nowadays say, "well-formed"). Examples of prohibited construction are

022, $+$, $(2 \{ 3)$, and 7/0. (These must, of course, be sharply distinguished from well-formed sentences such as $7 < 2$, which are rejected as false, not "ill-formed.")

Faced with the holiday task of analyzing the grammatical structure of this imitation quasi-language, a linguist would set himself two goals: (i) to construct a simple and comprehensive morphology (along the lines suggested by my preliminary division of the elementary symbols into four classes); and (ii) to devise a set of syntactical rules (using only formal criteria) which will generate just those complexes of symbols that the competent users of the arithmetical sub-language would accept as "well-formed" (grammatical or "sensible"). (He would, happily, be spared any investigations into "accidence," etc.)

Here, again, then, we have the by now familiar contrast between individual differences (*e.g.*, between 3 and 4) arising within a formal network of functional relationships. Here, too, is illustrated the basic principle that understanding how to use a symbol (or: knowing its meaning) involves knowing its place in the system of grammatical relationships, as well as those features of its application[28] that differentiate it from its grammatical partners.

Finally, this example neatly exemplifies a point that will concern us in our later discussion of "fictions."

The symbol 0, here as elsewhere, in mathematics may be felt to "behave queerly."[29] More important than the fact that any number whatever remains unaltered by the addition or subtraction of 0 is the "senselessness" of dividing by zero. For this last is a grammatical point, which requires, say, 5/0 to be treated as "ill-formed." If we think of it, however, as revealing something peculiar about zero itself, the "entity for which 0 stands," we shall easily mislead ourselves into fancying we have made a striking discovery. We may then be tempted to say that the answer when 5 is divided by 0 must be a number greater than anything that can be represented in our original notation. If at this point we introduce the symbol ∞ to mean "infinity," we shall simply be compounding our original confusion by a linguistic trick. Infinity, one might say, turns out

---

[28]An adequate analysis of the linguistic structure of arithmetical symbolism would demand examination of the uses of the numerals outside purely arithmetical contexts. We would need to describe how numbers are used for counting (men, sheep, and other non-mathematical entities) as well as for calculating. Such an investigation would belong to the *semantics* of this (sub-) language. I am deliberately neglecting semantical questions in this chapter.

[29]Consider, for instance, the trouble that children have in understanding the meaning of the zero exponent in X^0.

to be even "queerer" than zero and the remedy is worse than the disease.

Since 0 is, accordingly, subject to certain constraints from which the other members of class (*a*) are free (prohibition against being used as a divisor), it might plausibly be assigned to a special form-class in which it would be the sole member. But then parallel conditions would justify special treatment for 1 (as the reader can check for himself). How detailed we choose to make the "grammar" is partly a matter of convenience—of whether anything is to be gained by taking a closer look.

Grammar and Meaning

At several places in this chapter, I have stressed the interdependence of what might be called "extra-verbal" and "intra-verbal" meaning. (Linguists would prefer to say "lexical" and "syntactical" meaning.) Unless the word *vermilion*, for example, pointed beyond the language, reached out into the external world, it would have no practical utility. Like other words, it is an instrument for drawing attention to—recording, describing, conceiving, imagining, etc.—something "out there" that is not verbal.[30] When we paint a door vermilion, we change its *colour,* not its verbal description.

But this indispensable process of external reference, which is the open secret of the utility and importance of language, is a highly sophisticated and roundabout affair. Words need the cooperation of other words in the same linguistic system in order to achieve it. The idea that elements of "reality" are directly recognized as discrete entities and independently labeled (as tags might be attached to mineral specimens) is too simple-minded to survive reflection. *Vermilion,* as should be clear by now, belongs to a system of interrelated linguistic instruments, knowledge of whose connected functions is indispensable for their competent use. And when we use the word we implicitly assume and rely upon knowledge of such intra-linguistic relations: *vermilion* means, among other things, "*not* scarlet or crimson, etc." The word works by signaling contrast and difference; it sets the stage for grammatical elaboration and transformation. (Cf. the step from *That's vermilion* to *What colour did you say?*) We "grasp reality," make sense of what we experience or are told by means of a linguistic system, not by drawing from a hodge-podge of un-

[30]That this is not the only function of words will become abundantly clear in later chapters of this essay.

related words. This basic point may be reinforced by considering what is involved in learning to use and understand a given word.

Suppose we have tried to teach the meaning of the word *vermilion* to somebody who did not know it; and that we are now to decide whether the training has been successful, *i.e.,* whether the learner now *understands* the word.

Common sense will suggest the steps to be taken. Our learner may be presented with a series of cards uniformly coloured in different shades, with instructions to pick out those he recognizes as vermilion. Or he may be asked to find objects in the room of that colour. If he passes a number of such tests successfully, we might be satisfied that he did understand the word. We might say, in general: a person understands *vermilion* when he can recognize the presence and the absence of the colour in question.

The steps needed to teach anybody a colour name, and to test the success of his training, are, however, more complex than our simple story. Precautions are needed to forestall various possible misconceptions on the learner's part: he might think his attention was being drawn not to the colour of the cards, but to their shape, size, texture, or some other characteristic. (I assume that the training is deliberately non-verbal, for to use words in the teaching would only lead us to wonder how those words themselves were understood.) Even if the learner knows that only the colour of the samples is relevant, he might still mistake the teacher's intention by supposing that the intensity or brightness of the shade was what really mattered. Such obstacles to learning might be overcome by sufficiently varying the shape, size, texture, and other characteristics of the cards.

A similar story will fit many other words and expressions. A man is said to understand the word "plane-tree" if he calls nothing but plane-trees by that name; and to understand the word "cat" if he applies it only to a certain "small domesticated carnivorous quadruped in the habit of uttering a cry represented by 'miaou.'" (Words like "not" or "two" need a different and more complicated training.) A necessary condition for understanding a word is the ability to use it in the correct setting.

That the condition is not sufficient is easy to show. Suppose that some foreign learner of imperfectly related English has correctly passed the tests described above. It is still conceivable, however odd it might seem, that he is heard saying "I vermilion this wall," at a time when he is covering a wall painted vermilion with white paint. (How can we *exclude* this possibility?) Our confidence that the earlier training had succeeded would be rudely shaken if we found the learner was using a noun as a verb and, what is worse, using the word when the colour was rapidly *disappearing*.

If the reader feels certain that nobody who had a sufficiently thorough training could behave in this extraordinary way, let him consider why he thinks so. Is he perhaps implicitly defining a "sufficiently thorough" training as one which would guarantee acceptable behaviour in every situation? Such a training would, of course, exclude mistakes by definition. (If the learner speaks "eccentrically," the training must have been defective.) Then we could never be sure in advance that the training had been "successful." Yet if we define "training" more sensibly in terms of correct response to a limited set of test-situations, we have no guarantee against "eccentricity" in more complicated situations.

Minor and infrequent deviations from acceptable English usage for which we can find analogies in our own language might be written off as signs of incomplete mastery or of unfamiliarity with English idiom. But very startling departures from linguistic orthodoxy are conceivable. Faced with a notice painted in vermilion, our learner might say, "We shall have a vermilion concert soon." (Would we understand him? Would this necessarily show that we were dealing with a lunatic?)

A small number of such linguistic lapses might be explained away as symptoms of frivolity or an undisciplined imagination. But it might be simpler to conclude that he did not yet fully understand the word "vermilion." And all the time, test repetition of the training tests might still show no loss of skill in applying the word in simple situations.

Thus ability to say "This is vermilion" when, and only when, vermilion is perceived is an insufficient, though necessary, condition for understanding the word. Understanding involves, also, the ability to apply and withhold the word in novel and complex situations, and hence the ability to combine it correctly, and in the correct order, with other words. The learner has to know not only that in such and such situations he may say "vermilion"; he is also required to recognize that such combinations as *a vermilion concert* are forbidden. (And even so, we must make exceptions for metaphor and word-play.)

Briefly, then, *words are understood, not in isolation, but in interrelationship with other words*. We understand systems of symbols, rather than single words; a word is no more to be understood without understanding its linguistic associates than a hand can be shaken without touching a body.

This connection between meaning and syntax was already implicit in our account of primitive linguistic training when I spoke lightly of applying and withholding a word, as if no other accompanying symbols were needed. Certainly a teacher and a learner can arrange, by previous agreement, that mere utterance of the word "vermilion" shall record perception of the colour, while silence will count as inability to perceive the colour. But failing such arrangement, utterance of the word "vermilion" functions as affirmation of the colour's presence only if pronounced in a characteristically "assertive" tone of voice (with a marked fall in pitch towards the end of the word). And even this is unusual, the more normal form being "This is vermilion" or even "I see vermilion now."

Thus even learning to recognize isolated samples of colour involves learning to use certain related words such as the expression "This is . . . ." Such auxiliary symbols as the phrase "This is . . ." are used in approximately the same way in connection with all words referring to features of the immediate environment, while the wider set of associates with which a word may in general combine differ widely in composition from instance to instance.

MODERN LINGUISTICS AND DISTRUST OF MEANING

It is often said that "modern linguistics" (by which is meant especially the types of investigation, sometimes also called "structural linguistics," inspired by the example of Leonard Bloomfield)[31] eschews appeal to meaning and manages to perform grammatical analysis without any such appeal.[32] Some contemporary linguists do indeed regard *meaning* as a dirty word. But on the whole, the view that grammar can, or ideally should, be constructed by turning a blind eye to semantical questions rests on little more than ignorance of history and on conceptual prejudice.

As for mistaken history, any but the most careless reading of Bloomfield's epoch-making book will find the supposed founder of "meaning-free linguistics" testifying to the impos-

[31]See especially his highly influential treatise, *Language* (cited earlier).
[32]"Some linguists seem to have interpreted Bloomfield's position as ruling out all consideration of meaning in any context." (John B. Carroll, *The Study of Language*, Harvard University Press, Cambridge, Mass., 1953, p. 82.)

sibility of avoiding reference to meaning when performing linguistic analyses.

Typical remarks of Bloomfield are:

> The study of *significant* speech-sounds is *phonology* or *practical phonetics*. Phonology involves the consideration of meanings. (78)
>
> Only by finding out which utterances are alike in meaning, and which ones are different, can the observer learn to recognize the phonemic distinctions. (93)
>
> Only in this way will a proper analysis (that is, one which takes account of the meanings) lead to the ultimately constituent morphemes. (161)[33]

But one need not rely on Bloomfield's authority to see that appeals to meaning are essentially involved in phonemic and morphemic analysis and hence enter at the very portals of linguistic study.

The caricature of linguistics as entirely formal does have some grain of justification. Behind the far-fetched, if popular, allegation that modern linguistics does, can, or should ignore meaning is a methodological principle (largely fostered by Bloomfield's example) which might be formulated (with apologies to Occam) as: *meanings should not be invoked beyond necessity*. From this maxim spring two useful rules: *Whenever possible, rely upon differences of meaning, rather than substantive reports of meaning* and *Whenever possible, replace reliance upon meanings by the use of formal criteria*.

We have already seen how the search for phonemes, morphemes, and other units of linguistic analysis necessarily enlists the competent speaker's judgments concerning difference of meaning and lack of meaning (ungrammaticality).

The negative justification for the maxims proposed in the last paragraph is that the concept of meaning (or, rather, the large family of concepts for which the overworked word "meaning" stands) is an exceptionally confused and slippery one that linguists, philosophers, and others in pursuit of clarity and precision do well to shun whenever they can. (Even the more circumscribed concept of "identical meaning" can arouse bitter controversy: I have heard two distinguished linguists all but come to blows in public over the question whether *The Master beat the peasant* and *The peasant was beaten by the Master* have the same meaning. Questions of

[33] I take these quotes from the valuable article by Charles C. Fries, "The Bloomfield School," in *Trends in European and American Linguistics*, ed., Christine Mohrmann, Spectrum, Utrecht, 1961.

meaning are apt to generate spectacular manifestations of *furor academicus.*)

The point in justification for the methodical avoidance by linguists of semantical questions (for linguistic clean-shaving) is the comparative success that has actually been achieved by linguists who have obeyed the two subsidiary precepts stated above. Our earlier discussions of the foundations of phonemic and morphemic analysis showed that all we needed to get launched was the "competent-speaker's" recognition of *sameness* and *difference* of meaning. (Similarly, in elaborating a comprehensive grammar, the appeal is basically to an "informant's" recognition of ungrammaticalness—something that involves minimal reference to semantical questions.) As for the fruitfulness of "formal" criteria, the proof of that is in the superiority of modern grammars to those older "school-grammars" confusedly grounded in alleged apprehensions of fundamentals of meaning.

CHAPTER 3

THE PHILOSOPHY OF GRAMMAR

I SHALL CONSIDER here some, but by no means all, of the
general questions concerning grammar that suggest themselves to an inquiring mind. A number of the issues raised
will receive further examination in later chapters.

How Much of Grammar Is Conventional?

Everybody will freely concede that the phonemic system of
a language is conventional or arbitrary. Nothing about the
human purposes served by language, or about the "objective
reality" to which it aspires to refer, dictates the character of
the basic stock of phonemes or the nature of the rules governing their combinations. Any sounds that are easy to produce
with sufficient regularity for quick recognition will do; and the
resources of the vocal tract are rich enough to allow this condition to be satisfied in a vast number of different ways.
This verdict of arbitrariness is confirmed by the multiplicity
of markedly different phonemic systems actually used by different speech communities.

It is only an extension of the same insight to recognize the
arbitrariness of the connection between a word and what it
stands for. For so far as identifying the thing-meant it does
not matter what phoneme cluster (morpheme) is used, provided its connection with the corresponding meaning is fixed.
Thus it is that the animal called a *dog* in English is elsewhere
a *chien*, a *sabaka*, a *keleb* and so on. "The relation between
sound and thing is entirely artificial, and according to the

language so is the convention."[1] Even the so-called onomato-poeic words, that seem to imitate the sounds they represent, vary from one language to another: "The Englishman transcribes the crow of the cock as *cock-a-doodle-do,* the Frenchman as *cocorico,* the German as *kikeriki.* [A child might suppose that animals "speak" with different accents in different parts of the world.] The dog's bark is reproduced as *bow-wow* in English and as *ouâ-ouâ* in French. The sound of a shot is rendered as *bang* or *crack* in English and as *pum* or *paf* in Spanish."[2]

The point, though obvious, is worth emphasizing, because there is a lingering inclination to postulate some essential connection between word and thing. The proverbial old lady who thought it so clever of astronomers to discover the names of the stars has plenty of equally muddled contemporaries, as current superstitions about the number 13 amply show. Hotels regularly designate what would otherwise be Floor 13 as Floor 12A or Floor 14—as if changing the name changed the luck. Of course, given the prejudices of the guests, the practice is quite sensible: popular superstition may well create an indirect connection between 13 and bad luck. For if enough people think 13 is unlucky, an abnormal number of accidents might well occur on the 13th floor—or on Friday the 13th. A floor shunned by guests would be an unlucky floor for the management. And an eau de cologne labeled "13" will not sell as well as one bearing another number.

Leaving such oddities aside, we may take it as settled that choice of the basic phonemic elements and allocation of bundles of them to "things-meant" is arbitrary. Less obvious are the correct answers to the following questions:

1. Is the division of reality into *things nameable* in a given language also arbitrary? Or, to speak loosely, does reality have an "intrinsic grain" which any adequate language ought to respect? For example, is there an objectively correct way of analyzing the spectrum into "simple colours"? Or are all methods of division equally good?

2. Do the differences between the grammars of various languages show that grammar (that is to say, morphology and syntax) is as arbitrary as phonology? Or are there, beneath the superficial variety of grammars, some features of grammatical design imposed by the nature of reality?

The first of these questions, which raises perplexing philo-

[1]Entwistle, *Aspects of Language,* pp. 14–15.
[2]Stephen Ullmann, *Semantics,* Basil Blackwell & Mott, Ltd., Oxford, 1962, p. 86.

sophical questions about the nature of reality, may be left for our later discussion of "language and thought." It is clearly connected with the much-debated question of the extent to which the use of a given language influences the thought of its users.

However, I shall try to answer the second question at once.

THE ARBITRARINESS OF GRAMMAR

Is the character of a given grammar a clue to reality? Was Bertrand Russell right when he said,

> The study of grammar, in my opinion, is capable of throwing far more light on philosophical questions than is commonly supposed by philosophers. Although a grammatical distinction cannot be uncritically assumed to correspond to a genuine philosophical difference, yet the one is *prima facie* evidence of the other, and may often be most usefully employed as a source of discovery.[3]

By a "philosophical difference" Russell probably meant a distinction *in reality*. The lack of precision of the idea expressed by "distinction in reality" is unavoidable. Indeed, the difficulty of our question resides largely in the difficulty of making clear to ourselves what we are asking. For brevity, I shall call the correspondence to reality of an entire grammar or some feature of it its *objectivity*.

That grammar ought to be as objective as it can be made —ought to be closely modeled upon reality—is a view that has an ancient tradition behind it. Plato, who has some claim to be regarded as the father of Western grammatical theory, expressly based the distinction between a noun and a verb, which, so far as we know, he was the first to make explicit,[4] on a supposedly objective basis. He took a "noun" to refer to anything to which some action or condition was imputed and understood a "verb" to refer to whatever was thus imputed (or predicated). In short, his distinction was basically the one that philosophers still recognize between subject and predicate. "What is important in the history of grammar is that the distinction was justified on logical or philosophical

---

[3]*The Principles of Mathematics,* Cambridge University Press, 1903, p. 42.

[4]Robins, *Ancient and Mediaeval Grammatical Theory,* p. 17. Plato is thought to have been building on the work of Protagoras and others. I am much indebted to Robins in this section.

grounds, not formal or purely linguistic ones."[5] This philosophical or "logical domination of grammar"[6] has plagued the subject ever since. Priscian, whose treatise of Latin grammar became a favourite textbook in the medieval period, followed this tradition in defining a noun as "a part of speech assigning a common or specific quality to persons or things" and a verb as ". . . signifying action or being acted upon."[7] By the 13th century (and from the later medieval period to the Renaissance and beyond) considerable influence was exerted by writers on Speculative Grammar (theories about language in general) who ". . . proclaimed that there was *one* universal grammar dependent on the structure of reality and human reason."[8] The philosopher, according to these "Modistae,"[9] must criticize and, when necessary, improve the grammar that he finds in a given language. The philosopher-grammarian was to be a legislator, not a mere reporter.

The claim of speculative grammar that grammar ought to conform to reality presupposes some non-linguistic access to the structure of reality and regards any available grammar as being at best a flawed and distorting mirror of the universe. Indeed, nobody has ever had the temerity to claim that a given grammar can, in all its parts, accurately and objectively conform to "reality."

A fairly obvious counter-example to any thesis of the metaphysical adequacy of grammar is constituted by *gender*. That this is an obligatory grammatical category in French, Russian, and many other languages is obvious. Equally obvious is the fact that this does not mirror any "objective" feature outside language itself.[10] There is, for instance, no good reason why *flèche* (arrow) in French should be treated as

[5]Robins, p. 17.

[6]Robins, p. 18.

[7]Robins, p. 65.

[8]Robins, p. 77.

[9]So called because such philosophical grammars were usually entitled *De Modis Significandi* (On modes of signification), Robins, p. 80.

[10]Speakers whose native language is an Indo-European one tend to think of gender as somehow connected with sex. But there is reason to think that "Primarily gender has nothing to do with sex unless, perhaps, in the Dravidian languages" (Entwistle, *Aspects*, p. 191). The basic idea is that of subclassification of nouns by means of some more or less rational principle—often in terms of a contrast between animate and inanimate things, later extended by analogy, on the basis of mythical beliefs or by linguistic parallelism, to much wider classes.

"feminine" (assigned to the same class as *femme*) while *poêle* (stove) is masculine.[11]

Given that *some* features of a given grammar are arbitrary, non-objective, how are we to proceed in isolating its objective features—if it has any? There seem to be only two ways. If we follow the first, we argue from our supposed knowledge of "reality" to conclusions about what an adequate language must be like. This might be called an argument from ontology to grammar. (*Ontology* has the meaning of "knowledge of the nature of reality.")

There is a certain initial plausibility in this approach. Consider the analogous situation in making, for instance, a map of the earth's surface. Here it might be said that before we start we know enough about the earth to be able to lay down the conditions that any adequate map must satisfy. To take one example: Suppose two land masses, *A* and *B*, are represented by areas *a* and *b* in the map; then if *A* and *B* are really equal in area, they ought to be *shown* equal in *a* and *b*. In this respect, it seems, the map must conform to the surface it claims to represent. But if this argument is sound, why should it not be extended? Why not think of a language as a grand map of the universe and demand of it, as we do of the earth map, that it faithfully reflect reality?

Plausible as it may seem, there is a fatal objection to this line of thought. I was careful to say that the sections of the map, *a* and *b*, which stand for the land masses, *A* and *B*, respectively, ought to "show" *A* and *B* as equal in area. But it is certainly not necessary, nor indeed is it everywhere possible in a flat map, for *a* and *b* to *be* equal in area. For the flatness of the map produces distortions that must be compensated for by conventions of interpretation. Indeed, such conventions are all we need: it will be quite enough if we know how to "read" the sections *a* and *b* correctly, *i.e.*, in such a way as to inform us that *A* and *B* are equal. An element of convention enters necessarily, for a map, even a contour model, cannot result from the quixotic attempt to reproduce reality; it is necessarily a system of conventional signs which we have to learn to interpret as intended. Conversely, any map, no matter how unlike what it represents, is

[11]There is an amusing complication here: when *poêle* means frying-pan it becomes feminine—as if the only difference between a stove and a fry-pan were one of "sex." (Cf. Ullmann, *Semantics,* p. 183, for further examples and discussion of the ways in which differences of gender between homonyms obviate possible ambiguities.)

"adequate," in the only sense intelligible, if it supplies exclusively correct information.

Imagine that all the information conveyed by a given map is stated in words, providing what might be called a *verbal equivalent* (*V*) of the original map, *M*. Then *V* is just as "adequate" a representation of the earth as *M* was. Of course *V* may be harder to read or to grasp, but that does not affect the present argument. Now the words and sentences composing *V* are utterly unlike the earth's surface to which they refer; yet they serve, from a logical standpoint, just as well as the conventional map, are just as faithful a source of correct information.

A further point to be noticed about our analogy is that the rules of grammar might plausibly be said to correspond to such cartographic conventions as the use of lines of latitude and longitude. The question about the objectivity of grammar is strictly analogous to the question whether lines of longitude answer to anything in reality. And the sensible answer is that since we can *use* them to say true things (*e.g.*, about the relative positions of places in the earth's surface) that's the end of the matter. They are, in the suggestive old expression, "imaginary lines" serving a purpose—and the same can be said about the morphological lines drawn within a given grammar.

A second approach to the problem of the objectivity of grammar consists of trying to establish that some grammatical features are indispensable to any language whatever, if it is to serve its intended purpose. This might be called the argument from grammatical invariants.[12] Unlike the argument from ontology, previously considered, this new argument does not rely upon dubious, and unverifiable, assertions about what "reality" is "really like"; it hopes to get interesting results from a direct confrontation with language. (It might be viewed as a search for the *essence* of language.)

Yet this approach, also, seems fruitless. For the search for grammatical invariants, however plausible it has seemed to some theorists, comes to grief on the extreme variability of grammars. In order to appreciate this fully, anybody educated to speak an Indo-European language might be advised to become acquainted with some such exotic language as Kwakiutl or Navaho. He may then be startled to discover how parochial his grammatical habits are. Exposure to a

---

[12]"Invariant" is a technical term borrowed from mathematics, where it means something that remains *unchanged* in the course of transformations.

"wild" language can have a decidedly liberating effect as a prophylactic against what might be called grammatical sclerosis.

To take one important example: Some writers have had high hopes for the "objectivity" of the distinction between *subject* and *predicate*. For it might be supposed that any language must make a distinction, at least in normal sentences, between *what is being talked about* (the subject) and *what is claimed about it* (the predicate).[13] (Notice the a priori character of this argument!) Following Hockett, we might call "what is being talked about" the *topic* of the sentence, and "what is said about it" the *comment*. But in any reasonable interpretation of these words, the "topic" will not always coincide with the grammatical subject even in English,[14] while in Chinese a sentence lacking a "topic" is still one "of the favorite type."[15] (A grammarian needs *formal* criteria for "subject" and "predicate" and cannot rely upon speakers' intuitions about what is the topic.)[16] By the time we reach such examples as the Malay sentence: *datanglan anak-nya minta duit* "there came (there was a coming by) his son asking for money = his son came to ask for money,"[17] it seems as pointless to seek for the subject as it would be to do so in the familiar English sentence "it is raining."[18] It is salutary to

[13]"A few generations ago it would have seemed inconceivable to write a grammar, and particularly a syntax, without making extensive use of the terms Subject and Predicate. . . . These terms were thus considered as being of fundamental importance. Any doubts concerning their legitimacy or even their mere usefulness therefore betray a crisis of grammatical thought, a new departure in grammatical thinking. They affect the whole system of grammar and not merely part of it." (Manfred Sandmann, *Subject and Predicate*, Edinburgh University Press, 1954, p. 1.)

[14]In English and the familiar languages of Europe, topics are usually also subjects, and comments are predicates: so in *John/ran away*. But this identification fails sometimes in colloquial English, regularly in certain special situations in formal English, and more generally in some non-European languages. (Cf. Hockett, *Course*, p. 201.)

[15]Hockett, *Course*, p. 202. He cites the example of a Chinese sentence, roughly translatable as "very-much love(s) that girl," which "includes no topic at all, either in separate words or within the verb . . . ." (p. 203) and is not felt by Chinese to be elliptical.

[16]"It is, indeed, unfortunate that the grammarian has to use the word 'subject' which in ordinary language means, among other things, also 'topic' ('subject-matter')." (Jespersen, *Philosophy of Grammar*, pp. 146–147.)

[17]Quoted, with the translation, from Entwistle, *Aspects*, p. 178. Entwistle suggests that the verb should be regarded as the subject of a Malay sentence.

[18]Entwistle, however, takes "the phenomenon itself," *i.e.*, the rain, to be the subject of this sentence! (*Aspects*, p. 168.)

consider how one could separate the "topic" from the "comment" of a photograph. Once we see that information *can* be conveyed (as it were, in the form "That's the way things were") without the subject-predicate distinction, one can see that the inclination to regard this distinction as a linguistic universal is one more example of the tendency to ascribe metaphysical significance to our own linguistic patterns.

On the whole, then, the position we reach is as follows: (1) There is no reason to think that the grammatical system (morphology and syntax) of any known language[19] reflects the "grain" of reality. (2) On the contrary, there is good reason to think that the underlying ideas ("reflection," the "structure of reality") are confused ones that disintegrate upon critical examination. (3) There are, so far as it is possible to see, no grammatical "invariants"—distinctions and constructions that any language must observe on pain of ceasing to be a language. Grammar has no essence. (4) Thus the conception of an "ideal language," perfectly conforming to the nature of reality, is a will-o'-the-wisp that leads nowhere except into futility. (5) The grammar of any given language constitutes a set of conventions, a system of distinctions and relationships obligatory for that language. (6) Such a set of obligatory distinctions has a practical value in organizing and facilitating thought, communication, and understanding. (7) From a metaphysical point of view all known languages are equally "adequate" in the sense of being fit for the purposes for which they are intended:[20] roughly speaking, anything that can be said can be said in any language. Judged by the test of "global translatability" all grammars are equal—and none is more equal than others.

If the reader has never been tempted to think of grammar as a "mirror of the universe," he may wonder what all the fuss is about. The answer is that the seemingly academic debate between latter-day *modistae* (speculative grammarians) and their opponents (such as the present writer) has consequences which reach out to the foundations of thought and the character of the educational process.

To become convinced of the inescapable arbitrariness and essential variability of grammar is to be taught a valuable

---

[19]Some might wish to make an exception for the special "language" of symbolic logic. But even here there is little reason to think that the symbolism "mirrors" reality.

[20]Though this is by no means a negligible consideration. A good choice of symbolism can make enormous practical difference to the success of a science.

lesson in toleration. Nobody who has once seen this basic point will ever plume himself upon the superior "logicality" of the language in which he learned to think and to express his thought. He will be free, or as free as it is possible to be, of the besetting intellectual vice of inflating linguistic convenience into a set of metaphysical categories—or of imposing upon those comfortable in another linguistic culture the useful conventions of his own.

The Synthetic Resources of Language

Kangaroos cannot digest oysters. It may well be the case that this sentence has never been written or spoken before. Even if it has, the reader has almost certainly never encountered it—yet he understands it immediately. In this respect new sentences are strikingly unlike new words: if you meet the word *kookaburra* for the first time, you need to be told that it stands for an Australian bird with a characteristic cackling cry, and no amount of previous knowledge of the English language will enable you to anticipate that word's meaning. (At best, you might guess by the sound of the word that it had been borrowed from some aboriginal language.) But the sentence at the head of this paragraph, even if you see it for the first time, needs no explanation. In this respect, being regularly formed, it is quite unlike idiomatic sentences (*e.g.,* proverbs) whose meanings must be learned separately and independently, like those of individual words. Of course, this assumes that you know the meanings of the four separate words, *kangaroo, cannot, digest,* and *oyster,* and can recognize the grammatical pattern that can very roughly be shown as

Plural noun [subject]—(*can, cannot*) [verb modifier]—plural verb [habitual present tense, plural]—plural noun [object].

But even so, the sentence is not a mere bundle composed of four words (or, say, seven morphemes) plus a grammatical pattern: the familiar words are arranged to form a complex having a unified new meaning that is immediately grasped. In familiar mathematical terminology, one can say that the meaning of the novel sentence is a unique *function* of the meanings of the morphemes and their arrangement. We may well wonder how this is possible. Perhaps nothing about the remarkable social instrument that we call language is more wonderful than its capacity to generate the kind of novelty illustrated above.

I shall refer to the aspect of language that now concerns us as "the synthetic resources of language." Alternatively, we might speak of the powers of language-users to synthesize new linguistic compounds; but there must be some design features of the language system that make this remarkable power possible and it is with these that we shall be engaged. More specifically, I shall use the label to refer to the following facts, which hold for every known language: (1) There is no upper limit to the length or complexity of grammatical sentences. (2) From a finite number of words (or morphemes) infinitely many grammatical sentences can be constructed. (3) A competent speaker of the language knows in advance how to understand indefinitely many sentences that he has never considered or met.

To say that language has the "synthetic resources" listed above is to claim that it is an *open system*, whose design permits the construction from a limited number of word-elements (a finite vocabulary) of infinitely many intelligible complexes (an infinite set of grammatical sentences). The following are other examples of open systems: the tunes that can be played on a piano, chemical compounds, the truths of elementary arithmetic, the various possible games of chess. In each of these cases, a finite repertoire of elements and arrangements generates infinite diversity and novelty. For contrast, we may think of such "closed" systems as the traffic signs ("Stop," "Children crossing," etc.) posted at roadsides, where each component has an independent or idiomatic meaning.

Some writers refer to the "openness" of language as its "productive" or "creative"[21] aspect. But language is "open" or "creative" in all sorts of ways other than those singled out here for special attention. Users of language are free to invent new words, to invest old words with new meanings, to modify established syntactical patterns, to use the rhetorical devices of metaphor and irony, and to modify the stereotyped and routine ideas crystallized in the linguistic system. Even the relatively unmotivated, and spontaneous, choice of a sentence such as *Kangaroos cannot digest oysters* has an

[21]See, for instance, Noam Chomsky's valuable discussion under this heading in his *Cartesian Linguistics* (Harper & Row, New York, 1966), pp. 3–31. He concedes that the label "creative" is somewhat misleading (footnote 30, p. 81). Chomsky is one of the few linguists to have appreciated the basic importance of the openness of language. His discussion relates the relevant issues in illuminating ways to the unjustly neglected views of such outstanding Romantic thinkers as Schlegel and Humboldt.

important aspect of the "creative" about it. For all its fixity of structure at any given time, a living language has an inherent plasticity and capacity for growth and adaptation. (It is more like a developing organism than an inflexible machine.) But important as all this is, I shall neglect it for the time being. Our present concern, to adapt Chomsky's expression,[22] is with "rule-governed innovation" rather than with "rule-changing innovation."

Without the capacity for "rule-governed innovation," our ability to use linguistic signals would be limited to stock responses: we could make sense only of what we had heard before, like circus animals who can respond only to familiar commands—or like the tourist whose knowledge of a foreign language is confined to "phrases" learned as idiomatic and unconnected units.

It is not easy to understand how so basic a skill can be learned or embodied in a neural mechanism. Chomsky and his followers claim that current stimulus-response theories of learning are helpless to account for it. But it seems premature to assume, as Chomsky seems inclined to do, some "innate" capacity for innovation. True though it may be, such an account is hardly illuminating. The secret seems to reside in something no less fundamental than the apprehension of relationships in general. If so, that may be a reason why it is hard to come to grips with. To take a simple example: understanding the meaning of the word *on*—as in *The cat is on the mat*—means, among other things, to be prepared to understand combinations of the form X *is on* Y for an indefinite range of values of X and Y. A child or a foreigner would not be held to have learned the meaning of *on* unless, having previously learned the meaning of *the dog* and *the chair*, he knew without specific instruction what was intended by *The dog is on the chair*. Thus the requisite generalization and application to novel cases enters at the ground floor, as it were, with the basic understanding of relational words, including those that mark grammatical rules. It would be wrong to think of words as independent blocks which have, somehow and mysteriously, to be put together again in possibly novel ways to produce unified structures. We start with the "structures" (sentences) whose meanings are apprehended as wholes. As we begin to analyze these holophrases into elements that can be rearranged and re-

[22]N. Chomsky, "Current Issues in Linguistic Theory," in *The Structure of Language*, eds., J. A. Fodor and J. J. Katz, Prentice-Hall, Inc., Englewood Cliffs, N.J., 1964, p. 59.

combined, we learn at the same time how to reorganize them. Thus analysis and synthesis are inseparable aspects of the mastery of linguistic structure: to be able to divide is necessarily to know how to connect, and *vice versa*. If there is any residual "mystery," it is the basic one of how we perceive complexity in unity—how we ever manage to *see* parts related in a whole. But this mystery we must leave for psychologists and philosophers to wrestle with.

However we manage to perform the feat of perceiving productive relationship, we may be thankful that we can. For, returning to language (and anticipating our later discussion of the relations between symbol and thought), it is easy to see that without the "synthetic resources" of language, imagination and thought would be impossible. For to imagine what has not yet occurred, to think articulately about the possible though not yet actual, requires us to combine words or other symbols in novel ways. Only by so doing can we escape from the insistent present and free our minds to contemplate what *might be*. As an ironic footnote, we may observe that the "synthetic" aspect of language also opens the door to mendacity: it calls for a certain imagination to be a liar. Animals tied to a fixed repertoire of standard responses cannot *lie*, though they may engage in what we are pleased to call "deception." Such "deception," if we wish to call it that, is itself innocent in not being subject to the will of its agents. In the linguistic realm, as elsewhere, crime demands a certain power of imagination: in order to sin it is necessary to be able to *contemplate* evil.

Language Habits and Language Rules

In trying to understand anything as complex as language, it is natural to seek comparisons. We think: "Language is like . . ." (or, more dangerously, "language is nothing but . . .") and try to fill the gap by referring to something familiar, unproblematic, intelligible. In this way, thought about language easily comes to be controlled by some dominating model, whose basic ideas and assumptions are drawn from another realm in which they have proved their worth. There is, of course, nothing reprehensible in this useful strategy, but it has obvious risks. A model that is initially illuminating may end as a device for ignoring whatever fails to conform—in the spirit of "What I don't know isn't knowledge."[23]

²³From the famous epigram against Jowett of Balliol: I am Master of this college: What I don't know isn't knowledge.

For many 20th-century linguists, the dominating model is of language as *behaviour* (construed, as we shall presently see, in a notably restricted sense). Indeed, so obvious is it to many such thinkers that human speech *is* (not: *is like*) observable behaviour that they are usually unaware of employing a model at all. Now if "behaviour" meant no more than "something done," it would certainly be obvious enough that anybody who says something engages in "behaviour," does something. We might even concede with some qualms, that anybody who understands what is said also engages in "behaviour," in the sense of doing something. But this harmless interpretation of the view that speech is behaviour is as useless as it is innocuous: it is no more than a platitude in fancy dress. In practice, something more interesting and much more controversial is intended. Impressed by certain conceptions about scientific method, writers who emphasize speech as behaviour wish to do two things: to exclude such psychological terms as "intention," "purpose," "motive," and, of course, "meaning," because they do not refer to what is "publicly observable," and to banish any reference to linguistic "rules," "conventions," or "norms" on the ground that the business of science is to describe how things are, not how they ought to be. In short, such behaviouristic linguists, as they might be called, adopt the self-denying ordinance of refusing to see anything in language but the directly observable and the factual. (This attitude stems from stimulus-response theory in psychology and, less directly, from the philosophical tendencies labeled "positivism.")

This model can be clearly discerned in such a statement as the following:

> The only unimpeachable definition of a word is that it is a human habit, an habitual act on the part of one human individual which has, or may have, the effect of evoking some idea in the mind of another individual. A word thus may be rightly compared with such an habitual act as taking off one's hat or raising one's finger to one's cap: in both cases we have a certain set of muscular activities which, when seen or heard by somebody else, shows him what is passing in the mind of the original agent or what he desires to bring to the consciousness of the other man (or men). The act is individual, but the interpretation presupposes that the individual forms part of a community with analogous habits, and a language thus is seen to be one particular set of human customs of a well-defined social character (Jespersen, *Language*, George Allen & Unwin, Ltd., London, 1922, p. 7).

This kind of reference to "habit" and "act" is still so popular that the following quotation could easily be matched by another score in the same vein: ". . . the grammar of a language is simply an orderly description of the way people in a given society talk—of the sounds that people utter in various situations, and of the acts which accompany or follow the sounds."[24]

There is something distinctly odd, at first sight, in calling a word a "habit" as Jespersen did above. If an ordinary man were asked to list his habits, he might mention early rising or nail-biting but would hardly think of listing his active vocabulary. A word is not something that anybody does, and even uttering a word is not something done as a matter of habit. We do not pronounce the word "horse"—or, for that matter, the sentence "That's a horse" whenever we see a horse. It is a vitally important feature of speech that we are not trained to respond automatically by appropriate talk to a situation. We are always free to speak or to hold our tongues, to report truthfully or to deceive, and so on. Anything, on the face of it, less like a "habit" (if we take the word seriously) is somewhat hard to imagine.

I shall leave further discussion of this important topic to a later examination of behaviouristic linguistics—but the deliberate neglect of anything that is "prescriptive" or "regulative" in language can be conveniently discussed at once.

The notion to be examined is, roughly speaking, that there are no "oughts" in language: people say whatever they have been trained to say, or choose to say, and that's an end to the matter. The linguist is too good a scientist to tell anybody how he ought to speak—which may be left to such old-

---

[24] Bernard Bloch and George L. Trager, *Outline of Linguistic Analysis*, Waverly Press, Baltimore, Md., 1942, p. 6.

Notice also the characteristic emphasis upon "action" and "training" in the following statements: "Language creates and exemplifies a twofold value of some human actions. In its *biophysical* aspect language consists of sound-producing movements and the resultant sound waves and of the vibration of the hearer's eardrums. The *biosocial* aspect of language consists in the fact that the persons in a community have been trained to produce these sounds in certain situations and to respond to them by appropriate actions. The biosocial function of language arises from a uniform, traditional, and arbitrary training of the persons in a certain group. They have been trained to utter conventional sounds as a secondary response to situations and to respond to these slight sounds, in a kind of trigger effect, with all sorts of actions." (L. Bloomfield, "Linguistic Aspects of Science," in *International Encyclopedia of Unified Science*, ed., Otto Neurath, vol. 1, no. 4, University of Chicago Press, 1939.)

fashioned parties as schoolmasters, elocution coaches, and members of Academies. Indeed, there is nothing to tell: in language, whatever is is right—or, rather, there can be no question of right and wrong.

This attitude (for, as we shall see, it is really too confused to be called anything more) has become very popular among contemporary linguists. It is crystallized in the title of Professor Robert A. Hall, Jr.'s book *Leave Your Language Alone*[25] and in such remarks as:

"There is no such thing as good and bad (or correct and incorrect, grammatical and ungrammatical, right and wrong) in language."[26]

"All languages and dialects are of equal merit, each in its own way."[27]

" 'Correct' can only mean 'socially acceptable,' and apart from this has no meaning as applied to language."[28]

There seem to be two motives behind this extreme position: the conviction, already mentioned, that there is something reprehensibly unscientific—an abrogation of "objectivity"—in meddling with "ought" and "must"; and a strong revulsion against the attempts of philosophers and grammarians (*modistae*) to impose rules upon languages.

The first of these involves a confusion between investigating rules (or standards, norms) and prescribing or laying down such rules. Let us grant that a linguist, *qua* theoretical and dispassionate scientist, is not in the business of telling people how to talk; it by no means follows that the speakers he is studying are free from rules which ought to be recorded in any faithful and accurate report of their practices. A student of law is not a legislator; but it would be a gross fallacy to argue that therefore there can be no right or wrong in legal matters.

Now there certainly are clear examples of rule-governed practices—such as games, rituals, and practices having legal standing. Whether language is, at least in part, "rule-governed" cannot be settled in advance, but rather needs a

---

[25]Cornell University Press, Ithaca, N.Y., 1950. But even he might have shied away from calling it *Let Your Language Lay!* It was reprinted under the title *Linguistics and Your Language* in 1960 (Anchor Books, Doubleday & Company, Inc., New York).

[26]Hall, *Linguistics*, p. 6. Hall calls this and the next quotation "basic principles."

[27]Hall, p. 6.

[28]Hall, p. 13. Hall goes on to say that the "acceptability" of anything linguistic "is determined, not by reason or logic or merit, but solely by the hearer's emotional attitude towards it."

candid consideration of linguistic facts. And if it should prove to be so, there would be nothing unscientific about recognizing and describing it as such. On the contrary, it would be violating scientific method to shut one's eyes to such facts on the basis of some a priori prejudice.

Revulsion against the snobbery and prejudice of those who insist upon some ineluctable standard of linguistic propriety is a more respectable motive for proclaiming the equality of all languages. But it too is confused. One is entitled to smile or gnash one's teeth, according to temperament, at pedants who attach a factitious value to a drawled vowel and view as barbaric any deviations from the styles, themselves once regarded as "vulgar," which they long ago picked up from dogmatic teachers.

Tolerance and a liberal attitude towards innovation are as admirable in matters linguistic as elsewhere. But such tolerance, freely acknowledging, indeed welcoming, the scope for blameless variation in speech, need not be bolstered by the absurdly inflated view that "there is no such thing as . . . right and wrong in language." Whether one pronounces *tomato* with a short or a long *a* is a matter partly of taste, partly of choosing whatever will least impede the free interplay of speech and understanding: what will pass unnoticed in a Boston drawing room might well waste time in a Midwestern supermarket. Here the variations are comparable to fluctuations of fashion, and a severe insistence upon the "right" or "wrong" way to pronounce the word—*in vacuo*, as it were, and without reference to the expectations of the hearer—would be both humorless and unjustified. The case is quite different with such a sentence as *The men is home*. In this instance, the grammatical rules of English (or that dialect of English shared by the writer and reader of this work) unequivocally brand the sentence as wrong, ungrammatical. Tolerance and interest in novelty are here beside the point. Treating the man who says *The men is home* (unless he has some abnormal purpose, such as that of mocking a linguistic abuse) as merely eccentric in his habits—like a man who wears his cap back to front—is no more sensible than adopting the same attitude to a child who gets the wrong answer to his sums. We are as justified in using "right" and "wrong" of some matters in a given language (both provisos are important) as we are in arithmetic.

Does the issue matter, except to theorists, locked in high controversy about questions that leave the more naïve speaker indifferent and uncomprehending? Can it make any difference to the primary users of language (those who have no views *about* language) whether they treat deviations as eccentricities rather than breaches of rule? It can and does.

Consider the following parable. In the land of Erewhon, there are, returning travelers say, no games as we know them, governed by fixed rules of play freely accepted. But while the Erewhonians abhor the idea of being fettered in their amusements by arbitrary regulations, they love to *play*. This leads to foreseeable complications. When friends meet to "play at cards," each comes with his own pack, some marked with symbols we should recognize, others inscribed with representations of flowers, animals, or whatever pleases the individual fancy. Endless time is wasted, before play can begin, in arguing *how* to play and what is to count as "winning" for the particular occasion. And even if agreement is reached, the level of skill is deplorably low, for with constantly shifting conventions, there is no chance for theories of strategy to emerge.

Contrast now this babel with the position of anybody in the Western world invited to an evening's bridge. The very definition of the game guarantees that the play will proceed according to predetermined rules and conventions, known to all the players and accepted by all of them as binding. The individual player can count upon the acceptance of the rules (even if he tries to cheat!) in a way that he could not in the case of mere regularities of behaviour. For deviations from regularity must be accepted as brute facts; a breach of a rule has to be *corrected*. The existence and acceptance of the rules of bridge make possible the game as we know it and all the subsidiary activities of theorizing *about* the game, inventing strategies, teaching, and learning it. The game is partly constituted by the rules, *i.e.*, in the absence of rules it would not be what we understand by a *game*.

This parable, with suitable modifications, applies to the more serious business of speech. If the users of a language were not trained to recognize certain ways of speaking as right (correct, grammatical) and others as wrong, human communication would be a more chancy, a less tightly organized, affair than it is.

The view that I am here urging is that the use of a language (like that of any formalized game such as bridge) be recognized as a social practice with a code of demanded observance and an associated background of tradition. To be able to speak a language is to be able to speak it correctly and thereby to enter into the community of those other speakers, alive and dead, who have fashioned it or continue to preserve it while modifying it.

I hope that the following *caveats* will safeguard this view against some of the more obvious misinterpretations:

1. Conforming to a rule (being able to recognize breaches of it) is not the same thing as being able to state the rule: the former is, normally, much easier than the latter. It is the task of grammarians and other theorists of language to state the rules which users of the language learn to respect by imitation and correction. Nor need explicit knowledge of rules improve performance, though it is likely to have *some* effect upon it. By and large, linguistic rules are too complicated to be of much help to the primary users of language.[29] Anybody trying to learn a foreign language from a grammar book that aspires to be really accurate may echo Byron's comment on Coleridge:

> Explaining Metaphysics to the nation,
> I wish he would explain his Explanation.

2. Linguistic rules are not invariable: vocabulary and syntax suffer secular changes. But such changes can only exceptionally be made by fiat or decision. A linguistic innovator needs to modify a tradition, by persuading sufficiently many others to follow his lead. But traditions are notoriously recalcitrant to individual initiative, although revolutions, in styles of thought and expression as well as in political institutions, do occur. That linguistic rules ultimately change makes them, however, no less binding while they are in force.

3. I said before that to be able to speak a language is to be able to speak it correctly. But there are, of course, degrees of correctness, and there is no such thing as speaking a language perfectly. There must always be room, on the frontiers, as it were, even among the best authorities on usage. But a certain minimal conformity to rules of pronunciation, syntax, and meaning is a necessary condition for speaking a language even "badly" or "incorrectly." The idea of somebody "getting everything wrong" while speaking English makes no more sense than that of somebody playing the Moonlight Sonata but never hitting a right note. We recognize "error" by its presence against a background of rule conformity. This is why we cannot sensibly assert or deny

---

[29] If the reader doubts this, let him consult the rules for the use of *that* and *which* to be found in Fowler's *Modern English Usage* or other equally influential guides to correct writing.

that very small children are speaking "correctly." The sounds they produce are closer to expressive animal cries than they are to the highly conventional system that we understand by an adult language.

4. Throughout this discussion, I have been using "rule" in approximately the same sense as "regulation" or "prescription."[30] Now clear cases of regulations, such as the "Rules of the Road," are issued by competent authorities, having the power to enforce penalties for disobedience. It is therefore reasonable to ask for the authority and the power behind the rules which, according to the view proposed here, define "correct English." A child might ask: "Who *says* I must speak in this way? And what happens if I don't?" No doubt he will get poor marks in his schoolwork or get punished in other ways—but that is a poor answer to give anybody looking for some better reason than the power of those arbitrarily and temporarily controlling him.

There is no need to look for an external authority and arbitrary sanctions. Men can bind themselves by rules (as when they freely create a club or society controlled by regulations) or can find themselves already bound by rules through their participation in some social practice. Now this is the position of all those native speakers who reach the point of reflecting upon the nature of their commitment to the defining rules of their native language. They find themselves, as it were, already members of the club (the "speech community") of the speakers of English, or whatever language it may be. They are free, if they wish and can, to cancel their membership by withdrawing from the speech community and ceasing to speak its language; but they cannot remain members in good standing unless they recognize the constitutive rules on the whole. (Compare the absurdity of pretending to play chess while not giving a fig for *any* rule of the game.) For the specific rules of English usage define, at least in part, what it means to speak English. Obedience to the rules on the whole is a necessary condition for mastery of the language. The matter is even clearer when we consider the position of somebody undertaking to learn a *foreign* language, to whose use he is not already committed. Nothing compels me to learn Russian, but if I choose to, I must abide by the rules of Rus-

---

[30]The notion of a "rule" covers a number of importantly different senses. The reader who wishes to pursue this matter further will find a somewhat detailed analysis of various conceptions of rules in Chapter 6 of M. Black, *Models and Metaphors* (Cornell University Press, Ithaca, N.Y., 1962).

sian phonology, syntax, and semantics. For the Russian language *is* essentially the interlocking system of those rules.

It is not fanciful, therefore, to locate the authority behind linguistic rules in the reciprocal demands of the language users. The rules have such force as they have because the members of the relevant speech community (or such of them as are by general consent allowed a special position of authority) impose them upon themselves and others. And they cease to have such imperative force when nobody any longer minds or cares whether they are observed. So long as *some* people strongly object to the expression "He ain't," that can hardly count as "good or correct English," but a day may come when this seems no longer objectionable—and then the scope or range of "correct English" will have changed.

As for the sanctions discouraging and punishing abuses of "correct English," they are serious enough. Of course there are, happily enough, no legal punishments—even though some pedants might wish they existed. But there *is* a penalty for deviation from the norm of correct usage—the risk of misunderstanding. And that may be serious indeed, if something important turns upon mutual understanding (as in the case of the misread message that sent the Light Brigade on their fatal and pointless charge). Irresponsible divergence from the norm of correct usage introduces uncertainty into the message: we must pay special attention to the utterances of a child (Does he mean his father when he says "Da"?), a foreigner (What *could* he mean by saying he was "pulling my arm"?), or the kind of babbler who says whatever comes into his head—whereas the ideal of successful communication is to pass smoothly from the words to their meanings. Incorrect and careless speakers bleed their remarks of meaning in a way tending to corrupt and degrade language—to reduce it to a series of noises that mean anything or nothing. The ultimate "sanction" of correct usage, of conformity to the rules of the language, is the common interest of all members of the speech community in preserving the integrity and efficiency of the linguistic institution.

5. The foregoing analysis of the importance of the rules of standard English, or any other language, is not intended to be a defense of mindless conformity or a blanket *apologia* for linguistic conservatism. From one standpoint, the efficiency of language—to which I have several times referred—may be conceived as its swiftest intelligibility to the largest number of hearers. But this ideal, all too happily endorsed by advertisers, politicians, and other corrupters of intelli-

gence, tends to reduce language to its lowest common denominator. If he who runs can read, then what he understands must be precious little. (Any language that is widely used tends to hand on its slogans and clichés.) It is therefore not without reason that a poet refers to "the perpetually changing, muddied, maid-of-all-work, our *common language*,"[31] or half-despairingly describes his own medium, language, as "a public instrument, a collection of traditional and irrational terms and rules, fantastically created and transformed, fantastically codified, heard and uttered in many different ways."[32] The poet's predicament is, to a lesser degree, that of any serious speaker: the need to communicate *his* individual meaning through the battered medium of overworked words. Here the individual speaker's interest in conveying a special meaning appropriate to a unique occasion may well conflict with his general interest in maintaining the overall efficiency of the entire institution. Hence the efforts of poets and writers to renew language by *changing* it. But the bright novelties of one decade are likely to seem as dated as L'Art Nouveau nearly always becomes.

Fortunately, the rule-governed character of language, which I have been emphasizing in the last few pages, is compatible with, indeed demands, a wide exercise of initiative and choice by the individual speaker.

What Is Language? (*A Landing Stage*)

The extraordinarily ramified network of skills, habits, actions, conventions, understandings, which we bundle together under the label of "language," is too complex to admit of any simple summary. Consequently, my discussion, throughout this work, is unavoidably somewhat diffuse. The reader may therefore welcome, at this point, an attempt to highlight some of the more important "design-features" (some already discussed, others to be discussed later) exemplified by all clear cases of what we usually call languages.

I shall not try to provide a formal definition of "language" on the classical model of identifying its "essence" by distinguishing it from other things within a wider class (definition by "genus" and "differentia"); for this is probably impossible. My intention is the more modest one of directing attention to certain features, none of them individually necessary, which,

---

[31]Paul Valéry in *Essays on Language and Literature*, ed., J. L. Hevesi, Allan Wingate, London, 1947, p. 111.
[32]Valéry, p. 91.

when present together in sufficient strength, constitute what we should unhesitatingly describe as a language.[33]

1. *Language is rooted in speech.* I mean that nothing counts as a language in the fullest and clearest sense, unless it includes the production, reception, and interpretation of sounds originating in the "speech-tracts" of organisms.[34] This excludes secondary systems such as writing, Morse code, or the "hand-language" of the deaf,[35] which all in one way or another are parasitic upon or substitutes for a full language.

Two related points are worth stressing in this connection: speech is both economical and evanescent. A trivial amount of energy expended by a speaker produces comparatively massive changes in the hearer: spoken words have a "triggering" effect. (The ease with which words of some sort can be produced is responsible for the extreme loquacity of our culture and its high degree of "verbalization," with all its advantages and penalties.) On the other hand, a speech signal perishes as soon as it is produced. (Hence the need for "redundancy" in language and much else that we shall have occasion to discuss.) Thus, the transition from evanescent sound-signals to relatively permanent substitutes in the form of script—and, in recent times, tape recordings—marks a radical revolution in culture.

2. *The speech-act is directed, reversible, and self-regulating.* Speech is a social activity: it requires, in Samuel Butler's phrase, a "sayer" and a "sayee." (All speech begins in dialogue, though it easily declines into monologue.) In this, it resembles other social acts of cooperation or interplay, such as fighting, playing games, or making love. It differs from some such social acts, however, in being directed ("sent") to a particular receiver.[36] More important is the fact that the roles of speaker and hearer are interchangeable: we know what it would be like to be receiving the very same message

---

[33]A reader interested in the theory underlying this type of "range-definition" may wish to consult M. Black, *Problems of Analysis* (Cornell University Press, Ithaca, N.Y., 1954), pp. 24–37.

[34]For earlier discussion of the "primacy of speech," see above, pp. 13–14.

[35]See, for instance, William C. Stokoe, Jr., et al., *A Dictionary of American Sign Language on Linguistic Principles* (Gallaudet College Press, Washington, D.C., 1965). This careful and systematic presentation of the basic gestures and "grammar" of the "hand-language" of the deaf is very instructive for the light it sheds upon the importance of full speech and the deprivations resulting from its absence.

[36]Public notices, books, etc., addressed to "Whomever they may concern," are derivative from the primary situations in which we talk to an identified somebody.

that we send. Furthermore, we hear ourselves speak, while we speak—are constantly subject to "feedback." On this fundamental fact depends our capacity to think and feel ourselves into the situation of the other and in this way to establish the requisite community of understanding.[37]

3. *Language is an institution.* Behind the individual speaker there stands the *speech community* to which he belongs, with its massive resources of tradition and shared modes of life. The speaker inherits a social practice in the form of conventions and rules, from which he can deviate, but which he cannot ignore: speech is *rule-governed* activity.[38] With this is connected, as in the case of such other human institutions as the family, the law, warfare, etc., the arbitrariness and conventionality of the constitutive rules. Traditions, customs, practices, institutions are necessarily arbitrary to a degree, just because they are human creations.[39] Hence, also, the need to learn language: man is not born speaking, and will remain dumb if deprived of the proper social initiation.

4. *Language is a particulate system.* Any known language is constructed of ultimate particles ("phonemes") subject to intricate rules for composition. As explained in previous sections, the combination of the linguistic particles occurs at two markedly different levels: a finite stock of discrete phonemes combine, more or less arbitrarily,[40] into indefinitely many meaningful linguistic molecules (morphemes, words); these in turn, morphologically assorted into "parts of speech," can combine into indefinitely many sentences, of endlessly varied forms. (And any fuller account must at least recognize the more subtle relations between sentences and their components that belong to logic rather than to grammar.)[41]

---

[37]Experiments in which the speaker is artificially deprived of "feedback" show a marked degeneration of the speech act. For the consequences of breakdown of "interchangeability," consider the difficulties of communication between different generations of the same culture or between members of radically different cultures. The principle is: "I don't really understand what you are saying unless I can *imagine* saying it myself."

[38]See the previous section, pp. 67–76, for fuller discussion of this point.

[39]Primitive analogues of linguistic institutions can be found in many species of animals. Bird song must be taught to fledglings, and the patterns of animal cries have to be transmitted by indoctrination to each successive generation.

[40]But see my previous remarks on the restrictions upon phoneme association that are characteristic for any given language.

[41]See the further discussion of logic and its relation to grammar in Chapter 4.

This feature of the linguistic system deserves the utmost emphasis. It sets off a language in the fullest sense from such partial analogues as "animal languages." It is responsible for what I have discussed under the rubric of the "productive aspect of language." It permits a competent speaker to liberate himself from the "tyranny of the immediate present"—to say what has never been said before, to record what no longer exists, and to imagine what may never happen. It is the indispensable condition for history, science, and imaginative literature. "No difference between man and beast is more important than syntax" (Herbert Read).

5. *Language is meaningful.* It is designed to *express* the thoughts, wishes, attitudes, feelings, etc., of the speaker; to *evoke* similar or complementary echoes in the hearer; and it connects, at least part of the time, with a "world" that surrounds both speaker and hearer. Which is, of course, to say very little without further elucidation, some of which will be supplied in later chapters. (But no topic in our syllabus is more difficult than this one.)

6. *Language is plastic.* To a professional student of language, a linguistic system can often appear as exceptionally self-contained and, as it were, rigid. But this represents, at best, an approximation or a half-truth. The seemingly inflexible rules of linguistic performance are subject to a constant strain, due partly to the inevitable hazards of accidental deviations in thousands of cases from the prescribed norms; but also more fundamentally to the perennial tensions between the simplified, standardized, stipulations of the speech community and the interests of the individual speaker in serving his own specific and often deviant purposes. According to one's point of view, language can appear as one of the most rigid or one of the most malleable of human institutions.

CHAPTER 4

THOUGHT AND LANGUAGE

THE GROUND TO BE COVERED

IN THIS CHAPTER I propose to discuss a number of elusive but important questions concerning the relations between words and ideas. Bluff common sense is inclined to say, somewhat impatiently, that words should be treated merely as an indispensable means for expressing and transmitting thought. Sensible men, it seems, will treat words with scant respect, directing their intelligence and energy to ideas, rather than their verbal embodiment. Yet the relations between words and ideas are too intimate for this hearty approach to prove satisfactory. We are compelled, in the service of theoretical understanding and practical control, to raise profound questions about the logical relations between words and ideas. I shall, after a preliminary discussion of this basic issue, proceed to consider certain widely held and influential views concerning the alleged influence of the structure of a language upon the modes of thought of an entire culture (the so-called Whorf Hypothesis). From another perspective, the delicate issues evoked may be somewhat illuminated by considering the function of logic, both "formal" and "informal," in controlling and facilitating the processes of thought.

Thinking and Speaking

DEFINING THE ISSUES

The words a speaker uses in an utterance are one thing; the thought "behind the words" is another. The words may be adequate or inadequate to the thought; the speaker may wish to conceal at least part of his thought; and so on. It is natural, therefore, to ask about the relations between the two. Are they to be regarded as mutually independent, so that any thought might in theory be matched with any utterance? Or is the relation between the two closer and more intimate?

Before trying to offer even the crudest answers, it will be as well to raise some preliminary questions about the meaning of these large and imprecise questions. One way of understanding a question about the relation between one thing and another is in terms of their *causal* interactions. Taken in this way, the issue about the relations between thinking and speaking resembles a question about the relations between poverty and crime. We are then asking how far "thought" gives rise to speech and, still more interestingly, how far speech, in its turn, can causally influence thought. Some questions of this form will be considered in the next division of this chapter.

Another and more fundamental way of understanding the traffic between thinking and speaking concerns the *logical* relations between the two. Thus understood, our question resembles a question concerning the relations between a map and the terrain mapped. Indeed, it might plausibly be taken to be a special case of that question. A typical sub-question might then concern the possibility of "pure thought"— thought unexpressed in language or in any other symbolism. Again, we might wonder whether *thought* and *language*, however distinct, might not be "polar concepts" such as *husband* and *wife*, to take a much simpler analogue, providing complementary views of one and the same complex phenomenon. Such questions are quite distinct from those concerning causal influence, previously instanced.

So understood, the questions we have raised may seem somewhat remote from any practical interest. Yet our conception of the nature of language will be profoundly affected by any explicit or implicit stand we take on this matter of logical relationship. And so, less directly, will be our attitudes to such specific issues as the proper place of language teaching in education, the relative importance of textual studies in literature, the justification of propaganda, and much else.

Before embarking upon these troubled waters, we must linger a while longer to consider some duplicities of the key terms "thinking" and "thought." We can distinguish the following three, distinct but related, uses:

1. To refer to some ill-defined and vaguely delineated *process*, contrasted, for instance, with "hoping," "wishing," "daydreaming," and other "mental processes." The word is used in this sense when we say, "I am thinking about what to do," or, perhaps, "I am still thinking about what you said." In such cases, there is, typically, no ready answer to the supplementary question, *What* are you thinking? We are dealing with what might be called a *non-specifying* use of "thinking."

2. Sometimes, however, we do use "thought" or its cognate, "thinking," to refer to a definite mental episode, occurring at some particular time. We say: "The thought flashed across my mind—'he's dead!' " or, "I was thinking to myself, 'That's a strange thing to say,' but of course I didn't say so." In such examples, "thought" and "thinking" may be said to be used in an *episodic* sense, the reference being to some definite mental episode or event in a particular speaker's biography. Such "episodic" thoughts, as here understood, will be true or false—will have "truth-value." (I am ignoring, at least for the time being, more amorphous mental episodes.)

3. Finally, we shall need to recognize a use of "thought" to pick out what might be called the *cognitive kernel* of certain remarks. We say "I think *that he will come*" or "I thought *that I saw a bear* (but I was mistaken)" or "We both agree *that he should be given another chance.*" In each of these cases, the "thought" in question is identified by a clause commencing with the word "that" (a "that-clause"). Here we have, in what might be called a *propositional* sense of "thought," something more abstract than thinking as a process or as an episode. A propositional thought, expressed by a that-clause (or in the form of a complete sentence) can be shared by more than one person. And a thought, in this sense, is internal to its expression: to ask a man who has said "It's four o'clock" whether he thought it was four o'clock when he said so, could only mean that we took him to have been mistaken; it is clearly not a substantive question as to whether his utterance was backed by an episode of thinking: his saying what he did counts, by convention, as his having the propositional thought in question.

Of the three senses now at our disposal, the second and third are the more clearly relevant, though in different ways, to our initial question about the logical relations between thought and speech. And any answer we give will obviously depend upon which of the senses we choose to emphasize. It is one thing to ask the question about a thought (propositional sense) already identified by its adequate verbal expression in the form of a that-clause. It is another when we are considering less precise, possibly confused or inchoate, thought-episodes. But in either case, we are dealing, for present purposes, with "thoughts" (in either sense) that *can be put into words*. If it makes sense to talk about "thoughts too deep for words" we must here regretfully decide to ignore them. (Which is not to deny that thoughts might be suitably expressed in some non-linguistic medium. But if they are, they are potentially expressible in language also.)

TWO HERESIES ABOUT THE RELATIONS BETWEEN THOUGHT AND LANGUAGE

Two extreme positions, both much alive, in spite of their paradoxical flavour, will define the range of our own choice. The first is, approximately, an assertion of the complete separability of thought and its linguistic expression. A potential speaker can have a thought, it is claimed, before there is any question of how it is to be expressed: the relation between a thought and its outward manifestation is, in this respect, like the relation between a human body and its clothes. A body is what it is, quite independently of any suit that may cover it; and a thought is what it is, quite independently of its verbal dress. We may call this *the model of the garment*.

The second view flatly rejects this conception: to think of a "thought" as separable from its linguistic manifestation is as absurd as to imagine a human being without his body. Talk about a thought is just talk, from another perspective, about a certain kind of verbal complex. The relation between a thought and its verbal expression is like that between a melody and its embodiment in actual sounds: the same melody, transposed into different keys or played on different instruments, still retains its identity, but the idea of a melody separate from any acoustic representation is an absurdity. This might be called *the model of the melody*.

Thought is to speech as body to garment; thought is to speech as melody to sound: which of these conceptions is the better? This is like asking whether it is better to think of men as animals or as spirits: they are both and neither, as we please. Here there is no question of some objectively certifiable allegation of fact, but rather of a more or less fruitful comparison. (And that is why I have spoken of the rival conceptions as "models.") The decision to be made is whether it conduces better to understanding and illumination, on the whole, to emphasize the analogy between language and a separable garment—or whether more insight is to be expected from stressing thought's likeness to something intrinsic to its expression, like a melody. We might hope, in the long run, for perspectives more adequate than either of these (and the reader may be reminded here of the variety of approaches outlined in the first chapter); but if we must choose now, the model of the melody is preferable to that of the garment. My reasons for saying so I shall now try to explain.

MEANINGS IN THE MIND

An examination of the vast literature concerning the nature of language will show that discussion of this subject has been dominated for at least 2,000 years by what I have been calling the model of the garment.

The picture of the function of speech that emerges is both simple and plausible. A speaker's thoughts, as I have said, are taken to be logically quite separate from the words in which he clothes them. Hence, in speaking, his task is to express those thoughts—or, as some writers would prefer to say now, to "encode" them—in adequate words. And the hearer's task is the reverse one of passing from the words he hears to thoughts corresponding as closely as possible to those of the original speaker (to "decode" the message). Successful communication involves this double transformation of thoughts into words, and words back again into thoughts.

If speech is regarded in this way, it is natural, though not essential, to regard the speaker's original thought as the *meaning* of his verbal message. Taking this further step, innumerable writers have adhered to a conception of "meanings in the mind"—meanings that have to be transformed into audible or visible substitutes for transmission to the mind of another.

Thus we find Aristotle saying:

Spoken words are the *symbols of mental experience* and written words are the symbols of spoken words.[1]

Locke says:

[1] Hermeneia, 1, 16a2f, quoted from I. M. Bochenski, *A History of Formal Logic*, University of Notre Dame Press, Notre Dame, Ind., 1961, p. 48. Italics added.

. . . words, in their primary or immediate signification, stand for nothing but *the ideas in the mind of him that uses them,* how imperfectly soever or carelessly those ideas are collected from the things which they are supposed to represent (*Essay Concerning Human Understanding,* bk. iii, ch. ii, sec. 2, italics in original).

Similar ideas constantly recur in modern times. Collingwood says:

Understanding what some one says to you is thus attributing to him the idea which his words arouse in yourself . . . (R. G. Collingwood, *The Principles of Art,* The Clarendon Press, Oxford, 1938, p. 250).

And another modern philosopher of a different persuasion says:

Meanings are commonly conveyed by language; by series of ink-marks or of sounds. But it would at best be doubtful that meaning arises through communication or that verbal formulation is essential. Presumably the meanings to be expressed must *come before* the linguistic expression of them, however much the development of language may operate retroactively to modify the meanings entertained (C. I. Lewis, *An Analysis of Knowledge and Valuation,* Open Court, LaSalle, Ill., 1946, p. 72, italics added).

So it goes, in one text after another.

Thoughts "come before" the words in which they are clothed; words mean the speaker's thoughts that gave rise to them. A thorough examination of these important contentions would be impracticable here. I must confine myself to a few remarks that may help to explain why this dominant conception, so powerful for 2,000 years, is gradually losing its appeal.

Obviously, there must be some approximation to adequacy in a conception that has appealed for so long to so many diverse thinkers of the first rank. The common admonition to "Think before you speak!" implicitly testifies to the possibility of thinking *before* one speaks, and to the difference between speaking "thoughtlessly" or "realizing and meaning everything one says." Nor need we suppose that the thought that sometimes precedes speech itself takes the form of silent speech, as if every speaker had to rehearse to himself what he then proceeded to expose in public. Even when we do soliloquize in this way, it is rare for complete grammatical sentences to be used; everybody has his own argot of truncated words, sketched phrases, kines-thetic and visual images.[2] Silent speech is idiosyncratic—a kind of mental shorthand barely intelligible to another. (Compare the indecipherability of the scrawled notes and symbols that a thinker will record for his own benefit.) We must also recognize the existence and importance of still less articulate mental episodes in which the thinker gropes for expression and is swayed by dimly perceived intimations of significance, or promising roads to solution.

To deny all this, or its relevance to formal expression, would be closing one's eyes to an entire range of fascinating experience. But it would be a serious conceptual error to suppose that such varied mental activity must precede or ac-company speech; or to suppose that in the absence of such mental accompaniment, words lose their "life" and become meaningless; or that the meaning of words is to be sought in the "inner drama" played in the privacy of the speaker's mind.

It is, in the first place, preposterous to imagine that rapid speech is *always* accompanied by a parallel flow of mental images or "thoughts." A lecturer thoroughly familiar with his subject, an advocate skilfully developing an argument ex-tempore, are prime examples of speakers who "mean what they say."[3] Yet it would be altogether unplausible, as such speakers will confirm from their own introspection, to sup-pose that the flow of rapid speech is invariably accompanied by a parallel stream of "mental" events. Speech needs no mental correlate in order to be meaningful.

What is there to show, it may be asked, that the spoken words *are* meaningful, in a case where they are unaccompa-nied by the "mental drama"? Well, for one thing, there are the subsequent uses that the speaker can make of his utter-

---

[2]So far as I can trust my own introspection, thinking about the next move in a game of chess can take the form of a series of schematic images of possible positions, with the possible movements of the pieces appearing as imagined shifts in position. Verbal images appear to play almost no part. Yet it would be easy to *translate* this sequence of images into full sentences. A psychologist, himself a strong player, claims that "chess-thinking is typically non-verbal." But he does not deny that such thinking is in symbols. (Adrianus D. de Groot, *Thought and Choice in Chess*, Mouton, The Hague, 1965, p. 335.)

[3]Cf. the anecdote of the girl who, on being told to "think before she spoke," replied, "How do I know what I think until I hear what I say?" Her situation is not unusual: one important function of verbal expres-sion is to reveal to the author *what* he thinks. He thinks *in* speaking or writing: as Wittgenstein liked to say, one can think with a pen as well as in one's head.

ance. When he can comment upon what he said, elaborate it, defend it against objections, cite illustrations, and so on, that is excellent evidence that he meant and understood what he said. It is also excellent evidence of *what* his meaning was. (Where such a process of defense, elaboration, application fails, there is sufficient evidence of the thoughtless or meaningless use of words.) The "life" of the words, we might say, is not in some supposed mental afflatus, but rather in the capacity of the particular utterance to interact with, and to provide a point of departure for, further symbolic activity.

Finally, a dogmatic attempt to locate meaning in some supposed feature of mental acts is practically useless and theoretically pernicious. To seek the meaning of words in something supposedly occurring in the privacy of the speaker's mind is pointless. For if, by some miracle of technology, we could have access to the verbal and other images in the speaker's mind, we should still have to *interpret* those images before we could grasp the meaning: a "private," mental language is still a *language*.[4] And if we succeeded in translating the private language into, say English, we should still be faced with the problem of understanding *that*. Renewed recourse to mental scrutiny would get us no further. (Which is of course not to deny the value of an author's commentary upon his own writing. But such commentary will be ineffective unless expressed in words that are intelligible to another.) Focusing upon fleeting images and thoughts in the mind will not reveal meaning, whether to ourselves or to our hearers. It may, however, serve the purpose of emphasizing the inadequacy of the words we have used and lead to a search for better expression.

What is "theoretically pernicious" about this model is the support it gives to inclinations, always strong, to evade the difficult search for the meanings *in* words, in favour of an exploration of the never-never land of "mental life." Thus, instead of renewed attempts at a rich and imaginative understanding of the text before us, whether it be a casual utterance or a poem, we get speculative theories, usually impossible to verify, about "what is really going on" in the

[4]This point was clearly understood by medieval writers on language. "For medieval logicians this 'meaning' was a content of an individual mind, an inner utterance in an immaterial language; Ockham took this idea of mental language and its structure so seriously and so naïvely that he tries to determine which parts of speech, and which grammatical attributes like voice, case, and number, are to be found in the mental language." (P. T. Geach, *Reference and Generality*, Cornell University Press, Ithaca, N.Y., 1962, p. 54.)

speaker's mind, or about the motives that led him to say what he did. And thus attention is diverted from what in the end really matters, the articulated expression of thought. Of course, I do not wish to deny the value, if tactfully used, of knowledge about the author's life, the provenance of his literary work, the circumstances of composition, and all the other information that is the staple of those who write about the background of literature. Nor do I underestimate the technical and other difficulties of the policy of staying close to the text and constantly returning to it after explorations of the "background."

I have been recommending here a conception of thought as *immanent* or indwelling in its adequate symbolic expression. (The model of the melody.) Whether it is as illuminating as I think, the reader must decide for himself, bearing in mind always the platitude that a model is only a model; and that no model can be a substitute for the hard work of delineating and responding to the meaning of actual "texts."

LANGUAGE AS A HARNESS FOR THOUGHT

All thought, I have been arguing, strives toward symbolic and, ultimately, linguistic expression. Indeed, in the end, it is hardly possible to distinguish between thought and its verbal manifestation. A man is free to speak or not, as he pleases, free also to choose the words that satisfy him; yet the linguistic medium that he must use is "out there" and given, beyond his power to modify at will. However much the speaker may wish to express *his own* thought, he must make do with a social instrument, fashioned for other purposes than individual expression and often recalcitrant to personal desire. Hence the repeated revolts of great writers against the constraints and limitations of the language of their day. Those who write in the style of their fathers find it hard to avoid repeating their fathers' mistakes. Language, one might say, has a kind of inertia that limits the speaker's freedom to project a distinctive meaning; words, for all their flexibility, mean at any given time what they have come to mean through repeated use and the writer or speaker must do the best he can with these worn counters.[5]

[5]How galling this will be must depend upon the speaker's interest in spontaneity: in highly conventional situations, like the initial salutation of a letter, conventional formulas are a convenience. Yet I have known a man who could not bring himself to write "Sincerely yours" and ended his letter with "Am I sincere? Of course!" (But this device could easily become an affectation.)

Language constrains thought most plainly by the scope of what might be called the available vocabulary, the stock of words and phrases that will be readily understood by the intended hearer or reader. Obsolescent or unfamiliar words like *conspue, subfusc,* or *irenic,* however vivid or appropriate, can only be used for special effects: a writer who indulges in too many of them will lose his audience. This working vocabulary, amounting to no more than a few thousand words in all, is, however, based upon a crude analysis and classification of experience. It registers, as it were, a lowest common denominator of response.

While the eye can distinguish millions of different shades (and specialists have an elegant scheme for analyzing the "colour-solid" along the three dimensions of "hue," "intensity," and "saturation"), the simple colour words of ordinary discourse are only a handful, in somewhat haphazard logical relations. Of course, a skilled writer can convey a vivid characterization of a particular shade, but he has to take special pains to do so, relying upon simile or other figures of speech. But to "work hard" much of the time defeats the purpose of communication. Even more obvious defects of the "available vocabulary" can be seen in the realm of feelings and sentiments, where we must make do, for the most part, with such crude labels as "jealousy," "hatred," or "love" to indicate an incomparably more varied and more complex set of resemblances, oppositions, and relationships.[6]

More insidious is the extent to which the use of familiar words or expressions commits speaker and hearer alike to the acceptance of dubious presuppositions.[7] For the items in the "available vocabulary" of a given group at a given epoch

[6]Can anything be done to improve the situation? Probably not much. The reductive pressures of daily intercourse are too strong to offer much hope for the introduction of more adequate language. The best that can be expected, on the whole, is a more general awareness of the crude simplifications of the common vocabulary—and a greater familiarity with the works in which the great poets and scientists, in their different ways, highlight the complexities of human experience.

[7]One example, which can serve for many, is the stubborn fondness of spokesmen of the U.S. State Department for the phrase "Sino-Soviet bloc," long after the conflict between Russia and China was plainly visible. Arthur M. Schlesinger, Jr., records in his book *A Thousand Days* (Houghton Mifflin, Company, Boston, 1965, p. 415) some unavailing efforts to abolish this misleading usage. It would be hard to decide here whether a mistaken view generates the misleading cliché or vice versa. It is a safe guess that the availability and acceptability of the phrase at least facilitate the "thought." Think of the embarrassment that would result from its prohibition and the consequent need to think afresh.

typically embody far-reaching theories *about* the phenomena represented. For instance, to talk in the popular pseudo-Freudian jargon about "complexes," "repressions," and "unconscious motivations" is to accept, without examination, much dubious and unexamined psychological doctrine.

Behind such effects as these, we can dimly discern and guess at more general influences exercised upon thought by the overall pattern of a given language. Here we approach a theme that has received much attention in this century.

Language and World-View

INFLUENCE OF LANGUAGE UPON THOUGHT

Does the overall structure of a language channel the thoughts of its users in some far-reaching way? A number of distinguished thinkers have thought so. Some have gone so far as to claim that an entire metaphysics is embodied in a given language. Georg Christoph Lichtenberg said, "Our false philosophy is incorporated in the whole of language; we cannot reason without, so to speak, reasoning wrongly. We don't realize that to speak, no matter about what, is to philosophize." Similar views have been expressed by thinkers as powerful, though as diverse in their views, as von Humboldt, Cassirer, and Wittgenstein. The last was fond of saying that a given language is a "form of life."[8]

Languages can differ very strikingly in their vocabularies and grammars. Hence, if a distinctive "philosophy" or worldview is associated with a given language, we should expect the corresponding "world-view" to vary widely from one culture to another. Many anthropologists, impressed by the great diversity of the ways in which various societies solve their problems, find this corollary congenial. It seems to confirm the widely held view that human societies somehow "construct" the world of social experience out of a relatively undifferentiated and unstructured continuum. The following remarks are typical:

> Any language is more than an instrument for the conveying of ideas, more even than an instrument for working upon the feelings of others and for self-expression. Every language is

[8]See, for instance, his *Philosophical Investigations*, Basil Blackwell & Mott, Ltd., Oxford, 1953, pp. 8, 11.

also a means of categorizing experience. What people think and feel, and how they report what they think and feel, is determined, to be sure, by their individual physiological state, by their personal history, and by what actually happens in the outside world. But it is *also determined by a factor which is often overlooked; namely, the pattern of linguistic habits which people have acquired as members of a particular society*. The events of the "real" world are never felt or reported as a machine would do it. There is a selection process and an interpretation in the very act of response. Some features of the external situation are highlighted; others are ignored or not fully discriminated.[9]

Even skeptical critics find this initially plausible. And there is an appealing romantic charm about the idea of freedom to respond to "reality" in a variety of styles, reflecting different, but perhaps equally valid, modes of thoughts and feelings. We are all "relativists" nowadays and belief in "universal laws of Reason" or absolutes of any sort is likely to be regarded as dogmatic.

For one thing, even a slight acquaintance with different languages confirms the suspicion that a language is more than a neutral reflection of some independently given "external world"—more like a distorting mirror than a sheet of unflawed glass. For instance, an English reader has the feeling, confirmed by experts, that the "world" somehow looks and feels different if one thinks and writes about it in Russian. (A shift of view that eludes even the best translators and makes foreign fiction sound neither authentically English— nor authentically anything else.) We are not surprised to be told that the Malay language is "poetical, metaphorical, happier with proverbs than with abstract constatations" in a way that is "entirely fitted to the needs of a people concerned with the concrete processes of everyday living—fishing, gathering fruit and coconuts, begetting children, lying in the sun."[10] Again, it seems altogether natural to learn that a clas-

[9] Clyde Kluckhohn and Dorothea Leighton, *The Navaho*, Harvard University Press, Cambridge, Mass., 1946, p. 197. Italics added.

[10] Anthony Burgess, *Language Made Plain*, English Universities Press, London, 1964, p. 167. But Burgess goes on to mention "A new world of words, bewildering to the peasant," based largely upon borrowings from Arabic, Portuguese, and English, introduced for commercial and administrative purposes. "Cultures" are rarely as uniform as the outsider is inclined to think, and imputed correlations between language and "world-view" are correspondingly precarious.

sical language, such as Hebrew, offers a distinct resistance to its adaptation for the purposes of a modern society.[11]

But how are these vague, if stimulating, ideas about the "genius of a language" (to use an old-fashioned expression) to be rendered precise enough for verification? Is the "influence" of a language upon the thoughts and attitudes of its users to be ascribed to the distinctive nature of its vocabulary,[12] its commonplace expressions, the associations of "unconscious use," the tang and rhythm of ordinary speech, to syntactical structure? And how are we to tell? For provoking and controversial answers, I turn to the views of Benjamin Lee Whorf.

> . . . . the background linguistic system (in other words, the grammar) of each language is not merely a reproducing instrument for voicing ideas but rather is itself the shaper of ideas, the program and guide for the individual's mental activity, for his analysis of impressions, for his synthesis of his mental stock in trade. Formulation of ideas is not an independent process, strictly rational in the old sense, but is part of a particular grammar, and differs, from slightly to greatly, between different grammars. We dissect nature along lines laid down by our native languages. The categories and types that we isolate from the world of phenomena we do not find there because they stare every observer in the face; on the contrary, the world is presented in a kaleidoscopic flux of impressions which has to be organized by our minds—and this means largely by the linguistic systems in our minds. We cut nature up, organize it into concepts, and ascribe significances as we do, largely because we are parties to an agreement to organize it in this way—an agreement that holds throughout our speech community and is codified in the patterns of our language. The agreement is, of course, an implicit and unstated one, BUT ITS TERMS ARE ABSOLUTELY

[11]See, for instance, the charming article, "Reflections on Two Languages" (*Midstream*, New York, vol. xii, no. 8, October, 1966), by Aharon Megged, a distinguished writer and native speaker of Hebrew. Comparing Hebrew with Yiddish, Megged ascribes the "resistance" of Hebrew to its powerful "aristocratic" associations with ritual and holiness. If the Israelis had chosen to speak Yiddish, their "modes of thought and behavior would be different." For "the structure of a Yiddish sentence, the manner of its pronunciation, the linguistic associations, the flavor of each individual word are so remote from Hebrew" (p. 36). Similarly, one might speculate about how different life would be in the United States if everyone spoke Spanish.

[12]Each language contains words especially hard to translate, that seem to embody some distinctive and central concept of the culture. Cf., for instance, *on* in Japanese (very roughly: an obligation, burdensome to receive, demanding a reciprocal and balancing moral transfer); or *philotimo* in Greek (very roughly, again: self-esteem).

OBLIGATORY; we cannot talk at all except by subscribing to the organization and classification of data which the agreement decrees.[13]

The program formulated here would have little interest but for the attempts that Whorf made to apply it to specific American Indian languages, and notably to Hopi.[14] Let us see how the Hopi think about the universe, according to Whorf. They do not emphasize temporal relations, as Europeans do; nor do they make our familiar distinctions between time and space; instead they think in terms of two grand categories (which Whorf labels MANIFESTING and MANIFESTED), that may be roughly conceived as "subjective" and "objective." The subjective realm, that embraces the as yet unrealized future, is conceived as a spiritual domain of "burgeoning" and "fermenting" activity, embracing natural and animal phenomena as well as human behaviour; the "objective" realm consists, as it were, of the unchanging deposit, in the past and present, of this universal psychic activity. (Perhaps the relation between life and history is conceived on the model of a potter's design-in-the-head and the unchanging artifact that he ultimately produces? If all this seems unsatisfyingly vague to the reader, he must be referred to Whorf's own writings for further detail.) The Hopi, we are told, think of reality mainly as composed of *events,* eschewing the emphasis upon subject and predicate built into Indo-European language and thought. Objectively, events are identified by such features as outlines, colours, and types of movement; subjectively as "the expression of invisible intensity factors, on which depend their stability and persistence, or their fugitiveness and proclivities."[15]

Even in so crude a summary of the more detailed and more suggestive accounts supplied by Whorf and other anthropologists, a sympathetic reader may darkly discern un-

[13]John B. Carroll, ed., *Language, Thought and Reality: Selected Writings of Benjamin Lee Whorf,* The M.I.T. Press, Cambridge, Mass., 1956, pp. 212–214. Capitals in original.

[14]Benjamin Lee Whorf (1897–1941) was a greatly gifted amateur linguist, described by those who knew him as a "near-genius," by profession an engineer specializing in fire prevention, by avocation a linguist, anthropologist, and philosopher of language. His theories about the Hopi world-view were almost exclusively based upon information supplied by a single speaker of Hopi living in New York. (He paid a short visit to the Arizona Hopi reservation later.) Whorf undoubtedly achieved an extraordinary *tour de force* in reconstructing, on so narrow a basis, an interpretation of Hopi thought and culture that competent experts have praised for its faithfulness and insight.

[15]In Carroll, *Whorf,* p. 147.

familiar ways of patterning the universe, remote from our own familiar distinctions between past, present, and future, between "mental" and "physical"—and the like. But it is hard for even the most sympathetic reader to know how deeply such sophisticated renderings of a "world-view" really influence the thought ways of philosophically unsophisticated users of the language. (How many English speakers recognize the shards of Aristotelian metaphysics preserved in such words as "essence," "specific," "substance," "entity," and the like?) And when we come to the supposed linguistic "reflections" of the delineated "world-view," the course of the argument becomes dubious indeed. Writers who share Whorf's general views about the relations between grammar and culture are apt to draw inferences from selected grammatical features, emphasizing some as significant while neglecting others as irrelevant. But no firm criterion has ever been offered for such discrimination. One anthropologist, for instance, will discover the notion of the "given as undifferentiated content"[16] built into certain general features of the nouns of a given language. The Wintu use the same word for *red, redness,* and *red-mass;* "the care which we bestow on the distinction of number is lavished by the Wintu on the distinction between particular and generic";[17] and this distinction, in turn, is regarded by them as "subjective." Well, this interesting way of handling ultimate categories may indeed be characteristic of Wintu thought, for all that any outsider can tell; but it may be doubted whether it would ever have been discovered as a "reflection" in their grammar if the theorist had not already known what he expected to find. So long as communication between members of radically different cultures remains as crude as it is apt to be at best,[18] the perception of patterns of thought embodied in the formal

[16]Dorothy Lee, "Linguistic Reflection of Wintu Thought," in her *Freedom and Culture,* Prentice-Hall, Inc., Englewood Cliffs, N.J., 1959, p. 122.

[17]Lee, p. 122.

[18]"If the Wintu offers me an English word in translation for a Wintu one, I rarely have any way of knowing exactly what the word means to him. When he says that *watca* is to *weep,* for example, is he, like me, thinking of the whole kinesthetic activity with all its emotional implications, or is he merely concerned with the sound of keening, as I think he is?" (Lee, p. 126.) (And here one may wonder what Miss Lee means by "keening"!) Yet this frank recognition of limitation is immediately followed by a sentence which runs: "Whenever I find a group of words derived from the same root, *I can clearly see* that they point to a preoccupation with form alone" (italics added). What is thus "clearly seen" by some will seem murky enough to others.

structure of a language will remain a controversial and speculative exercise. And even if some reliable procedures for conducting this kind of investigation were to be evolved, it would be a further and a very difficult step to argue from such formal features to the existence of causal influence upon the thought habits of the language users. (The existence of diverse philosophical systems, all expressed with equal facility in such a language as English or German, must cast doubt upon the possibility of any *simple* causal relation between grammar and thought.)

On the whole, the verdict of competent anthropologists and linguists upon Whorf's suggestive ideas is that until some other "near-genius," with a talent for exact thought, succeeds in deriving some reasonably precise hypotheses, there is little scope for profitable argument.[19]

Some interesting attempts have been made to determine the validity of Whorfian ideas in their application to the influence of terminology upon visual perception.[20] But the results remain inconclusive, if suggestive for future scientific research.

Language and Logic

SOME CONTROVERSIAL ISSUES

Every responsible speaker or writer is conscious of certain logical controls to which his thought and expression must submit. It is, for instance, easy to fall into inconsistency, but few thinkers are bold enough to glory in self-contradiction. Walt Whitman might invoke poetic license to cry, "I contradict myself? Very well, I contradict myself!" but even he, in a

[19]See, for instance, *Language in Culture,* edited by Harry Hoijer (University of Chicago Press, Chicago, 1954), a valuable report of a conference largely concerned with Whorf's position. The lay reader will find in this book much fascinating anecdotal material, *e.g.,* about the Navaho colour system which does not discriminate between blue and green, but distinguishes two sorts of "black" (p. 96); the curious inability of the Bororo of Brazil to "note the features common to all parrots" (p. 8), and their capacity to count as high as thirty-eight, using only words equivalent to our "one" and "two." As to what such *curiosa* demonstrate in the end, the experts remain in doubt.

[20]See, for instance, the careful experiments reported in Roger W. Brown and Eric H. Lenneberg, "A Study of Language and Cognition," reprinted in *Psycholinguistics,* ed., Sol Saporta (Holt, Rinehart & Winston, Inc., New York, 1961). The authors discovered some suggestive correlations between what they call the "codability" of colours in English (roughly, a statistical factor answering to the ease with which the colours can be named) and the ability of subjects to recognize colours. Somewhat similar results have been obtained with Zuni Indians.

more sober moment, might have agreed that unabashed inconsistency corrupts rational discourse.[21] The very possibility of conveying information depends upon the speaker's choice between saying something and saying its logical opposite; and the hearer receives information because he knows that the speaker made—or at least intended to make—such a choice. Similarly, a clock gives information about the time because it shows, say, four o'clock, when it *might* have shown something else. But imagine a clock that, on being tapped, swings from four o'clock to some other hour, and then on being tapped again, shows some other time, and so on without end. Such a clock would obviously be utterly useless; because it would indicate *any* time at random, it would not "tell the time" at all. Now the same can be said of a human speaker. If he is willing to change a remark about the time to another and conflicting remark, and then in turn to change that capriciously, his words are as uninformative as the signal of the erratic clock. Conformity to the demands of consistency is required in order to lend definiteness to utterances. To the extent that these demands are violated, linguistic signals become unreliable and uninformative.

Where does the ideal of logical consistency derive its authority? How is a challenge to this ideal (perhaps in the name of "existential freedom" or some other catchword of the day) to be met? One traditional answer invokes "Laws of Thought" or a "Realm of Logical Necessity." There is, for instance, said to be a "Principle" or "Law" of Contradiction (to the effect, in one version, that no proposition can be both true and false) whose truth is to be perceived by an exercise of "intuition." Just as we can see certain spatial relations with our eyes, so, it has been said, we possess the power to "see eternal truths with the mind's eye." The basic principles of logic—and mathematics, too—are accessible to the "insight" of an unprejudiced and unclouded mind. To those who have the wit to understand them, the "first principles" of logic are

---

[21]There are familiar *forms* of utterance which, superficially interpreted, seem to be self-contradictory. But paradoxes, such as "Even the most unselfish of men is still selfish in his own fashion," must permit unparadoxical paraphrase. We could make no sense of an attempt to say, literally, and without qualification, that an unselfish man is, at the same time, and in the same respect, selfish—nor could we make sense of the assertion that some physical object was, at one and the same time, and in the same respect, green all over and red all over. These remarks apply even to the notorious philosophies of Hegel and others that seem to revel in contradiction. Upon closer examination, "contradiction" in such contexts is conflict, struggle, or something else that differs from logical contradiction.

"self-evident" and neither need nor can receive any further justification.[22]

Whatever truth there may be in this traditional conception, it has come to be increasingly felt by some thinkers to be inadequate as an account of the nature and authority of logic. Talk about "mental vision" seems incurably metaphorical and the mental processes needed in order to ensure the postulated acts of "mental insight" remain, in the traditional view, unsatisfyingly mysterious. As an alternative, it has been argued that the "Laws of Logic" have more to do with language than earlier thinkers would have admitted. This modern conception (a controversial one, to be sure) obviously falls within the scope of the present work. In order to explain its scope and promise, it will be necessary to remind the reader of certain important, if familiar, features of elementary logic.

THE NATURE OF LOGIC

The features of logical reasoning that I wish to recall may be sufficiently illustrated by the simple and basic type of argument known, since medieval times, as *Modus Ponens*.[23] Consider, therefore, the following argument: "This is a metal. If this is a metal, it will conduct electricity. Hence, this will conduct electricity." Obviously, the correctness (or "validity") of this trifling argument in no way depends upon the truth or falsity of its premises. Indeed, in the form in which it has been here presented, the reader is unable to know what "This" is, and hence unable to tell whether the first premise is true; yet he is perfectly able to recognize the argument as valid. And it is no less obvious that the argument's validity depends in no way upon its particular subject matter or topic (the

[22]This is the view associated with the philosophical attitude known as Rationalism, and powerfully argued by such thinkers as Aristotle, Descartes, and Leibniz—to mention only three famous names. The view that the fundamental principles of logic and mathematics are "a priori"—independent of experience—and self-evident inspired the hope of finding similarly a priori principles in the natural sciences and in ethics, politics, education, and theology. Conversely, the failure of such efforts, and the increasing recognition, forced upon scientists, that supposedly self-evident principles, such as that of universal causation, need to be revised, have discredited the rationalist program. It seems at least plausible that if we have been forced to recognize "non-Euclidean" geometries, belief in a single and unmodifiable logic might also be merely a hangover from earlier dogmatisms.

[23]With the approximate meaning of "the affirmative mode." In the traditional terminology, it is contrasted with *Modus Tollens,* a simple argument involving one if-then premise, and another premise in which the first part of the if-then premise is *denied,* rather than affirmed.

conduction of electricity by a metal). We could change the "topic" radically and still have recognizably the same type of argument as in: "James is a bachelor. If James is a bachelor, he pays high taxes. Hence, James pays high taxes." In short, the *validity* of the original argument depends, not upon its content or substance (its "topic" or "subject matter") but rather upon a certain form that can be made prominent, either in the following clumsy way:

> *Something-or-other. If that something-or-other, then such-and such.*
> *Hence, such-and-such.*

or, more concisely, as follows:

> *P. If P then Q. Hence Q.*

It is convenient to replace the expression "if-then" by a symbol, such as an arrow, and so to represent the form of the argument as:

> *P. P→Q. Therefore, Q.*

In this representation, the letters *P* and *Q* function as *variables* or "place-holders," eligible for replacement by any sentences expressing full propositions (provided the same replacement is made each time the same letter occurs). The original argument has been stripped of its substance in order to reveal its logical skeleton. Since the validity of the argument depends only upon the form thus revealed,[24] we can at a single stroke appraise the correctness of a vast class of formally similar arguments. Recognizing *Modus Ponens* to be valid, we know, once for all, that any argument, whatever its topic, will be valid if it is of that form. Thus the extraordinary range of logic (and, for that matter, mathematics, too) is connected with the fundamental tie between validity and form. Grasp of logical forms permits immediate mastery of an infinitely large class of concrete embodiments of such forms.

Outside the pages of logic texts, it is rare to find arguments set out with full and explicit formality. We say "This is a metal and metals conduct electricity . . ." leaving our hearer to understand the conclusion intended to be drawn. Thus the existence of logical connections between propositions—some of them perhaps unstated—has important consequences for

---

[24] Thus, for instance, the similar but clearly different form: *P. Q→P. Therefore,* Q is obviously invalid.

the notion of linguistic "implication" discussed elsewhere in this work. Roughly speaking, a speaker or writer is held responsible for any conclusions that can be derived by valid reasoning from any propositions that he asserts (whether explicitly or by implication). In this way, the hidden network of logical connections (of which we have uncovered only a corner in our illustration) lends discourse an extra complexity and richness. In speaking, we submit willy-nilly to appraisal, judgment, and possible amendment on the basis of the *logical implications* mediated by the hidden network of logical connections between propositions. A speaker is like the driver of a car who, choosing one route from many, finds himself then required to follow roads whose existence he never suspected. Or like a player in some game, whose rules have been determined by others, in which a simple act like kicking a football may have unexpected conventional consequences. Hence the value of logical analysis (the painstaking teasing out of logical relations of agreement and disparity) for revealing to the speaker or writer the deeper meaning of what he utters. Logical criticism may sometimes seem tiresomely pedantic and fussy[25]—and certainly there are uses of language to which it is inappropriate—but in its proper place it is an incomparable technique for the improvement and organization of thought.

THE AUTHORITY OF LOGIC

When we are confronted with a perspicuously valid argument, we receive an impression of inexorability. "All men are mortal and I am a man, so I *must* die too." Here, the presence of the word "must" expresses the recognition of what is usually called "logical necessity." But what do we really mean when we call the conclusion of a valid argument necessary? If there is compulsion here, what is its source? And what, if any, are the sanctions behind it?

Such questions as these are puzzling because our clearest notions of compulsion and necessity arise in quite different contexts. "I must do as he says (otherwise I shall lose my job)"; "I must help him in his distress (or suffer the pangs of remorse)." In such cases, it is possible to resist the "compulsion" expressed by the "must" if one is willing to suffer the penalty for disobedience. But what is the "penalty" for drawing an invalid conclusion? To reply that the thinker would then be reasoning illogically seems to amount to no more

---

[25]A student once protested to his professor: "I don't mind your splitting hairs; it's when you quarter them that I want to stop."

than *labelling* the default with a disapproving epithet. One could, to be sure, argue, on the lines previously sketched in this section, that logical inconsistency corrupts language.[26] Thus, it might be argued, the penalty for writing or speaking inconsistently is deterioration and ultimate destruction of the linguistic medium without which thought, and its expression and transmission, are impossible. (This assumes that the man to whom the defense is addressed already has a genuine interest in thinking and its verbal embodiment.) As a general defense of the ideal of logical consistency, this line of thought has some merit, but it will not explain why a particular argument should be accepted. Similarly, one might defend the practice of truth-telling on general utilitarian principles; but this would leave open the question of why somebody should not lie on a particular occasion, when the damage to the institution might be negligible.

A more promising answer might take the following form. Consider the procedure to be followed in determining whether some expression in a "dead language" really answers to what we mean by *"if . . . then."* Suppose we find the writers of this language sometimes linking propositions by the words *"ok . . . ak."* Then it is clear enough that we should not count *"ok . . . ak"* as meaning the same as our own *"if . . . then"* unless *P* and *ok P ak Q* committed the users of the language to the assertion of *Q* (rather than, say, *not-Q*). In short, we take acceptance of *Modus Ponens* to be a necessary condition for identifying the *"ok . . . ak"* locution as meaning *"if . . . then."* If we were to find the members of the investigated culture treating somebody who said *P* and also *ok P ak Q* as if he had also said *not-Q*, we should have conclusive evidence that *"ok . . . ak"* must be translated as *"if . . . then not,"* rather than as *"if . . . then."*

Applying these ideas to our own language, we can now say that the use of *"if . . . then"* in *Modus Ponens* is part of the meaning of that expression. To teach a child how to use the expression *"if . . . then"* is, among other things, to teach him to be ready to treat the assertion of *P* and *if P then Q* as committing himself and others to the assertion of the con-

---

[26]It can be proved that an explicit contradiction (of the form *P-and-not-P*) logically implies anything whatever. So, if a speaker is held accountable for all the logical implications of what he says, the presence in his discourse of a single contradiction renders him as useless as the fickle clock previously discussed. Because he implies everything, he says nothing. Yet this line of argument is persuasive only to somebody who already accepts the rules of valid reasoning. For in order to *prove* that a contradiction implies everything we must use logical principles.

clusion *Q*. Hence, the proper answer to somebody who asks "What would happen if I made the conclusion of an argument in *Modus Ponens* not-*Q* rather than *Q*?" should be: "In that case, you would not be using the expression '*if . . . then*' correctly." Of course, the questioner might not wish to use the expression correctly, but that is another story. There is in a sense nothing to prevent his changing the language, if he is willing to run the risk of the misunderstanding that might ensue.

More generally, then, the authority of logic derives from the rules of language that determine the meaning of the "sentential connectives" such as "if . . . then." Such rules, considered merely as rules of language, are, from a certain standpoint, arbitrary,[27] but once we use them, we use them. The somewhat mysterious sense of "necessity" we recognize upon being presented with the conclusion of a valid argument arises from our prior commitment to speaking our own language correctly.

From this standpoint, the "rules" of logic are analogous to the rules of grammar. Both are constitutive of the language that they help to define. Both, in the end, have no other source than our interest in speaking and making ourselves understood. What has been traditionally called "grammar" concerns the licences and constraints upon the combination of words within single sentences; while what has been traditionally called "logic" concerns the linkages between groups of sentences and their components. But philosophically viewed, this difference may seem somewhat unimportant.[28]

THE MECHANIZATION OF THOUGHT

The "formal" character of valid argument, to which attention was drawn above, has important technical consequences. We have seen that the logical structure or "form" of a simple argument can be made prominent by doing two things: replacing the sentences or clauses referring to the specific "subject matter" of the argument by *variables* (letters, serving as "place-holders" for possible substitution); and replacing the

---

[27]The reader should be warned that the issues arising from this "linguistic conception" of logic are too complex to receive adequate discussion in this brief report. Fuller treatment may be found in Chapter 5 of M. Black, *Models and Metaphors*.

[28]There remains, however, the question, too formidable to be discussed here, of why it is easy to accept a view of the relativity of grammar— as previously argued in this essay—and very difficult to accept a corresponding thesis of the relativity of logic.

distinctive "sentence connectives" whose properties are in question ("if . . . then," "either . . . or," "not . . . unless," and so on) by distinctive symbols. When this has been done, the original meaningful sentences, of which typical arguments are composed, are transformed into symbol-groups (variables tied together by the special logical signs) whose meaning no longer needs explicit attention. Just because the rules of valid argument that are sought in logic depend only upon the form of arguments, we are entitled to abstract from the meaning of specific arguments in order to attend solely to the visual designs of symbol combinations, constructed in such a way as to exhibit logical form. The derivation of valid conclusions from given premises can then be regarded as if it were a kind of game, where the question of meaning does not arise at all. So, the task of logic can be roughly described as that of finding rules and procedures for deciding when initial "positions" in the logic game ("axioms") can be transformed into other positions ("theorems") according to accepted rules of transformation.

It is by no means obvious at the outset that this program for the investigation of logical relations, in abstraction from propositional meaning, has any hope of success. One might have expected that the "logical game" would prove too complicated to be mastered. In fact, however, the game of logic, at any rate in its simpler branches, has proved to be a good deal easier than bridge or chess.[29] Moreover, the bold technique of replacing meaningful propositions by symbol-groups, manipulated without reference to their meaning, releases the investigator's mental energies for the new tasks of studying the properties of the formal system itself. Once the "game of logic" has been "formalized" by the invention of suitable symbolism, we are in a position to think *informally* about it. Such informal thought about logic can then, in its turn, be formalized, and provide material for still more sophisticated investigation at a higher level.

Here we have a striking instance of one of the most remarkable features of language, its "reflexive" capacity to become its own subject. This is absent from other forms of

---

[29]The reader will find the illuminating details in any of a number of modern texts of logic. The following may serve as an example of the kind of unexpected result that emerges from the formal study of logic. Form a complex sentence structure having the form $P \equiv (P \equiv (P \equiv ... \equiv (P \equiv Q)$, where the sign $\equiv$ stands for "if and only if." Then it can be proved that this form will invariably represent true propositions if and only if the $\equiv$ occurs an odd number of times. Here, a simple rule emerges from an intricate web of logical relations.

representation, or present only in a rudimentary and uninteresting form. There is no sense to the idea of "music about music"; and maps of maps, or paintings of paintings, have little interest. By contrast, the power we have to talk about talking, by inventing auxiliary devices for the crystallization of linguistic and logical structure,[30] is at the heart of the creative power of language. The interplay between the informal "insight," expressed in unformalized language, and the formal or "mechanical"[31] properties, codified in a symbol system, deserves more attention than can here be provided.

It may have occurred to the reader that what has been said in the foregoing paragraphs about the formal character of elementary logic applies just as well to mathematics. Indeed the power of mathematics depends strongly upon the abdication of meaning (the temporary inattention to anything but the formal structure of symbols) which I have been emphasizing in connection with logic. It is characteristic of modern mathematics, as it is of modern logic, to treat entire systems of thought as "games," lending themselves to "metamathematical" investigation of their global structure. The familiar word "calculus" (derived from the *small stones* used in reckoning on the abacus) may remind us of how deeply concern with the formal is embedded in mathematics —that paradigm of abstract thought. To *calculate* is to replace the concrete objects of thought by symbolic surrogates (pebbles, abacus beads, or signs) that can then be manipulated according to fixed rules of procedure. And all abstract thought may be held to involve some such "calculation," broadly conceived. Not the least service of language is its power to facilitate such calculation and abstraction.

NON-FORMAL ARGUMENT

It is easy to produce examples of arguments that do not seem to be formal in the sense of that word already ex-

[30]The "language" (or special terminology) in which a given language is talked *about,* is nowadays often called a "meta-language," while the language talked about is called the "object language." It is possible to have a "meta-meta-language," a "meta-meta-meta-language," and so on without end.

[31]The possibility of "programming" logical and mathematical problems on computers depends upon the possibility of formalization. For a computer or any other machine cannot think in the "informal" sense. But it is perfectly able to follow rules for the manipulation of "game-positions" according to fixed and predetermined rules. And even if a computer is only a "swift moron," it can perform certain mechanical operations of search and classification more efficiently and much more rapidly than the human being who designed it.

plained. For instance: "Johnson was in Chicago at noon on January 1; therefore he could not have been in Washington at the same place and time." If we try to replace the meaningful words or clauses of this argument by "variables," according to the technique for showing logical form already explained, we shall not yet succeed in revealing the principles on which the validity of the argument depends. Here it might be said that further, unstated, assumptions must be brought into play. Anybody offering our illustrative argument no doubt thinks correctly that a man cannot be in two places at once, and also thinks that Chicago and Washington are different places. Once these two premises are added to the original argument (together with some obvious ones, like "Johnson is a man") the amplified argument does lend itself to the exhibition of logical form.[32]

The crucial additional premise, "A man cannot be in two places at once," is, however, a *necessary truth*, as philosophers say. Its truth does not depend upon experience or upon particular facts that might have been otherwise, but (it might be held)[33] merely upon the meanings of the words of which it is composed. It might be held, therefore, that this premise contributes nothing substantial to the original argument, though there is certainly no harm in stating it. On this view, the argument, "Johnson is now in Chicago; hence he cannot now be in Washington," is valid as it stands, without benefit of additional unstated premises. If so, we shall have to recognize that arguments can be valid, even though they be not exhibited as instances of perfectly general forms.[34]

But even on this view, which the present writer endorses, there is no reason to abandon the connection between logic and the rules for the uses of words that was presented in the previous section. For it might be held that learning how to use words like "place," "time," and "person" requires initiation into a complex network of logical connections between them. Thus a man who does not clearly understand that we are supposed to use these words in such a way that it is forbidden to

[32]An argument that needs unstated premises in order to be presented in full is called by logicians an *enthymeme*.

[33]It would technically be called an ostensibly *synthetic a priori truth*. Some theorists would deny that such truths arise entirely from connections between the meanings of their constituents. They would urge that such truths "reveal something about the nature of the universe."

[34]The reader should be warned that perhaps the majority of logicians and philosophers would deny this. The dominant view is that all argument is valid in virtue of logical form and that arguments that seem to be exceptions must be treated as being enthymemes.

say that a man can be in two different places at the same time is to that extent unsure about how to use these words. He might be compared to a beginner at chess who knows how to move the pawns forward but is uncertain about the rules for capturing with pawns. In formal argument, I would urge, we rely upon this hidden network of connections between meanings. We pass from one point to another in the linguistic web by means of paths that all together define what the language is.

LOGICAL GRAMMAR

The conduct of arguments that are more complex than the simple ones used as illustrations in the previous section is greatly hindered by two pervasive features of natural languages (languages that have grown, like Topsy). On the one hand, distinctions marked by the grammar may not correspond, or may no longer correspond, to differences in thought. An obvious example is the obligatory distinction between genders, required in many languages, that may have reflected earlier, mythological, conceptions about the universe, but no longer answer to any distinction that a contemporary speaker would wish to make. (There is no intelligible reason for regarding wisdom as "feminine" in French or a child as "neuter" in German.) Gender is like the vermiform appendix in the human body—a survival that is only a nuisance.

This tiresome phenomenon of *pointless grammar*, as it might be called, is encountered throughout all languages that have not been artificially constructed for limited purposes, like the symbolism of mathematics.

> Whether a verb is *syntactically* active or passive depends on its form alone; but the same idea may be expressed sometimes by an active, sometimes by a passive form: A precedes B = A is followed by B; A likes B = A is attracted by B. The passive Lat. *nascitur* has given way to the active Fr. *naît* in the same sense and is rendered in English sometimes by the passive *is born*, sometimes by the active, *originates*, *comes into existence*. . . . There is thus nothing in the ideas themselves to stamp verbs as active or passive (Otto Jespersen, *The Philosophy of Grammar*, George Allen & Unwin, Ltd., London, 1924, p. 165).

Pointless grammar, one might say, renders language unnecessarily complicated for the purpose of clear and exact thought. But the complementary defect of deficient complexity is more common and all the more dangerous for being so easily overlooked. Grammatical similarities between sentences or their component expressions very often mask important differences in meaning.

> Language disguises the thought; so that from the external form of the clothes one cannot infer the form of the thought they clothe, because the external form of the clothes is constructed with quite another object than to let the form of the body be recognized. The silent adjustments to understand colloquial language are enormously complicated. (Ludwig Wittgenstein, *Tractatus Logico-Philosophicus,* Routledge & Kegan Paul, Ltd., London, 1922, p. 63, with some alterations in the translation.)

A full exploration of the implications of this important thesis of the disparity between the structure of thought and the superficial grammar of the language in which it is expressed would require a book longer than the present one. (A good deal of what has come to be called "analytical" or "linguistic" philosophy in the West might plausibly be viewed as an attempt to put Wittgenstein's insight—also previously stressed by Bertrand Russell and others—to useful work.) A single illustration must suffice.

Consider the following simple sentences:

> (A) *I am sleepy.*   (B) *I am healthy.*

Considered from the standpoint of simple grammar (the kind of thing that children are taught in school) the two sentences are altogether alike in structure and would be parsed in the same way. But as soon as we begin to consider the normal contexts of utterance, the relevant procedures or confirmation, and the associated implications, interesting differences soon appear.

A might be imagined said late at night—perhaps with a yawn. It is designed for expressive uses (as well as others): the tone of voice in which it is uttered is directly relevant, in a way which is not true—or not true to the same extent—of *B*. *A* might be uttered in solitude, as an *expression* of weariness, but one can hardly say the same for *B*. (The latter would almost certainly need a specific question in order to be produced. "Do you think you could stand the climate?" "Yes, I am healthy.")

In the case of *A*, the situation in which I have imagined it uttered would make any further attempt at confirming its truth absurd—it would be like "confirming" a yawn. But in the case of *B*, there are familiar tests that might be applied to determine whether the speaker was in fact making a true statement about his state of health.

With respect to *B*, the following supplementary questions might be raised (partly in an effort at further elucidation of meaning): "Have you always been healthy?" "Are you taking any steps to remain healthy?" "Can you say as much for other members of your family?" "Are you sure you have not simply been living in a healthy climate?" The parallel questions, attached to *A*, with "sleepy" replacing "healthy," result in patent absurdity.

Anybody who uttered *A* would be committed to some such utterance as "I have to make an effort to stay awake"—so that the remark "I am sleepy but I have no difficulty at all in remaining wide awake" would sound paradoxical; there is no parallel implication for *B*. Anybody who says *B* implies that he is not, at the time of utterance, suffering from a disease; there is no parallel implication for *A*.

The reader can easily produce further contrasts of this sort for himself. It seems plain enough already that a close examination of the linguistic roles of the two sentences (in the imagined contexts) soon reveals striking differences. A philosopher might summarize the result of the inspection we have outlined by saying that *A* is the expression of a momentary state of the speaker, while *B* is a report or assertion concerning a complex and continuing condition of that speaker (or perhaps of his body). But these formulas, useful as they might be as reminders, do little justice to the subtle and complex differences of use we have tried to exhibit.

In a wide sense of "grammar," the differences in use of the two sentences might still be called grammatical. But in that case, we should have to distinguish, with Wittgenstein, between "surface grammar" and "depth grammar." Exploration of context, confirmation conditions, implications, and the like must be taken as belonging to depth grammar.[35]

[35]The techniques for exploration of "depth grammar" may be summarized as description of context of utterance, formulation of conditions of validation (where appropriate), elaboration of meaning by means of relevant supplementary questions, and tracing of logical implications. Utterances that reveal parallel patterns under all these heads may be said to have the same linguistic (or logical) form—in an extended sense of "form." It is seldom profitable to pursue this program in great detail: we are usually interested in concealed *differences* of logical form and can stop as soon as they are convincingly demonstrated.

FICTIONS

The totality of rules that determine the correct use of a given word or expression may be said to specify the *grammatical form* of that word or expression; and two words subject to parallel rules may be said to have the *same grammatical form*. Two words having the same grammatical form can be substituted for one another in all sentences in which they can correctly occur, without violation of grammar or logic. (For example, "red" and "blue" can replace one another in this way; and so can "three" and "five"; but not "red" and "three" or "blue" and "five." It is grammatically correct to speak of "a red sunset," and equally so, however false, to speak of "a blue sunset"; but *"a three sunset" violates grammar, and *"three plus blue makes five" sins against grammar or logic, as we please. "Red" and "blue" have the same grammatical form, which differs from the form shared by "three" and "five.")

Words having markedly different grammatical forms (*i.e.*, subject to very different rules for use and association) are unlikely to be confused with one another: it would take a lunatic to think of red as a kind of number, or of five as a kind of colour. When there is *partial* similarity of form between the words, so that many though not all linguistic rules apply equally to both, there may be serious risk of resulting conceptual confusion, as the following examples will illustrate.

Let us begin with a trivial example of possible confusion arising from misconception of grammatical form. The expression, "The average American," in some respects resembles such an expression as "The tall American," or even a personal name such as "John Brown." We can, perhaps, say of both the average American and Brown that each of them is more than five feet tall, can read English, has been to grade school, and so on indefinitely. But if we press the underlying linguistic analogy too far, we shall end with seeming absurdities: the average American will prove to be partly male and partly female, to have a fractional number of children, to profess several religions, and the like. Such paradoxical remarks are harmless enough if we remember their intended meaning, recalling, for instance, that to say that the average American has two and a half children is only to express in convenient shorthand the result of dividing the number of American children by the number of American adults. Should, however, some simple-minded person (a child, perhaps) suppose that the average American had some identifiable surname, lived in a particular house, and was subject to the draft, he would be seriously misled by a superficial linguistic analogy. This particular muddle is too gross to be likely to occur; but others, almost equally blatant, have been responsible for much confused doctrine.

The average man is very commonly called a *fiction*. This term, though well established, is unfortunate in its implication that the average man (or any other "fiction") is unreal, nonexistent, like Mr. Pickwick or other fictitious characters. Jeremy Bentham, who exploited the notion of a fiction with much success, defined the idea as follows:

> A fictitious entity is an entity to which, though by the grammatical form of the discourse employed in speaking of it, existence be ascribed, yet in truth and reality existence is not meant to be ascribed.[36]

It is hard to see how this definition can be usefully applied. Does the language in which we speak of the average man "ascribe" existence to him? Who is to say? As to whether the clear-headed speaker intends to ascribe existence to the average man, that depends upon the sense in which "existence" is understood. If the intention were that the average man exists in just the same way that any flesh-and-blood person does, that would imply inexcusable confusion of thought. But a reasonable case could be made for saying that the average man exists (or: is real) in his own fashion, since we can objectively determine his properties. There is no need to assume that everything that exists, or is real, must occupy a definite position in space and time. Bertrand Russell once said:

> People often assert that man is mortal; but what is mortal will die, and yet we should be surprised to find in the "Times" such a notice as the following: "Died at his residence of Camelot, Gladstone Road, Upper Tooting, on the 18th of June 19—, Man, eldest son of Death and Sin." *Man*, in fact does not die; hence if "man is mortal" were, as it appears to be, a proposition about *man*, it would be simply false. The fact is, the proposition is about men.[37]

I suppose that Man might die if all men were exterminated. Russell seems to think that it is philosophically preferable to

---

[36]Quoted from C. K. Ogden, *Bentham's Theory of Fictions*, Routledge & Kegan Paul, Ltd., London, 1932, p. 12. This book contains much fascinating material on Bentham's position.

[37]*The Principles of Mathematics*, Cambridge University Press, 1903, pp. 53–54.

talk about men rather than about man; but his persiflage does not show that any mistake is committed in speaking about man. Nor has he shown that Man is unreal or a "fiction" in some pejorative sense.

If we are to improve on Bentham's definition, it seems advisable to attend to a *fictitious use* of a given expression. More explicitly, we might say:

> An expression *E* is used fictitiously in a given context if it is subjected to grammatical (syntactical and semantical) rules appropriate to an expression of analogous grammatical form, but not appropriate to *E*.

According to this proposed definition, a fictitious use of an expression always involves a breach of given grammatical rules. In general, this is to be condemned, but there may be special cases, as we shall eventually see, in which the grammar is deliberately violated in order to serve a useful and defensible purpose.

The following is a simple example of an indefensibly fictitious use of an expression:

> "I see nobody on the road," said Alice. "I only wish *I* had such eyes," the [White] King remarked in a fretful tone. "To be able to see Nobody! And at that distance too! Why, it's as much as *I* can do to see real people, by this light!" (*Through the Looking-Glass*).

If this seems fanciful, consider the strange case of the Frenchman, Radulfus, who, at the end of the 13th century, followed the same fantastic path.

> This man had the idea—whether in earnest or jest is hard to decide—that the Latin word for no one, *nemo,* was the name of a person. He hunted for passages in the Bible and other authorities in which this Nemo was mentioned, and actually discovered that Nemo was the true son of God. He preached sermons about him, attracted believers, and founded a sect of worshippers of Nemo, *Neminiana secta.* Unintentionally or intentionally, Radulfus became a laughing-stock.[38]

This extreme instance nicely shows the evils that may result from the fictitious use of expressions. If a writer seriously treats "Nobody" as the proper name of some person (ignoring the respects in which the rules for using that word differ

---

[38]Karl Vossler, *The Spirit of Language in Civilization*, Routledge & Kegan Paul, Ltd., London, 1932, pp. 41–42.

from the general rules for using nouns or pronouns), he will soon find himself ascribing extraordinary properties to the "person" he has thus conjured into existence.

Nobody can be in two places at once, nobody can give birth to himself, nobody can square the circle; but if Nobody were, *per impossibile,* a person, he could be ubiquitous and self-creating and could perform impossible tasks like squaring the circle! In general, it will be found that the uncritical use of fictitious language creates monsters: violation of grammatical logical rules is transformed into fantasies about the nature of reality.

Abuse of fictitious language is a more insidious fault than the crassness of my illustrations might suggest. It is, for example, fatally easy to fall into thinking of numbers as "extraordinary" or "peculiar" objects, that are "eternal," outside space and time, and so on. It is at least plausible, though still controversial, to suggest that this Platonizing conception of the nature of numbers arises from the kind of inattention to differences in grammatical form that I mentioned in the last paragraph. To realize that the "names" of numbers have a grammar importantly different from the names of physical objects is to be forewarned against the danger of illegitimate inference, having no better basis than willful blindness to grammar.

Let us pursue this interesting case a little further. It is obvious that in such a sentence as "Two men entered," the word "two" is an adjective, and equally obvious that the sentence can be transformed, without alteration of meaning, into "A man entered and another man entered." The first point distinguishes "two" from nouns such as "Robinson" that are plainly *names;* the second point marks an important difference between numeral adjectives and others, such as "red," that do not permit corresponding paraphrase. Both together suffice to cast doubt upon the notion that numbers are "peculiar sorts of objects."[39]

Whenever illegitimate use of fictitious language is suspected, the method of *elaboration,* or paraphrase, suggested in the last paragraph may be useful. *Spelling out* a fictitious

---

[39]These brief remarks cannot settle this fundamental issue in the philosophy of mathematics. The great Frege did not commit an elementary blunder when he eventually came to the reasoned conclusion that numbers were, after all, objects of a certain sort. But he needed a long and intricate argument to reach that conclusion and never remained altogether happy with it.

use of an expression will sometimes suffice to reveal the underlying error.[40]

I must not leave the impression that the introduction of fictions is always reprehensible. Consider the mathematician's practice of saying that "parallel lines *intersect at a point at infinity*." Here there seems to be a flat violation of the definition of parallel lines as those that *do not* intersect, however much they are prolonged. To remove this contradiction by an understanding that "intersect at a point at infinity" shall mean the same as "do not intersect" may seem to a layman a very capricious way of distorting language. There is an excellent point to it, however.[41] However dangerous the procedure might be in the hands of those who leap to metaphysical conclusions about the "peculiar properties of infinity," the gains in organization and manageability of the realm of geometric relationships are too substantial to be easily sacrificed. There are solid reasons for the mathematician's repeated invocation of mathematical fictions.

A parallel defense might be mounted for lawyers' affection for fictions. Treating a corporation *as if* it were a person (while remembering all the time that it is not!) permits the extension to a new domain of a corpus of legislation, concerning personal property and the like, without creating an altogether new system of laws. (The dangers of thereby circumventing the rights of legislative bodies have often been pointed out.)

The last word may be left to Bentham:

> What is here meant is, not that no such fictions ought to be employed, but that to the purpose and on the occasion of instruction, whenever they are employed, the necessity or the use of them should be made known. . . . Why? In the first place, to prevent that perplexity which has place in the mind, in so far as truth and falsehood being confounded, that which is not true is supposed to be true; in the next place, by putting

[40]A man was once asked by his small son to explain how it was that, by means of radio, somebody singing in Chicago could be heard in New York. His answer ran: "You know that if you step on the tail of a cat, the squeal comes out at the mouth. Imagine a tremendous cat with its tail in Chicago and its head in New York. That's what radio is like. Except that there is no cat!" Some explanations invoking fictions (like the appeal to "centrifugal force" in elementary mechanics) are really no better than this.

[41]The fictitious phraseology removes the need to distinguish the special case in which lines do not intersect from the general case in which they do. More importantly, it permits Euclidean plane geometry to be "mapped" upon projective geometry, and in this way provides the mathematician with powerful tools of research.

it as far as possible in the power of the learner to perceive the use and the value, as well as the nature of the instruction communicated to him, to lighten the burden of the labour necessary to be employed in the acquisition of it.[42]

THE LIMITATIONS OF FORMAL LOGIC

Logical techniques derive their formidable power from the strategy of suppressing specific meaning in favour of the exhibition of form by means of variables and symbolic operators. The same is true, in a more limited way, even of what was called, in an earlier section, "informal logic." The success of logic (and mathematics, also) in organizing thought and releasing mental energy for more sophisticated tasks at higher levels of analysis (investigation of the structures of "metalanguages") depends essentially, as we have seen, on such emphasis upon form, in abstraction from content. But this character of the formal sciences of logic and mathematics leads to certain difficulties when application to concrete material is in question. That 2 and 2 make 4—to take a very simple example—is established wholly *within* arithmetic, by mathematical calculation, and needs no reference to an untidy environment in which objects do not always preserve fixed outlines or stay still long enough to be counted. It follows that questions about the *application* of arithmetic— questions about when it makes sense to treat things as fit to be counted as 2 and 2 more—do not themselves belong to the formal context of arithmetic, but must be left to the informal intelligence and judgment of the investigator. The corresponding point applies to logic, even in its most simple and obvious application to concrete argumentation. The validity of *Modus Ponens* is wholly secure within formal logic: it would be senseless to deny that if P is asserted and also *if P, then Q*, the reasoner is committed to asserting Q rather than *not-Q*. But when we come to use this simple and fundamental rule for appraising a fragment of actual discourse, we have to decide whether the words used for stating a relation between two thoughts can properly be rendered as the logician's "if . . . then" (which, like other technical concepts, is a "trimmed" version of the common-sense idea that originally inspired it).[43]

[42] Quoted from C. K. Ogden, *Bentham's Theory of Fictions*, p. xliii.

[43] This happens regularly in the transition from common sense to science. The *mass* of the physicist does not answer exactly to any conception of the man-in-the-street; and similarly, the connection symbolized by the logician's arrow, "→", differs, in certain subtle ways, from what the ordinary man would understand by the words "if . . . then." Such deviations are, of course, not introduced capriciously. They serve technical purposes of ease of manipulation and generality of treatment.

And we have to be satisfied that the propositions we need to designate at different points of the text by the *same* symbol, "*P*", really can be taken as having the same, or approximately the same, meaning. Thus the use of logic inescapably involves the determination of semantic issues that may sometimes be trivial but, in hard cases, may call for rare tact and insight. Words, and the ideas they represent, are not the sharply defined entities that would best answer to the logician's simplified models: they characteristically shift their contours from one use to another. If this is ignored, what results from the application of logic is not an illuminating revelation of underlying structure, but a mere distortion and caricature.

It hardly needs to be added that there are vast and important realms of discourse that are not primarily concerned with argument, in the narrow sense of that term, or with the promulgation of literal truth-claims. When the poet says, "Truth is Beauty, Beauty Truth—That is all ye need to know" it would be philistine stupidity to question solemnly whether the identity of truth and beauty can really be accepted—or whether, even if the two were identical, that interesting fact would be "all" that we would need to know. A sympathetic exegesis of the poet's communication will require more subtle tools than this.

In short, to state the obvious, "Logic is not enough" (but the same can be said of anything!). With all the cavils and qualifications that we have noted above, it remains true that logic (and grammar, too) are invaluable means of learning a part of the truth about language and the thought it embodies. Those who, in a muddled way, bewail the "tyranny of logic" or regard it as a "straitjacket confining thought" betray only their ignorance of the nature of logic and of the nature of language and thought.

CHAPTER 5

THE MANY USES OF LANGUAGE

SPEECH AS A PURPOSIVE ACTIVITY

WORDS MAY BE UTTERED IDLY, for no particular reason and with no end in view: we can doodle with sounds as with marks on paper. But this is exceptional. Normally, we speak in order to achieve some purpose; and that is why we can appraise the success or failure of acts of speech, judging them by reference to what we try to accomplish when we speak. Speech, like much other human activity, is purposive. But then, what are the purposes intended to be served by speech? If a demiurge set out to create language, what would he be trying to achieve? What would be his criteria of success or failure?

Setting these questions aside as too sweeping to be manageable, let us begin, instead, by asking about the purposes of particular utterances. When you or I produce a particular sentence, what do we try to achieve?

This simple question can be answered in a baffling variety of ways. A man may speak in order to impart information, to deceive his hearer, to show friendliness, to ease social tension, to relieve his feelings, to show sympathy or some other attitude—and so on, indefinitely. Yet there might, after all, be some principle underlying this superficial variety of actual purposes served. We may remind ourselves of the many ways in which even a relatively simple instrument, such as a hammer, can be used: as a doorstop, a paperweight, a weapon, or in the sport of hurling the hammer. In spite of this variety of uses, there is a simple answer to the question, What is a

115

hammer used for? Its *standard* or *normal* use is simply to hit things; and all the other uses mentioned are incidental to that single primary purpose[1] that the tool was designed to serve. Similarly, it is reasonable to expect to find some single primary purpose of speech, to which all the other uses it actually serves might be regarded as incidental, subordinate, or derivative.

SPEECH AS THE EXPRESSION OF THOUGHT

Most writers on speech and language have in fact discerned a single unifying purpose expressible in the formula: "Speech is used for the expression and communication of thought."

Consider, for instance, the following definition of language supplied by the Eleventh Edition of the *Encyclopædia Britannica*: "the whole body of words and combinations of words as used in common by a nation, people or race, for the purpose of expressing or communicating their thoughts; also, more widely, the power of expressing thought by verbal utterance." (The reference to "nation, people or race" might trouble anthropologists and politicians today.)[2]

Or compare the following remark from Locke's *Essay*: "The comfort and advantage of society not being to be had without communication of thoughts, it was necessary that man should find out some external sensible signs, whereof these invisible ideas which his thoughts are made up of, might be made known to others" (bk. iii, ch. ii, sec. 1).

These two statements, which could be matched by a hundred others, agree in stressing the expression and communication of *thoughts,* and both, by implication, assign to language this single purpose. No doubt, Locke and many others of the same opinion would freely concede that language is in fact often used in many other ways, but these uses they would treat like the conversion of a hammer into a doorstop—things incidental, but not intrinsic, to the nature of language.

"The primary and standard use of language is to express and to communicate the speaker's or writer's *thoughts.*" This plausible doctrine—let us call it "Locke's formula"—can be understood either in broad or in narrow senses which we need

[1] I shall ignore throughout this discussion the finer distinctions in meaning between "use," "purpose," and "function." Although these words differ in meaning, what is said by using one of them can usually be expressed by means of the others.

[2] 1964 edition has wider definition: "An arbitrary system of vocal symbols by means of which human beings, as members of a social group and participants in a culture, interact and communicate."

to distinguish. Consider such familiar utterances as "Please close the window" or "How do you do?" I have argued in a previous chapter that it seems impossible to identify the speaker's "thoughts" in these cases, without using the utterance itself. The speaker can paraphrase, in the first example, by saying "I wanted him to close the window," but he said *more* than this when he made his request. And it is even harder to isolate an independent "thought" expressed by "How do you do?"

If Locke's formula is to cover such cases as these, "thought" must be taken to mean approximately the same as "whatever the speaker wished to communicate." Approximately only, because, as we shall see, we must allow for and attach due importance to the *unintended* message. This is the "broad sense" to which I have referred. But then a thought, in this indefensibly extended sense, can very well be a feeling, an intention, and much else. It is misleading and unhelpful to use "thought" to cover all those things. On this broad interpretation, language serves many purposes: the way is open for a *multiple* theory of linguistic uses.

By contrast, the narrower interpretation of Locke's formula takes a "thought" to be *something that can be either true or false* or, in the terminology of modern logic, something "having a truth-value." Then, "It is four o'clock" and "Copper is a metal" and "Twice two is four" do express "thoughts," while "Please close the window" and "How do you do?" and almost any line of poetry do not.

The use of an utterance to express a thought, according to this narrower conception (something that is necessarily true or false), is commonly identified as a *cognitive use* of language.[3] The existence of such cognitive uses is obvious enough; but equally so is the existence of any number of non-cognitive uses, in which words are used to express feelings and attitudes, to transmit orders, to bind the speaker to future performance, and so on. How could these have been overlooked? It is hard to understand, in retrospect, why so many able thinkers should have been able to persuade themselves that the cognitive use of language was its only standard use, meanwhile turning a blind eye to "non-cognitive functions" as unworthy of serious investigation.

---

[3]The word "cognitive" has the force of "pertaining to knowledge," with the underlying idea that if the hearer accepts a true "thought" conveyed to him by the speaker, he may acquire knowledge. Although I use this well-established terminology, I hope to end with some better ways of drawing useful lines between different functions of language.

There is a fairly obvious trap here, into which too many acute minds have fallen. A question about the primary use (or: purpose, function) of an instrument as simple as a hammer is readily answered in a single formula. But even something as simple by comparison with language as, say, paper, is designed to serve a multitude of purposes: it has the primary functions of being used for writing, for wrapping parcels, for lining compartments and packages, and so on. Paper, unlike a hammer, has multiple uses.

Given the obvious complexity and versatility of language, and the enormous variety of purposes to which words seem to be put, it might be expected that language would, from the very outset, be recognized as having a multiplicity of uses. In fact, however, there is an ancient tradition of regarding language as an instrument with a single primary use—more like a hammer than like paper.

One reason for this curious phenomenon in the history of thought may have been a dominating interest in the "rational" aspects of language (and a correspondingly narrow conception of rationality), reinforced by the general feeling that language, in its proper use, ought to be exclusively concerned with the formulation and transmission of truth-claims. A general exception has always been made for fiction and poetry. But the existence of poetry has always made the cognitive theorists uncomfortable. Some writers give the impression that if poets don't care about expressing "truths,"[4] they really ought to. Today, however, no serious students of language would be happy with this monolithic conception. A striking feature of 20th-century studies of language has been an increasing realization of the central and crucial role of "noncognitive" aspects of language, in fields as diverse as aesthetics, ethics, philosophy, education, and politics. In place of Locke's oversimplified formula, the modern linguist would be readier to agree with the famous remarks of Wittgenstein:

> But how many kinds of sentences are there? Say assertion, question, and command?—There are *countless* kinds: countless different kinds of use of what we call "symbols," "words," "sentences." And this multiplicity is not something fixed, given once for all; but new types of language, new language-games, as we may say, come into existence, and others become

[4]Part of the trouble in discussing this fundamental question, which would need careful attention in a more extended treatment, is the slipperiness of the word "truth." Are ethical dicta and mathematical theorems—to consider only these—to be regarded as "true" in the same way that a weather report is?

obsolete and get forgotten (*Philosophical Investigations*, p. 11).

Wittgenstein uses the expression "language-game" here in order "to bring into prominence the fact that the *speaking* of language is part of an activity, or of a form of life" (*Philosophical Investigations*, p. 11). As examples of such types of linguistic activity, he proceeds to give the following (p. 11–12):

> Giving orders, and obeying them—
> Describing the appearance of an object, or giving its measurements—
> Constructing an object from a description (a drawing)—
> Reporting an event—
> Speculating about an event—
> Forming and testing a hypothesis—
> Presenting the results of an experiment in tables and diagrams—
> Making up a story; and reading it—
> Play-acting—
> Singing catches—
> Guessing riddles—
> Making a joke; telling it—
> Solving a problem in practical arithmetic—
> Translating from one language into another—
> Asking, thanking, cursing, greeting, praying.

And he adds the significant comment:

> It is interesting to compare *the multiplicity of the tools in language* and of the ways they are used, the multiplicity of kinds of word and sentence, with what logicians have said about the structure of language (p. 11-12, italics added).

"What logicians have said about the structure of language," in Wittgenstein's phrase, is what I have been referring to as "Locke's formula" in its narrower interpretation—the claim that language consists essentially of the expression of thoughts having truth-value, *i.e.*, what logicians call *propositions*. The inadequacy of this view as a general conception of the functioning of language is sharply underlined by Wittgenstein's choice of examples. But this valuable reminder of the diversity of language uses can only be a beginning. Recognition of diversity provokes the desire to find patterns of organization: We shall naturally wish to arrange the "multiplicity" of language uses in some manageable order—to develop principles of organization that can be applied for relating, comparing, and contrasting varieties of linguistic practice.

Many thinkers have tried to provide workable schemes of this sort. One of the aims of this chapter will be to report upon and to criticize such proposals.

It is only fair to warn the reader at the outset that the basic questions involved in analyzing the functions of language are troublesomely complex. Since no answers have yet been found that are generally accepted by competent experts, this chapter must necessarily be at least as controversial as any other sections of this work.

INFORMATIVE USES OF LANGUAGE

In some ways the most intelligible use of an utterance is to *tell* the hearer something. But not all uses of language fall under this description: our eventual aim will be to contrast these cases with others—notably with the use of utterances to express and communicate feeling.

However, this gets us very little further, since a moment's reflection suffices to show the great variety of linguistic acts that we commonly lump together as telling somebody something. Consider, for instance, the following sheaf of requests:

> Tell me the time, please.
> Tell me your name.
> Tell me how to open this parcel.
> Can you tell me the chemical composition of insulin?
> Tell me what to do now.
> Tell me what he said.
> I would like you to tell me the meaning of *Angst*.
> Please tell me what you are trying to achieve.

If what is told is called "information," we must recognize at once that the word covers a heterogeneous set of things: facts, procedures, structure, advice, meaning, intention, and so on. One thing in common in all the cases cited, however, is the presumed initial ignorance of the hearer who is to receive the information in question. On the assumption that the speaker already has the desired information, succeeds in adequately expressing it, and is correctly understood by a hearer who accepts what he is told (large assumptions indeed), the linguistic transaction will be successful and knowledge will pass from speaker to hearer. Hence, the suitability of the label, "cognitive use," as explained earlier in this chapter.

SAYING AND IMPLYING

In order for knowledge to pass without a hitch from speaker to hearer, the latter has to understand and accept a good deal that is not normally stated "in so many words." He cannot accept what he is told—and hence, when all goes well, come to know it as true—unless he *trusts* the speaker to the extent of taking him to be honestly and adequately talking about what he knows.

Now the indications of the speaker's credibility and reliability in the given situation—if present at all—are commonly not verbal: the hearer has to rely upon facial expression, tone of voice, the nature of the topic, and so on, for clues to the essential supplementary information that he needs. All this must somehow be conveyed to the hearer, but normally it is not stated. We may say that the speaker implies that he is to be "trusted," though he does not normally say so.

This is neatly shown by the paradoxical effect of an utterance in which the speaker seems to deny his own credibility or trustworthiness. It may be true that arsenic in small doses is harmless and true also that a particular person, *S*, does not believe this. There is nothing paradoxical about saying "Arsenic is harmless in small doses, but *S* doesn't believe it." But if *S* himself were to say, "Arsenic in small doses is harmless, but I don't believe it!" the hearer would be hard put to it to make sense of what he heard.

An understood convention for the serious and literal use of unqualified assertions is that the speaker, in the absence of contrary indications, purports to believe what he says, and presents himself as saying it *because* he believes it. Hence to say something, with a straight face, and in the same breath to disclaim belief in what is being said violates the background conventions and makes nonsense of the activity in which the speaker is ostensibly engaged.[5] It may be compared to the action of a tennis-player who goes through the motions of serving, but without using a ball! Here, too, an observer would "fail to understand."

The speaker's credibility, as we may say, for short, may sometimes be asserted: he may state reasons why he should be believed, though if he does, he tends to raise suspicions, as protesting too much. But if he does say "You can trust me because I was an eyewitness," or "I know what I am speaking

---

[5] Another reason why an utterance of the form "Arsenic in small doses is harmless, but I don't believe it" sounds so paradoxical is that we are puzzled to discern any *point* in the utterance: it is hard to see why anybody should want to say this or to understand what he would hope to achieve by saying it. That is why we should be inclined to treat it as a joke, or as a cryptic way of implying something mysterious. Now the point of an utterance is normally implicit—it has to be understood, without being formulated.

about, having just consulted a dictionary," corresponding questions about reliability will arise in connection with *these* additional remarks. No utterance is self-vindicating.[6]

There is no escape from the conclusion that the efficacy of spoken communications rests in the end upon the transmission of nonverbal signs of credibility. No amount of talk can certify the speaker as worthy of trust unless there are independent indications that he is.

Modifying a familiar expression, we may therefore say that all successful transmission of knowledge depends upon the hearer "reading *behind* the lines"—somehow receiving a sufficient and correct understanding of the entire setting in which the words occur. Isolated from any context allowing for this supplementary and essential interpretive underpinning, words, however eloquent and well-chosen, fail to produce their desired effect. If I simply hear the words, "It's four o'clock," I shall understand the message without being so foolish, if I can help it,[7] as to believe it without knowing who said it, and why, and in what circumstances.

We have arrived at what might be called the principle of context dependence: the words used, however central and important, must be regarded as only a part of the total speech act. To concentrate upon the audible or visible symbols, to the exclusion of what is invisible and inaudible, is no more sensible than forgetting that nine-tenths of an iceberg is out of sight.

Ordinary men hardly need to be told this: from infancy on, they have learned to attend to tones of voice, facial expression, and contextual features as crucial signs of intent. They follow, without benefit of academic injunction, the maxim that "Who the speaker is, and how he says what he says, and why he says it, are as important as what he says." Linguists, however, tend to neglect the context—possibly because the procedures used by skilful hearers and readers in "reading behind the lines" are too subtle and variable for ready analysis.[8]

---

[6]A scholar, reproached for verbal mystification by his children, once agreed to raise his thumb whenever he was merely joking. But how were they to tell that he wasn't sometimes raising his thumb as a joke? Would another gesture help?

[7]Mere repetition of truth-claims, out of context, has some tendency to induce belief, as advertisers have long ago discovered. But even they seldom rely upon brute repetition and try to simulate normal conditions by establishing the credibility of the advertiser.

[8]To tough-minded theorists, my insistence upon "reading" what is "invisible and inaudible" will smack of paradox and mystification. They will insist upon being shown in detail how the feat is accomplished. The demand is reasonable and could be satisfied in an ampler discus-

READING BETWEEN THE LINES

Relevant facts about the speaker, such as his possessing items of information that he wishes to convey faithfully, may be said to characterize the *speaker's situation*. And this notion, in its turn, can be generalized to speech acts in which the purpose is not to convey information, but to do something else. In general, the "speaker's situation" may be taken to refer to his intentions and to whatever powers and capacities are relevant to such an intention. In the case of somebody telling a joke, the intention, roughly speaking, may be to amuse; in the case of what Malinowski has called "phatic communion,"[9] the intention may be to establish easy relations with the hearer; and so on. The point that was made in the previous section can now be succinctly stated in the following manner: information about the speaker's "situation," which is essential to full understanding of the message conveyed,[10] is normally implied, not explicitly stated.

The task of "reading behind the lines" to the speaker's situation is one that regularly arises in the interpretation

sion. There is no need to postulate some mysterious power of divining the speaker's honesty and reliability; but the story of how we discern the signs by which we discern these qualities is necessarily somewhat involved.

[9]"*Phatic communion* . . . a type of speech in which ties of union are created by a mere exchange of words." (B. Malinowski, "The Problem of Meaning in Primitive Languages," Supplement I in C. K. Ogden and I. A. Richards, *The Meaning of Meaning*, 3rd ed., Routledge & Kegan Paul, Ltd., London, 1930, p. 315.) Malinowski means the use of language in "free, aimless, social intercourse" (in *Meaning*, p. 313)— including such things as "inquiries about health, comments on weather, affirmations of the supremely obvious state of things" and the like.

[10]The importance of attention to the context of utterance has been eloquently argued by Malinowski: "A statement, spoken in real life, is never detached from the situation in which it has been uttered. For each verbal statement by a human being has the aim and function of expressing some thought or feeling actual at that moment and in that situation, and necessary for some reason or other to be made known to another person or persons—in order either to serve purposes of common action, or to establish ties of purely social communion, or else to deliver the speaker of violent feelings or passions. Without some imperative stimulus of the moment, there can be no spoken statement. In each case, therefore, utterance and situation are bound up inextricably with each other and the context of situation is indispensable for the understanding of the words." (In *Meaning*, p. 307.) [He overstates a good case, however, when he says that "the utterance has no meaning except in the *context of situation*" (p. 307).] What I have called the "speaker's situation" is a part, but only a part, of what Malinowski calls the "context of situation."

of spoken—or, for that matter, written—utterance. But even when this preliminary task has been satisfactorily performed and it is clear enough what the speaker is trying to do and how far he is qualified to do it, there normally remains a further task of "reading between the lines" of what he says. It would be short-sighted indeed to regard "what is being said" as being fully expressed by the words he uses.

The existence of this important phenomenon can be brought home by the following simple examples, all sufficiently familiar. They have been chosen to illustrate the wide variety of types of relevant implication.

VARIETIES OF IMPLICATION

1. A newspaper correspondent characteristically writes: "The Polish prime minister has been strengthening the regime's repressive measures against the Catholic Church." Here, the writer has not "said, in so many words," that there is a Polish prime minister (one and only one man holding the highest executive position); nor has he said that the "regime"[11] has already tried to repress the Church; yet both of these things are implied. That is to say, the new information offered, whether correct or not, proceeds on the assumption, intended to be shared by the reader, of the existence of the officer in question and the character of previous measures taken by his government. Were these assumptions to be rejected, the explicit communication would become pointless: the "Polish prime minister" cannot be doing anything if there is no such person, nor can "repressive measures" be strengthened when no such previous actions have occurred.

Here we have an example of what philosophers have come to call *presupposition*[12] in a technical sense of that word. By

[11]Notice the disparaging suggestions of that word, which would never be applied to the writer's *own* government.

[12]In European languages, the presuppositions are easily inserted by using adjectives or subordinate clauses, in place of full sentences. Instead of saying outright, "The rose is red and beautiful," we say "The red rose is beautiful." And instead of saying explicitly, "The battle was won and then the victors mourned" we can say, more concisely, "After the battle had been won, the victors mourned." Any competent speaker knows how to expand such compressed sentences into their longer and more explicit forms. So long as we are dealing with such standard ways of expressing implications, there is no argument, in most cases, about what the presuppositions really are.

means of certain standard grammatical devices,[13] the speaker is induced to accept as true some assumptions, often exceedingly questionable, which then serve as the indispensable basis for the new information presented. If the "presuppositions" were brought out into the open, they might appear in the form of a sort of preamble: "Whereas there is a Polish prime minister (as you are supposed to know) and whereas his government has previously taken repressive measures against the Church . . . [you are now told that such-and-such]." But of course this would be insufferably pompous and verbose. And besides, it is rhetorically much more effective to insinuate the crucial assumptions into the hearer's mind without focusing attention upon them.

The relevant presuppositions commonly take the form, as in our example, of assumptions about something's *existence*. For we can, without much violence, conceive of most utterances as either attributing some property to a supposedly existing thing (a single *subject*) or else attributing some relation to a number of supposedly existing things (a set of subjects).

In order for this to work, the subjects in question must be taken to exist by writer and reader alike. One of Mrs. Beeton's recipes began: "First catch your hare, then cook it." Similarly, we might say, "First catch your subject(s); then say something about it (them)." I ignore, to avoid complications, the kind of situation in which, as in fiction, the writer is talking about imaginary objects or situations. If the writer fails to "catch" his subject, *i.e.*, if he cannot gain his reader's assent to the presupposition of existence, the intended communication becomes "null and void," like a bet on a horse that is "scratched." One would normally say, in such a case, that the utterance was neither true nor false—that it becomes, as it were, a "non-starter." But where the intent to convey the presuppositions is central to the communication, the speaker might still be charged with deceit, or falsehood. A man, knowing himself to be a bachelor, who starts off by saying *"My wife . . ."* could be fairly accused of lying by implication.

This common and important device is the more subtle when the relevant presuppositions run through an extended discourse. It is a nice problem in the theory of literature to

[13]Current interest in this topic was aroused by a paper of P. F. Strawson, entitled "On Referring" (*Mind*, 1950), and is still lively among specialists. See, for instance, the comprehensive report by Isabel C. Hungerland, "Contextual Implication" (*Inquiry*, 1960), or my own examination of some of the associated philosophical issues, "Presupposition and Implication," in Black, *Models and Metaphors*.

investigate how far such presuppositions can be "bracketed" by a sympathetic reader, willing to engage in "suspension of disbelief" for the sake of aesthetic or other values incorporated in the literary work. Can an atheist really understand Milton's *Paradise Lost?* Is he in a position to appreciate it fully?

2. I turn now to a characteristic example in which the presence of the implied communication does not turn upon the use of a standard grammatical device.

> "He's taking advantage of me and he knows it." How could he help but know it, if he were? But the woman didn't mean that. She spoke in code. She meant, "I don't intend to tip," as when she said, "the service is frightful in this hotel," and "that man has an insolent look" (Thomas Sterling, *The Evil of the Day,* Simon & Schuster, Inc., New York, 1955, p. 26).

This is a substantially different type of case from the one previously considered. There is no grammatical or semantical rule that would allow one to read "He's taking advantage of me and he knows it," out of context, as meaning "I don't intend to tip." To get that reading, the responsive hearer must make an imaginative leap, aided, no doubt, by previous knowledge of the speaker. Yet the meaning might be plainly intended, though in the situation depicted perhaps it was not. If the speaker's husband were to reply, "My dear, I think you should tip him, just the same," he would be responding appropriately to the unspoken communication. And if he said instead, in the infuriating manner of so many husbands, "How could he help knowing it?" she might reasonably retort, "You knew very well what I meant!"

All of us "speak in code" in this way, to use Sterling's happy expression, and perhaps oftener than we commonly realize. Nor are the means by which such specific implications (unformulated messages) are conveyed difficult to discern. Sometimes it is the tone, or some other perceptible feature of the utterance, that supplies the clue:

> "Is anything wrong, Abbe?" he asked. "Have I offended you?" "No," Abbe replied, in the tone women reserve for answering such questions, the tone implying that what is wrong is so obvious that to ask the question is to compound the wrong (Don Mankiewicz, *Trial,* Harper & Row, New York, 1955, p. 177).

Some implication! as Churchill might have said—yet no doubt fully justified in context. More commonly, however, the hearer relies upon some oddity, incongruity, or disparity between the standard meaning of the words used and the nature of the situation in which they occur. The diversion of the utterance's regular meaning invites "decoding." If somebody says, "A newspaper published *not a hundred miles from Washington* regularly prints stories it knows to be false" the oddity of the italicized phrase nudges a sensitive hearer to find the hidden, but intended, message. The same device is operative in irony, sarcasm, and other forms of "transposed utterance."

Fully spelled out, the hearer's inference would take the form: "He would not say *that*, unless he intended such-and-such"—and we are off in pursuit of the submerged and partly concealed message that, unlike the official and standard meaning of the words used, may be what counts most.[14]

3. Not long ago, Professor Arnold Toynbee, in the course of protesting against American atomic policy, and especially its insistence upon withholding from allies the processes for manufacturing atom bombs, coined the slogan, "No annihilation without representation." This relatively simple example of concentrated implication may serve as a sufficient reminder of the literary devices by means of which a skilful writer can achieve compression, energy, and the interaction of meanings.

The effect of the slogan depends strongly upon its implicit reference to the famous slogan, "No taxation without representation." To a reader lacking knowledge of this original, or of the historical setting in which it was used, Toynbee's phrase might seem no better than a mandarin affectation. But with a sufficiently informed and alertly responsive reader, the four words can generate a rich and complex thought. At the risk of labouring the obvious, the implications might be spelled out in some such way as this: "If to be taxed without consent was thought sufficient to provoke a war for independence, how much more so the prospect of terrible destruction. You Americans are rejecting your own founding principles by such high-handed and arbitrary action against your friends and allies." And so on, *ad lib*. The lameness of such a para-

---

[14]If the reader thinks that reliance upon the "unspoken message" is restricted to familiar and literary discourse and is absent from formal scientific writing, he may be invited to reconsider. It would be easy to show that the most sober and straightforward scientific report relies very heavily upon the reader's "uptake"—his capacity to "read between the lines" and to understand a great deal that is not explicitly said. For better or worse, this is unavoidable. The quixotic effort to "say everything explicitly" would lead to intolerable prolixity and would, in any case, be self-defeating. Every utterance, no matter how laboured, trails clouds of implication.

phrase is patent: the effect of Toynbee's memorable phrase depends precisely upon *not* saying explicitly what, stated in plain language, might seem banal, at any rate open to serious question as a line of argument. But in implying what he intends, rather than arguing explicitly in its favour, he succeeds in establishing a wider perspective; invokes, effectively enough, some wider historical considerations.

4. Finally, a more extended and more subtle illustration:

> The day of the Master's study with its vast mahogany desk on which the blotting paper is changed every day, its busts of Daunty, Gouty and Shopkeeper, its walls lined with indexed bookshelves, one of which is reserved for calf-bound copies of the Master's own works, is over for ever. From now on the poet will be lucky if he can have the general living room to himself for a few hours or a corner of the kitchen table on which to keep his papers. The soft carpets, the big desks, will all be reserved by the Management for the whopping liars (W. H. Auden, "Squares and Oblongs," in *Poets at Work*, Harcourt, Brace & Co., New York, 1948, p. 176).

The phrase, "Daunty, Gouty and Shopkeeper," is arresting. Why do Dante, Goethe, and Shakespeare figure here in such transparent disguise? Is this a mere whim of a poet, amusing himself by word-play with no ulterior motive? This seems unlikely, with so scrupulous a writer as Auden. For one reader, at least, the phrase invokes the invisible presence of the little skivvy, dusting the absurdly predictable busts, and echoing in her own fashion "the Master's" borrowed values, her own mispronunciation unintentionally parodying the great man's own ignorance of what he publicly honours. The reading might be challenged as fanciful,[15] but that something like this effect was intended seems reasonable enough. Correct or not, the reading is of the *type* that writing of this sort can legitimately demand of its competent readers. Shorn of the implications and suggestions, the writer's thought declines into decorated banality.

---

[15] A student, perhaps too much influenced by the techniques of the New Criticism, once made much in an essay upon this passage of the connection between the three writers and the rise of bourgeois values in Europe, discerning a Marxist criticism as controlling the sense of the entire paragraph. This was no doubt going too far. Yet whatever a perceptive reader can discover in the passage may be either taken to have been intended—or at least, this may be assignable as included in its purport.

INFORMATIVE USES RECONSIDERED

In a previous section I said that "the most intelligible use of an utterance is to *tell* the hearer something," *i.e.*, to convey information. This conception of language, at first sight absurdly restrictive if intended to cover all uses of it, can, after our excursion into the topic of implication, be seen to have greater resources than might be supposed. If we count as part of the "information" all that can be conveyed by implication and suggestion—the unspoken side-comments, the indications of the speaker's "situation," conveyed by his tone and choice of language, and so on—the informative content of even simple utterances becomes so rich that it is plausible enough to view the transmission of information, in this extended sense,[16] as the main burden and object of speech.

Yet, however much we stretch "information" to cover implications as well as explicit "message," the exclusive identification of speech with transmission of information will still operate as a distorting theory, preventing us from understanding the full resources of language.

For one thing, there are plenty of speech acts in which the notion of "conveying information" or "telling somebody something" seems off the mark. The speaker may not know whereof he speaks, and may not pretend to, and so the question of transmitting knowledge hardly arises: he may be doing no more than guessing, expressing an opinion, or predicting some future event of whose occurrence he cannot be certain. Or he may simply be recording something as a future reminder (notes and minutes). Or again, the hearer may already be familiar with what he is told and cannot therefore be taken to *learn* anything. Or again, something may be formulated as a hypothesis for the sake of exploring its consequences, with no thought of asserting it as true.

What is common to all such cases, and to the many others that might be cited, is that the speaker presents *something that might be true or false* (whether in order to assert it as true, or merely to wonder about it, to explore its consequences and the like). Whenever this occurs, we might perhaps speak of the *propositional use* of speech, with the implication that some *proposition(s)* (something having "truth-value") are presented for consideration, though not

[16]Once again, the warning is needed that in anything but this kind of preliminary survey a good deal of attention would have to be given to a careful discrimination of the various senses in which the overworked word "information" is being used in this chapter.

necessarily asserted. Yet, propositional uses of speech by no means exhaust the resources of language. Consider the following lines of Roy Campbell (directed against some of his contemporaries):

> They use the snaffle and the curb all right,
> But where's the bloody horse?[17]

Is the poet saying "something that might be true or false," and hence uttering some propositions? Well, no doubt he is accusing his targets of pedantic restraint at the expense of content—which might, in some broad sense of the words, be held to be either true or false. But to leave the matter at that would be fatuous. The lines are a verbal *assault*, an act of aggression, comparable to a blow; and they effectively express attitudes (contempt? rejection?) finely manifested in the words used, which could only crudely be captured in a prose paraphrase. It would be myopic indeed to suppose that the major intention of the utterance was to "tell the hearer" something (to use our original formula). The example demands a different type of analysis.

With this illustration, we are on the brink of our promised discussion of "non-cognitive" uses of language. I shall begin by describing earlier and somewhat crude attempts to introduce the notion of "emotive meaning," and I shall end with some suggestions for a more supple set of adequate "speculative instruments."

THE EMOTIVE RESOURCES OF WORDS

In their "informative" aspect, words—or, rather, the utterances in which they are used—serve to indicate and to characterize objects, qualities, events, situations, either explicitly or by implication. Commonplace and routine utterances may have no other function: "The train is arriving now" draws the hearer's attention to the train (whose existence is presupposed, as we have seen) and merely tells him something true or false about it.

Very common, however, are the more complex cases in which "information" about the ostensible subject of utterance —or, as we may say for brevity, the *reference*[18]—is inter-

---

[17]"On Some South African Novelists" in *The Collected Poems of Roy Campbell*, Curtis Brown Ltd., 1949, p. 198.

[18]I am ignoring the more technical sense of *reference*, in which it is contrasted, by philosophical students of language, with *sense*. "Reference," as here used, is a mere device for avoiding long-winded phrases containing "information."

woven with the expression of feeling and attitude. Somebody exasperated by boredom might say "That damned bone-shaker is just creeping in." He might then be held to be saying, in part, the same (giving the same information, making the same reference) as he would have done by using the cooler utterance already cited. Obviously, he says a good deal *more*—a point which will concern us later. But now the disparaging force of "bone-shaker" is central to the import of the utterance. And so are the plainly discernible feelings (contempt? impatience?) conveyed by it.

The emotive force of an utterance, as it may provisionally be labelled, depends in part upon the speaker's tone. (Cf. such comments as "He sounded irritated.") But independently of the speaker's own contributions to the emotive force, the words he uses may have regular capacities to produce a given emotive effect.

This point is neatly illustrated by the existence of approximate synonyms, roughly agreeing in reference, but differing substantially in their "emotive powers." To use a stock example: the verb "to be firm" may be conjugated as "I am firm, you are stubborn, he is pig-headed." In a similar vein, it has been said that "Animals sweat, men perspire, women glow!" Practical men are well aware of the capacities of what Bentham called "passion-kindling epithets." Not without reason does a trade journal addressed to businessmen advise its readers:

Instead of saying *Profit and Loss Account* say *Income Account.*
Instead of saying *profits,* say *income* or *earning.*
Instead of saying *added to surplus,* say *reinvested in the business.*

Apparently, profit by some other name does smell sweeter. Any newspaper will provide such examples as the preference of the Miami Chamber of Commerce for "sea-mist" in place of humidity. ("This so-called humidity is one of Florida's great health-building assets," an official spokesman once said.) Or, for a more serious example, consider the difference made to the procedure described in the United Nations Charter as "the concurring votes of the permanent members," when it is referred to by Americans as the "veto" or by Russians as "the rule of unanimity." A "distinction without a difference"? Hardly. The reference is the same in all the three cases, but the emotive force differs appreciably.

Such emotive coloration supplies a regular motive for

euphemism when conventionally unpleasant subjects are in question:

> Once I carried out a critical experiment on a large audience in the Community Church of Boston, an assemblage that may be classed as "liberal." Discussing obscenity, I said: "If I were to talk on the subject of sexual relationships and to use the words 'organs of generation' none of you would be at all disturbed. If I now turn Greek for the moment and say for the external organs of generation 'phallus' and 'lingam,' even those of you who know the meanings of these words will still sit quietly in your seats. But if I now turn Latin and so use the words 'penis' and 'vulva,' I see you squirming in your seats, some of you blushing, others with your heads down, and I hear a few titters—you are really uncomfortable. So I will turn English, say of the thirteenth century, and use the terms that nice people used in those days—good four-letter Anglo-Saxon words." I paused, "If I did, the police would arrest me and you would never forgive me. Yet these four-letter words, so redolent of obscenity and so devastating to your peace of mind, mean nothing more or less than the words you and the police permit me to use."[19]

A fine example, but a lame comment. To regard these alternative descriptions of the sexual organs as having precisely the same meaning is to don gratuitous blinkers.

The reader can easily find more examples for himself of the omnipresent phenomenon of "emotive coloration."

> Apart from technical, and especially scientific, language, which by definition is outside ordinary life, the expression of an idea is never free from some emotional tinge. In the affective gamut there is no note corresponding to the absence of emotion, but only to feelings which differ from each other (J. Vendryes, *Language,* Routledge & Kegan Paul, Ltd., London, 1925, p. 138).

To which the author adds the useful point that the deliberate suppression of signs of emotion, *e.g.,* when talking about a traffic accident, is really the manifestation of emotion (p. 164). The very "neutrality" of scientific discourse when dealing with subjects of grave human concern (*e.g.,* in current discussions of how many millions of deaths may be expected from alternative nuclear strategies) is an emotional affront to a sensitive reader.

[19]Abraham Myerson, *Speaking of Man,* Alfred A. Knopf, Inc., New York, 1950, p. 104.

The importance of the topic has been widely recognized, and for a long time:

> But by those [epithets] which are of the disparaging cast, prodigious is the mischief caused, when considered from the moral point of view. By a single word or two of this complexion, what hostility has been produced! How intense its feeling! How wide its range! How full of mischief, in all imaginable shapes, its effects! (Bentham's *Handbook of Political Fallacies*, ed., H. S. Larrabee, Johns Hopkins Press, Baltimore, 1952, pp. 143–144).

Yet the emotive powers of words, if potentially mischievous, also have their beneficent aspect. To reduce speech to "neutrality," if that were a realistic goal, would result in the utter destruction of poetry and literature. Our task, however, is neither to celebrate nor to deplore the emotive resources of language, but rather to seek a better understanding of them. For which purpose we turn first to a consideration of the theories about it that have been most influential in the early part of the 20th century.

THE DOCTRINE OF EMOTIVE MEANING

The term "emotive meaning," now thoroughly but perhaps unfortunately entrenched in discussions of language and related topics, owes its currency to the writings of I. A. Richards. Concerned in his early work to argue for an autonomous function for poetry, independent of any "statements" made by the poet (in our terminology, any "information" or "reference" conveyed in a poem), Richards was led to distinguish between "referential" and "emotive" meaning.

> A statement may be used for the sake of the *reference*, true or false, which it causes. This is the *scientific* use of language. But it may also be used for the sake of the effects in emotion and attitude produced by the reference it occasions. This is the *emotive* use of language (I. A. Richards, *Principles of Literary Criticism*, Routledge & Kegan Paul, Ltd., London, 1925, p. 267).

And a later writer, who has made influential use of this idea, says:

> Emotive meaning is a meaning in which the response (from the hearer's point of view) or the stimulus (from the speaker's point of view) is a range of emotions (Charles Stevenson, *Ethics and Language*, Yale University Press, New Haven, Conn., 1944, p. 59).

Both of these definitions presuppose a causal theory of meaning, which we shall have occasion to criticize later. In its "cognitive" or "referential" or "descriptive" aspects, an utterance is supposed to *cause* in a suitably trained hearer a range of corresponding beliefs; while in its "emotive" aspects it likewise causes a range of feelings or "attitudes," regarded by Stevenson and other defenders of the sophisticated form of this doctrine as a *disposition* to have the corresponding feelings.

Reverting to our original example, we might say that, on this view, the utterance, "The train is arriving now," will normally arouse a certain corresponding thought (true or false) in the mind of the hearer; while the emotively charged utterance, "That damned bone-shaker is just creeping in," besides arousing thoughts, will also have a tendency to arouse feelings. Which feelings? Why, those that would normally be vented by the use of "damned" and "bone-shaker," etc.

All writers on this subject recognize the difficulty of identifying the feelings in question except in terms of their appropriate verbal expression. It will be noticed that we are concerned with compatible and indeed interdependent uses of the utterance in question. Whether there can be such a thing as an emotive effect altogether independent of the transmission of any information or reference is a much-debated and still unsettled question.

The view outlined above is initially plausible for linguistic theorists who are satisfied to explain meaning in terms of causal effects. Those, like the present writer, who find this approach defective, will, however, need to make a distinction between the *emotive influence* of words and utterances and their possible *emotive meaning*.[20]

That emotively charged language can sometimes arouse feelings can hardly be questioned. No doubt Eliza Doolittle's use of the epithet "bloody" in Shaw's *Pygmalion* succeeded in shocking the play's earlier audiences as much as it was intended to, and all eloquence depends upon "arousing the passions," to use the old-fashioned phrase. But it seems at best doubtful whether such causal effects can usefully be considered as part of a word's meaning. The crucial point is that we can *understand* emotive language, whether or not we are

[20]The need to make some such distinction has come to be widely recognized. Thus Monroe C. Beardsley contrasts "emotive import" or capacity to affect the hearer's feelings, with "emotive purport," capacity to convey information about the speaker's feelings (*Aesthetics*, Harcourt, Brace & Co., New York, 1958, p. 118). The first of these is what I have called "emotive influence."

swayed by it: we don't need to share the feelings expressed in "Bitch" or "Kraut" (happily enough) in order to discern the intended force of these derogatory epithets.

The outline of a view more satisfactory than the causal theory of emotive import might run somewhat as follows. All feelings and all emotive attitudes have a natural tendency toward outward expression. Such expression, whether it takes the primitive form of gesture or the most sophisticated form of verbal utterance, is not normally produced for the sake of informing a hearer, nor, *pace* Richards, for the sake of arousing similar or complementary feelings in him.

A man who frowns with displeasure is not usually engaged in telling somebody anything: the frown is not a *sign of* displeasure, although it can be treated as such by a spectator, the truth being, rather, that frowning is a way of *being* displeased. Now the same can be said in general of the expression of more subtle and more sophisticated affective attitudes: the attitude, we might say, is embodied in the words used, however hard it may be to account for this theoretically. The feeling, the emotion, the attitude, is presented tangibly to the hearer or spectator, who is able to "read" it *in* the words.

We must, therefore, recognize a kind of symbolic representation substantially different from what we have already noted as the "propositional use" of words. In the latter, the words are, as it were, external to and independent of the thought expressed, the two being clearly distinguishable. But the feeling *expressed by* felicitous words can no more be separated from them than can the attitudes conveyed in a Seurat painting of a picnic in the park. We respond to the affective values by a kind of sympathetic insight of which we should be hard put to give an adequate analysis; but it is beyond dispute that we can more or less adequately discern the embodied feelings. The point to be stressed is that adequate response to the emotive aspects of discourse, whose importance can hardly be overstressed, is far less a matter of brute undisciplined arousal of feelings than the causal theory, in its cruder forms, would tend to suggest.[21] Since we can *under-*

---

[21] Richards himself has, on more than one occasion, protested against the vulgarized uses to which his early doctrine has been put, and especially against the common pejorative use of "emotive." In his most recent writings on the topic, he has tried to substitute for the earlier dichotomy between "emotive" and "referential" a more complex scheme of analysis in which, for instance, distinctions are made between the jobs done by words in "indicating," "characterizing," "realizing," and "influencing." The third of these comes close to what I have been loosely referring to as the capacity of emotive language to *place* the embodied feeling before the reader.

stand the feelings expressed in language, the way is open to exposition, exegesis, and criticism. Nothing, except our own inadequacies, the lack of suitable "speculative instruments," to use Coleridge's phrase, and the intrinsic difficulties of having clear ideas about the emotional ranges of experience, prevents our intellectual mastery of a poem, no matter how much infused with feeling, to any desired degree of explicitness. Which is not, of course, intended to imply any derogation of all such "non-cognitive" aspects of the poem, its rhythm and "verbal music." However much it is explained, the poem remains a unique verbal artifact that has to be experienced and enjoyed.

SOME USES OF EMOTIVE MEANING

Earlier forms of the doctrine of emotive meaning arose, as already explained, as part of an effort to assign an honourable function to poetry, whose autonomy and dignity seemed to be threatened by earlier positivistic theories of the "meaninglessness" of all but "referential" uses of language. It seems, in retrospect, that Richards and those who agreed with him conceded too much to the philistine in treating poetic utterances as "pseudo-statements" whose function was to arouse a comprehensive and harmonious system of emotional and attitudinal responses. A major weakness in this approach to poetics was its tendency to divert attention from the poem itself toward hypothetical and undetectable "responses"—in short, to confuse literary criticism with unavailable and largely fictitious psychology.[22] There are few literary critics today who would regard this as a promising avenue to the unsettled problems of poetics.

More stir, not to say scandal, continues to be caused by certain applications of the doctrine of emotive meaning to moral philosophy. It has long been recognized that the force of such ethical remarks as: "It is wrong to lie" is not satisfactorily captured in any "neutral" referential paraphrase.[23] For the ethical utterance I have cited is regularly

[22]See, for instance, the powerful attack upon this position in the essay by W. K. Wimsatt, Jr., included in his book *The Verbal Icon* (Noonday Press, New York, 1958), under the title, "The Affective Fallacy." It should be added in fairness to Richards and other "emotivist" critics that their practice was notably superior to their official doctrine. A reader of Richards' fine explications of particular poems will find surprisingly few traces there of his views about emotive meaning.

[23]This is the basic insight behind G. E. Moore's famous discovery of the "naturalistic fallacy." He argued that any analysis of "wrong" as,

used to *condemn* lying and to arouse in the reader corresponding attitudes toward the act. From this insight arose the doctrine of the absence of cognitive content in ethical judgments:

> In saying that a certain type of action is right or wrong, I am not making any factual statement, not even a statement about my own state of mind. I am merely expressing certain moral sentiments. And the man who is ostensibly contradicting me is merely expressing his moral sentiments. So that there is plainly no sense in asking which of us is in the right. For neither of us is asserting a genuine proposition (A. J. Ayer, *Language, Truth and Logic*, Dover Publications, Inc., New York, 1946, pp. 107–108).

This view of ethical judgments, as this passage shows, seems to invite a facile relativism, which is one reason why it gives so much offense to those who still hope to find an "objective" basis for morality. That this objection can be met, at least in part, is one outcome of the more careful emotive theories of ethics since elaborated by Charles Stevenson and others.[24] But it is fair to say that current work of this sort, successful as it has been in overcoming the earlier crude contrasts between "emotive" and "factual" language, still suffers from the absence of a more fully elaborated and generally accepted linguistic doctrine.[25]

THE DIMENSIONS OF LANGUAGE

The moral of the somewhat confused discussions of "emotive meaning" that have been surveyed in the preceding sections is that any useful conception of the manifold powers of language will have to operate with more complex and more discriminating distinctions than any crude opposition between "emotive" and "referential." What distinctions will ultimately establish themselves as satisfactory will depend, of course, upon the end in view. Of the making of distinctions, there can

---

say, "not conducive to the greatest happiness of the greatest number" or "tending to hinder the preservation of the species" or the like would still leave the "open question" whether the state-of-affairs thereby invoked should itself be regarded as right or wrong. No referential or "descriptive" analysis of basic ethical terms will do.

[24]See especially Stevenson's *Ethics and Language*, cited earlier. A valuable comprehensive survey is Avrum Stroll's *The Emotive Theory of Ethics* (University of California Press, Berkeley, 1954).

[25]The work of R. M. Hare, in his books *The Language of Morals* (The Clarendon Press, Oxford, 1952) and *Freedom and Reason* (The Clarendon Press, Oxford, 1963) show the benefits of a more adequate analysis of linguistic functions. But much still remains to be done.

be no end: it would be easy but pointless to construct a critical apparatus as unwieldy as Peirce's fantastic machinery of 77 categories of signs.[26] If our aim is to assist and enhance the fullest understanding of speech and writing, the critical apparatus provided ought to be simple enough to be easily remembered and applied, while flexible enough to avoid constraining the resourceful interpretation of given texts, for which no predetermined machinery can be a substitute.

A promising beginning might be made by recognizing, in general, three different, if related, aspects of language and speech.

Consider as simple a case as that of John Doe, at the breakfast table, asking his wife to "Pass the butter, please." Considering this utterance in its concrete setting, we can distinguish in turn its relations to what we have called the "speaker's situation," its relations to the intended effects upon the hearer, and its relation to its symbolized meaning. When we concentrate upon "what the speaker *says*" (allowing, as we always must, for elusiveness of the crucial word "says"), we are attending to the third of these aspects: the illustrative utterance *formulates* a certain meaning, capable of being elaborated by a paraphrase. But the speaker in his actual situation will have certain beliefs, attitudes, feelings which may, more or less intentionally, and more or less explicitly, be *expressed* in his utterance. And, after all, the main point of the breakfast-table request is not to convey a formulated meaning (to have the hearer *understand* what is being said), nor to convey, less formally, the speaker's attitudes and desires, but rather to get something done. We may say that the utterance is intended to *evoke* a hearer's response.

If the main "point" of the request for butter resides in its power to evoke a desired response, *via* the transmission of formulated and expressed desires, in other cases the stress, according to circumstances, may be rather upon the expressive aspect—as when someone says "What a beautiful day," not to convey information or to get something done, but merely to "relieve his feelings." In formal, scientific, or mathematical prose, however, emphasis is squarely upon the "presentative" dimension: the reader knows that the original writer had beliefs and attitudes, however thin or abstract, revealed in his choice of topics, his structuring of the argument, and

---

[26]The exact number might be disputed. By piling one trichotomy upon another, Peirce ended with a scheme, couched in barbarous jargon, that quite obscured his important initial insights. No subsequent theorist has used more than fragments of this baroque construction.

his style; and he knows also that the purpose behind the communication is to induce certain ideas and beliefs in his own mind; but the situation is conventionally conceived impersonally as one in which the standard *meaning* of the words used takes precedence over everything else (as if one angel were writing and another were reading).

In general, we might, therefore, distinguish between the *expressive*, the *presentative*, and the *dynamic*[27] aspects or dimensions of an utterance, where the use of the words "aspect" and "dimension" is intended to mark the important point that we are not trying to isolate mutually exclusive classes, but are emphasizing different ways in which utterances work (as solid bodies can be compared according to the three dimensions of length, breadth, and width). Some utterances may be specialized in one dimension rather than another (as expletives are intended mainly to express feelings, imperatives to achieve certain actions, and so on); but the general rule is that all three aspects, though distinguishable, are present and effective together. An utterance lacking all "expressive" and "dynamic" aspects is as impossible to conceive as a body that is all length, without width or breadth. In intricate cases, where, as in poetry, the speaker or writer simultaneously relies upon a number of linguistic powers, the interaction of all three aspects is of the highest importance. For instance, a perceptive reading of a poem demands lively awareness of the interplay between the poet's attitudes, modified and controlled by the presented meanings of the words used, and his imputed or merely pretended attitude toward his reader.

All of this, even if developed more carefully and more fully than space here permits, could be only a beginning. For one thing, we should be faced at once with the delicate and unsolved task of distinguishing within the "presentative" dimension between different ways in which a "meaning" can be placed before an audience. The case I previously labeled "informative," in which a *proposition* is presented, so that the meaning is straightforwardly true or false, is clearly only one of those that arise. It would be necessary to try to explain how a poet manages to display or exhibit a "meaning" without making a literal truth-claim about that meaning

[27] I have been influenced here by the suggestive tripartite scheme of analysis developed in Karl Bühler's book *Sprachtheorie* (Gustav Fischer, Jena, 1934). In his book Bühler distinguishes between *Ausdruck, Appell,* and *Darstellung,* which correspond, approximately, to the expressive, dynamic, and presentative functions here distinguished (p. 28 and passim).

—how he manages to "bracket" the truth-claim in the interest of some more subtle, less explicit, "statement." This is perhaps the hardest unsolved problem of poetics.

Further complications would be introduced by the necessity of distinguishing within each dimension, as we have done already in a preliminary way, between the explicit and implicit. And running athwart this already sufficiently complex scheme of analysis there is the distinction, constantly to be borne in mind, between what *the words* mean (conventionally express, conventionally evoke) and what the speaker means (expresses, evokes) *by means* of those words—between the lasting powers that the words possess and the particular ways in which speakers in given concrete settings play upon and avail themselves of these linguistic resources.

If something like this proposal proves serviceable for the purpose of improved "interpretation," we shall be led to ask of any given text a series of interrelated but distinct questions: What does the explicit utterance "say"? And in what modes of "saying"? What does this same utterance "express"? What kind of influence does it bring to bear upon the reader? How much of all this is explicit, and how much, and in what ways, are these effects to be counted as merely suggested or implied? How much is intended, how much merely revealed, without the speaker's consent? How far does all this come about as a matter of standard linguistic convention? And how much results from the distinctive contributions made by the speaker in the given context and setting?

And if these questions, for all their number, are still only a prelude to the complex act of interpretation, that is but one more indication of the extraordinary depth and richness of the phenomena here under discussion.

SPEECH ACTS AND PERFORMATIVES

I shall conclude this survey of the multiple uses of language by outlining a somewhat different approach that, under the influence of John Austin,[28] is increasingly attracting the attention of linguistic theorists. The investigations here to be discussed concentrate not so much upon the functions of words and utterances (as in the previous sections of this chapter) as upon the nature of the various acts that may be performed by means of speech.

[28] See especially his posthumous book, based upon lecture notes: J. L. Austin, *How to Do Things with Words* (The Clarendon Press, Oxford, 1962).

It is obvious enough, once attention has been drawn to the point, that there is a class of utterances whose main point is to *do* something, rather than to "say" something *about* something (or to express, to evoke, etc.). To take the stock example, a man who, in a suitable situation, says, "I promise such-and-such," is not merely telling his hearer something (though no doubt he is doing that, too): he *is* promising. And if nobody were ever in a position to promise *by* using the formula "I hereby promise" or some other formula serving the same purpose, there would be nothing to refer to in such informative uses of the same word as "He promised yesterday." (Where there is no question of the speaker himself making a promise.) Similarly, the umpire who says "Out!" or the judge who says "I sentence you to death" cannot be regarded as primarily engaged in informing his hearer: in both cases something is being done that could not be accomplished except by the use of some conventional linguistic formula. When a speaker counts by convention as doing something other than, or more than, "saying something," by uttering a form of words, we are dealing with what Austin calls a *performative* use of words (or a *performative* utterance). Thus a duly accredited clergyman who, having performed the previous ritual correctly, ends by saying, "I pronounce you man and wife" has, *in* that linguistic act, married the persons concerned. (One useful sign of such a performative use of language is, in English, the use of the verb in the "present" tense but not in the so-called "continuous" present tense— "I promise" rather than "I am promising." Unfortunately, this is neither a sufficient nor a necessary condition of a performative use.)

Performative utterances do not admit of the attribution of truth or falsity: think of the absurdity of responding to "I warn you not to do it" with the retort "You are lying!" But of course, performatives, like other utterances, admit of appraisal in terms of criteria of correctness. The analysis of what "correctness" can mean in such cases; or, to take another problem, the distinction between the conventional consequences of a performative (which Austin calls its "illocutionary force") and the effects actually induced in a hearer (its "perlocutionary force") are among the many interesting questions opened up by this new approach. For details the reader may be referred to Austin's own writings. The notion of "performative utterance" promises to afford important new insight into the uses of language in law, in ordinary life, and in many other contexts.

A WARNING

There is even less general agreement about an appropriate analysis of "the many uses of language" than about other branches of our tangled subject. This is unfortunate, given the importance, both practical and theoretical, of such analysis and the reformed terminology that might result. But disagreement is unavoidable, in the absence of comprehensive and accurate theory concerning the inter-relations between intention, feeling, perception and other basic concepts in philosophical psychology. Unsupported by such fundamental inquiry, present classifications of the uses or functions of language, such as those sketched in the preceding chapter, must be treated as exceptionally tentative and controversial. It is, indeed, a bad sign in this area when a technical term has a popular vogue: such popularity nearly always produces crude simplification, offensive to the idea's original promulgators. A particularly crass case of this is the popular currency of the term "emotive," whose rhetorical benefits are in inverse proportion to its clarity. A danger of opposite tendency is that a comparatively clear and fruitful, if somewhat ill-defined term, like Austin's "performatives," gets so battered and qualified by philosophical criticism that it becomes virtually discredited for all practical purposes.

Plainly, however, a sound and effective analysis of the multiple functions of language is sorely needed. In no part of our subject, it might be predicted, would general agreement, based upon authentic insight, produce more immediate and lasting benefits.

CHAPTER 6

LINGUISTIC ABUSE
AND LINGUISTIC REFORM

Distrust of Language

FOR ALL its obvious imperfections, language at its best is a
superb instrument for expression and communication. Since
familiarity blunts the wonder, it is a useful intellectual exercise to consider the consequences of any widespread deterioration in the effectiveness of language.

There is a terrifying mental disorder, known to psychia-
trists and experts on speech disorders as "semantic aphasia,"
in which familiar words lose their meaning and become mere
sounds. A glimpse of this pathological condition can be obtained on a small scale by overworking some familiar word.
If the reader will try repeating aloud a great many times
the word "cat," say, he should reach a point at which that
monosyllable becomes "opaque" and is heard as a sound in
its own right. He may then have the disturbing experience
of finding that the sound, temporarily deprived of its ordinary meaning, appears as alien as *koshka*,[1] or any other
name for a cat in a foreign language. Normally, of course,
we do not attend to the sounds we produce and, in a sense,
fail to hear them.

Semantic aphasia can be regarded as an acute form of a
more widespread incapacity to understand language, a kind
of "meaning-blindness," analogous to colour blindness, that
appears sporadically even in healthy persons. Let us imagine

[1] The Russian word for cat.

143

that such meaning-blindness, now happily exceptional, were to reach epidemic proportions. It is clear that everything we call civilization would grind to a standstill. All printed matter would become worthless, and as memories of craft and skill began to fade, all collective human enterprises would collapse. Deprived of all information beyond the narrow circle of immediate experience, men would be unable to think or to make intelligent provision for the future and would rapidly degenerate to a merely animal level. Since the existence and successful use of language make this nightmare of the general destruction of meaning only a science-fiction fantasy, one might expect the wisest of men to celebrate the power and the wonder of this incomparable human endowment.

In truth, however, the testimony of the wise is quite different, amounting, on the whole, to a surprising indictment of the imperfections of language. Logan Pearsall Smith's complaint may stand for a hundred others:

> I stood there awhile and meditated on language, its perfidious meanness, the inadequacy, the ignominy of our vocabulary, and how Moralists have spoiled our words by distilling into them, as into little vials of poison, all their hatreds of human joy.[2]

Such radical criticism of language must, indeed, be as ancient as language itself. If it is true that "in the beginning was the Word,"[3] we may presume that soon after the beginning there was a wise man of the tribe already bemoaning the inadequacy of the Word, and laying plans for the invention of a better one.

In some cases, indeed, the distrust of language goes so far as to deserve the name of logophobia. We find Bishop Berkeley grumbling that "Most parts of knowledge have been so strangely perplexed and darkened by the abuse of words, and general ways of speech wherein they are delivered, that it may almost be made a question whether language has contributed more to the hindrance or advancement of the sciences."[4] It is hard to believe him in earnest when he

---

[2] *All Trivia*, Harcourt, Brace & Co., New York, 1934, p. 64.
[3] The translation of *logos* as "Word" in the opening passage of St. John's Gospel is a famous crux of scholarship. The word bears the sense of "inward thought" as well as "the expression of thought." Goethe's Faust chose to render the passage as "In the beginning was the *act*" (cf. Ullmann, *Semantics*, p. 173).
[4] *Principles of Human Knowledge*, Introduction, 1st ed., sec. 21.

therefore resolves to abstain to the best of his ability from the use of language: "Since therefore words are so apt to impose on the understanding I am resolved in my inquiries to make as little use of them as I possibly can: whatever ideas I consider, I shall endeavour to take them bare and naked into my view. . . ." As well might he have resolved to outdo the nudists by sloughing off his own body: I do not know that he wrote any less in consequence of his resolution.

John Locke was so impressed by "the errors and obscurity, the mistakes and confusion, that are spread in the world by an ill use of words" as to wonder whether "language, as it has been employed, has contributed more to the improvement or hindrance of knowledge" (*Essay Concerning Human Understanding*, bk. iii, ch. xi, sec. 4). And if testimony to the same effect is desired from the moderns, we have Santayana asking "Why should philosophers drag a toy-net of works, fit to catch butterflies, through the sea of being, and expect to land all the fish in it?" (*Works*, Triton edition, vol. viii, p. 21) or Alfred North Whitehead saying that "Language is incomplete and fragmentary, and merely registers a stage in the average advance beyond ape-mentality"[5] and characterizing "uncritical trust in the adequacy of language" as one of the "two main errors to which philosophic method is liable." According to the immensely influential views of Ludwig Wittgenstein, "all philosophy is critique of language."[6]

Few of these writers go as far as the speaker who is said to have exhorted his hearers to "clear their minds of words" (though Berkeley comes close); and perhaps none of them would want to say with Brigham Young, "I long for the time that a point of the finger, or motion of the hand, will express every idea without utterance."[7] Criticism of the imperfections of language, when pushed to this extremity, leads to the kind of absurdity satirized by Jonathan Swift in his account of "A Voyage to Balnibarbi":

The other, [project] was a scheme for entirely abolishing all words whatsoever: and this was urged as a great advantage in point of health as well as brevity. For, it is plain, that every word we speak is in some degree a diminution of our lungs

[5]*Adventures of Ideas*, The Macmillan Co., New York, 1933, ch. 15, sec. 8, p. 291.

[6]*Tractatus Logico-Philosophicus*, 4.0031. The same emphasis upon language as a source of radical philosophical error dominates Wittgenstein's even more influential later work.

[7]*Journal of Discourses by Brigham Young*, Liverpool, 1854, vol. 1, p. 170.

by corrosion, and consequently contributes to the shortening of our lives. An expedient was therefore offered, that since words are only names for *things,* it would be more convenient for all men to carry about them such things as were necessary to express the particular business they are to discourse on. And this invention would certainly have taken place, to the great ease as well as health of the subject, if the women in conjunction with the vulgar and illiterate had not threatened to raise a rebellion, unless they might be allowed the liberty to speak with their tongues, after the manner of their forefathers: such constant irreconcilable enemies to science are the common people. However, many of the most learned and wise adhere to the new scheme of expressing themselves by *things,* which hath only this inconvenience attending it, that if a man's business be very great, and of various kinds, he must be obliged in proportion to carry a greater bundle of *things* upon his back, unless he can afford one or two strong servants to attend him. I have often beheld two of those sages almost sinking under the weight of their packs, like pedlars among us; who, when they met in the streets would lay down their loads, open their sacks, and hold conversation for an hour together; then put up their implements, help each other to resume their burthens, and take their leave.

But, for short conversations, a man may carry implements in his pockets and under his arms, enough to supply him, and in his house he cannot be at a loss; therefore the room where company meet who practise this art, is full of all things ready at hand, requisite to furnish matter of this kind of artificial converse (*Gulliver's Travels,* part iii, ch. 5).

The chorus of condemnation from so many eminent logophobes is sufficiently impressive to deserve closer examination.

PRACTICAL REASONS FOR DISTRUST OF LANGUAGE

There are grounds enough for any serious thinker or responsible reader to be on his guard against the traps set by the language in which thought is expressed. A great legal theorist once said:

In most of the domestic broils which have agitated civilized communities, the result has been determined or seriously affected, by the nature of the prevalent *talk:* by the nature of the topics or phrases which have figured in the war of words. These topics and phrases have been more than pretexts: more than varnish: more than distinguishing cockades mounted by the opposite parties (John Austin, *The Province of Jurisprudence Determined*, ed., H. L. A. Hart, George Weidenfeld & Nicolson Ltd., London, 1954, pp. 55–56).

It is easy enough to think of illustrations—of wasteful litigation arising from ambiguity, great wars turning upon the equivocal meanings of treaties—the endless and depressing story of human misunderstanding. Words have an almost frightening power: if Karl Marx had been denied a desk in the British Museum, the Bolsheviks might never have been able to seize power in Russia. As another writer has said, "I do not know which is the more striking—the clumsy inadequacy of words, or their world-shaking power. So long as men remain emotional creatures, they will continue to be taken, like rabbits, by the ears" (F. L. Lucas, *Style*, Cassell & Co. Ltd., London, 1955, p. 22).

Even in the less emotionally charged contexts of science and scholarship, the first requisite for intellectual advance is often an improvement, by no means easily achieved, in the relevant terminology.

> For the first tool needed by any analysis is an appropriate language; a language capable of describing the precise outlines of the facts, while preserving the necessary flexibility to adapt itself to further discoveries and, above all, a language which is neither vacillating nor ambiguous (Marc Bloch, *The Historian's Craft*, Alfred A. Knopf, Inc., New York, 1953, p. 157).[8]

Some of the complaints against the imperfections of language that I have quoted may be regarded as instigating programs of practical reform. When writers bemoan failure to communicate or to understand, the very complaint suggests a practicable remedy, however hard this may be to achieve with reasonable success. Such linguistic disabilities as ambiguity, vagueness, the improper use of emotive language, defective definition, inadequate terminologies, reliance upon anthropomorphic metaphors, entanglement by verbal issues, serious as they are, are all in principle capable of correction. (I shall be discussing some of the appropriate strategies in a later section.) When William James, complaining as so many philosophers do in like case, that he had been grossly misunderstood in his famous essay "The Will to Believe," asked, rhetorically, "of what insane root" his contemporaries had eaten to be capable of such incomprehension, he cer-

[8]This is a fascinating discussion of the problems faced by historians in devising a suitable language.

tainly thought that if they had taken more pains they would have been able to understand him. I call such criticism of language "practical," because the defects can in principle be corrected by suitable measures, well within the power of articulate and intelligent human beings to achieve. In this respect, disparagement of the resources of language is like dissatisfaction with the efficiency of automobiles or any other human contrivance. The cure for inadequate language is the invention of better language.

THE ALLEGED GAP BETWEEN LANGUAGE AND REALITY

The more acute forms of logophobia (pathological fear of language) arise from deeper anxieties. Induced by what looks like a reasonable conviction of the radically distorting nature of any language, no matter how satisfactory for ordinary practical ends, it might be called metaphysical criticism. As we shall soon see, such metaphysical criticism cannot be answered by *any* practical measure of improvement. From this standpoint, language necessarily distorts and misrepresents: it suffers, as it were, from an original sin that no amount of amendment can expunge.

The attentive reader will already have detected a suggestion of this metaphysical *malaise* in Berkeley's reference to "*general* ways of speech," in the passage from him that I have used above. What especially troubled Berkeley, as it has troubled many thinkers before and since, is the inescapable presence in language of widespread abstraction. We call somebody a man, or a husband, or a salesman, or a Democrat, but such general terms as these simply classify the individual with others more or less closely resembling him. It is easy to come to think that the individuality of the man in question—what marks him off as a unique person from everything else without exception—must inevitably elude any such heaping up of general labels. Each man has an inclination to say "I am not *just* a man, a husband, and so on—but, as it were, myself!" Such a feeling of something radically inadequate about the attribution of general characters may also be reinforced by a conviction of the arbitrariness of the classes into which we lump together persons or other objects for ease in reference and communication. From this it is but a step to the philosophical position known, in its many varieties, as *nominalism*, the view that in reality all things are individuals. It is fair to say that popular distrust of language is inspired strongly by some such nominalism, however imperfectly articulated.

A crude nominalism of this sort is often to be found, nowadays, expressed by overenthusiastic devotees of the popular movement known as General Semantics.[9] When we are exhorted to eschew such a general term as "cow" in favour of individual names—"Bessie," "Mollie," and the like—or are solemnly told by no less an authority than Stuart Chase that "fascism is only a word," unreflective nominalism reaches a laughable pitch of absurdity. Given the unavoidable presence of abstraction in language, the only sensible policy seems to be expressed in Whitehead's dictum, "Seek abstraction and distrust it."

It is, to be sure, easy enough to create a mood in which language, even at its best, seems hopelessly inadequate to the complexity of reality. "Million-fuelèd, nature's bonfire burns on" (Hopkins)—and language, by contrast, seems thin, oversimplified, unsubstantial, a mere smoke screen of words. As Locke put it, words "interpose themselves so much between our understandings, and the truth which it would contemplate and apprehend, that, like the medium through which visible objects pass, the obscurity and disorder do not seldom cast a mist before our eyes, and impose upon our understandings" (*Essay Concerning Human Understanding*, bk. iii, ch. ix, sec. 21).

Let us try to recapture the mood. Look attentively at any common object, say an oak leaf, and you may easily be

[9]General Semantics was an educational movement established in America after the first World War by the Polish Count, Alfred Korzybski (1879–1950), whose aims are still actively fostered by the International Society for General Semantics. Korzybski held that widespread and systematic distortions in human reactions to sign-situations, and especially those involving the use of language, had produced endemic "un-sanity," for whose cure he recommended some complex therapies. The most controversial of these is his—as I think unnecessary —rejection of "two-valued" conventional logic. His techniques, which some disciples have found applicable to fields as diverse as dentistry and marital relations, notably stress the importance of a critical approach to the use of abstractions. But Korzybski himself never made the crass blunder of supposing that language could dispense with the use of abstractions. In popular use, "semantics" has become a word of power like "the blessed word Mesopotamia," and "a question of semantics," used in a disparaging sense, means hardly more than a verbal issue. This is a far remove from Korzybski's elaborate constructions. The reader who wishes to pursue the matter further might consult S. I. Hayakawa, ed., *Language, Meaning and Maturity* (Harper & Row, New York, 1954), an anthology drawn from the journal *ETC*, which continues to publish interesting articles on popular semantics.

seized with an intense conviction of the irremediable poverty of language. That quite particular green, with the light reflecting and modifying the hue; the contrast between the colour of the veins and the stalk; the sharply etched, plainly perceived, yet indescribable outline; the special feel of the surface and the contrasting roughness of the underside; the earthy (what a poor word!) yet faintly aromatic scent; and so on and so on.

How on earth is one to reproduce all this in language? If one stares at the leaf as a painter might, only a painting begins to seem adequate, and even the best painting must fall short of the reality. And then, the leaf is only a tiny fragment of the experienced world, full of a "blooming, buzzing confusion" of scents, sounds, and feels. Consider the impossibility of rendering in words even such familiar experiences as the first taste of water after thirst, or the smell of a ripe limburger cheese. Whatever language we use for description now seems abstract and thin, by contrast with the immediacy and concreteness of lived experience. Where reality is a web of specific, particular, individual things, each with its own tang, language now appears as a disembodied ballet of abstractions.

This feeling of the alienation of language from reality is to be found vividly expressed in Sartre's first novel, *La nausée* (*Nausea*) where his hero, Roquentin, moves to a climax of metaphysical distress as he realizes the gap that exists between language (and hence, thought itself)—and things as they really are. He stares at a seat in a streetcar: "I murmur: 'It's a seat,' rather like an exorcism. But the word remains on my lips, it refuses to settle on the thing." And again "Things have broken free from their names. They are there, grotesque, stubborn, gigantic, and it seems ridiculous to call them seats or say anything at all about them."

It will be noticed that Roquentin is tempted to retreat into silence. This is, indeed, the only final resting point for anybody obsessed with the notion of an insurmountable gap between language and thought on the one hand and "million-fuelèd" reality on the other. For no practical reforms or improvement of language can help: to "purify the language of the tribe"[10] will still leave it a language, that is to say, incurably abstract and selective. But the metaphysical complaint against language is, precisely, that it is language and not reality itself. The quixotic attempt to purge language of

---

[10]Eliot's translation of Mallarmé's *Donner un sens plus pur aux mots de la tribu* . . . (from *Le Tombeau d'Edgar Poe*).

abstraction can end only in reducing it to a series of meaningless noises. Mysticism is just around the corner—the mysticism of "Whereof one cannot speak thereof one must be silent."[11] But the consistent mystic really ought to maintain silence, answering questions like Kratylos, by wagging his finger, or using the flapper of the Zen Buddhist to beat down attempts at intelligible conversation. There is nothing more ridiculous than a garrulous mystic.

Like other philosophical conceptions, the picture of language as a barrier or distorting medium (or, alternatively, of the supposed "gap" between language and reality) will seem inevitable to some minds and fantastically implausible to others. For those to whom its truth seems inescapable, the following considerations will probably have little weight. But they deserve attention for all that, since an important confusion about the nature and function of language is at issue.

I have already hinted that the supposed "obstacle" to the adequate representation of reality in language is of an absolute, metaphysical, or "logical" nature, not to be removed by any practical measures. It may be usefully compared to the supposed absolute "gap" between present and future, that cannot be overcome by any human contrivance—since the future, when we reach it, will inevitably then be what we call the "present." But if there is felt to be a *logical impossibility* of adequate representation, that is because those who think they detect it have a confused idea of what representation is. The complaint about the inadequacy of our linguistic means for describing a leaf, to revert to our earlier example, reduces upon inspection to a demand that the *description* of the leaf shall evoke the full *experience* of seeing, touching, and smelling the leaf. If it is not this, then it is a special case of the "practical" complaint about the poverty of our vocabulary or the ineptitude of our powers of expression. But then the difficulty might in principle be removed. If winetasters can make themselves understood to one another, a corresponding terminology could in theory be developed for talking about leaves, with any assignable degree of precision and accuracy. Now, to be sure, it is logically impossible for this demand to be met: the verbal description will never have the specific shape and scent or the other

---

[11]The famous concluding remark of the *Tractatus Logico-Philosophicus*. Wittgenstein, however, meant this to apply only to would-be metaphysical remarks, that seek to express the "essence of the world"; the mysticism I am here considering applies more radically to *all* attempts at intelligible discourse.

qualities of the leaf itself (indeed it is absurd to talk as if it might); nor will it evoke those qualities in imagination. But then why should it? The purpose of language in point is not to evoke reality, as perhaps representational painting hopes to do, but *to say true things about it*. And to accomplish this, it is essential that the representation should be distinct from the thing represented. Language cannot be saddled with the absurd task of reduplicating reality.

With this simple distinction clearly in mind, we can now see that the underlying image of the "barrier" between language and reality is a symptom of conceptual confusion. In any intelligible sense, a barrier is an obstacle that can be imagined removed, as a fence or a wall may be removed to facilitate entry. But the supposed "barrier" between language and reality is one of those "superhard" barriers, one might say, like the supposed barrier between present and future, or between one person and another, that loom so large in fruitless philosophical discussions. It may be paradoxical, but it is true, that a "barrier" that it is logically impossible to remove is not, in any interesting sense, a barrier at all. That this is so can be seen, from another angle, by considering how a critic of language claims to know that there is a "gap" or a "barrier" between language and reality. He must, it seems, know a good deal about reality in order to know, as he claims, that language does not and cannot fit it properly. But then if he speaks at all, he refutes himself from his own mouth; and if he consistently says nothing, there is nothing to answer. The fact is that the skeptic, like all humans, cannot long remain silent, and in speaking he illustrates that we can know enough about reality for our purposes. What we cannot do—and would not dream of attempting in our less confused moments—is to reduplicate reality in words. It is a fundamental mistake to suppose that the task of language is to try to make two worlds out of one.

We must, in truth, abandon all hope of modeling language upon a Reality that can be independently scrutinized without the assistance of thought and language. For better or worse, men, as soon as they can think at all, are committed to thinking in words; to bewail this or to view it with alarm is to lament the existence of thought itself. Perhaps Reality with a capital R will always elude us; but there is no need, quite the contrary, to suppose therefore that we are in any way prevented from exploring the nature of any number of realities (with a small r). Nor need the improvement of language, or urgent practical importance as that is, wait upon the resolution of metaphysical problems.

Failures of Communication

I propose in this section to survey some of the reasons why language often fails to be as efficient a means of communication as might be desired. The sign of such failure is misunderstanding—whose most obvious source is ignorance of the standard meanings of words. (But recourse to a dictionary will go far to correct this.) More troubling is lack of requisite background information, experience, and training. (There is no point in discussing painting with a blind man.) Lack of knowledge and lack of *rapport* between speaker and hearer raise general educational problems which, for all their importance, cannot be discussed here. I wish rather to consider some of the obstacles to understanding which may still block understanding even when the words used are familiar and the *rapport* exists. Failure to communicate, even in a situation as favourable as this, can be traced in part to certain important general features of language, such as "polysemy," "homonymy," and "synonymy," which will be explained presently. My object is to provide a preliminary survey of these features and to outline some measures that can be taken to cope with them.

Let us assume, for the moment at least, that the immediate purpose of a given speech-act is to convey to the hearer precisely one of the infinitely many complex meanings that can be expressed in the particular language that is being used. If we further assume that the meaning of the total utterance is uniquely determined by the meanings of the words of which it is composed and by their grammatical arrangement, we are led to the ideal expressed by many writers of "each word having a uniquely correlated meaning." For instance C. K. Ogden and I. A. Richards, in their influential book, *The Meaning of Meaning* (10th ed., Routledge & Kegan Paul, Ltd., London, 1949; originally published 1923), prescribe as one of the prime requisites for a satisfactory symbolism (with language as a special case), the "Canon of Singularity" that "One symbol stands for one and only one Referent" (p. 88).[12]

[12]Here, "referent" can be taken to be roughly equivalent—but only roughly—to "meaning." It is ironic that Ogden and Richards fail to be faithful to their canon in the very act of formulating it. For a careful analysis of their somewhat sprawling argument will show they mean different things by "referent" at different times.

It is obvious that whatever reasons may recommend it, this principle of one word, one meaning, need not be followed in successful communication. Consider the following example: The word *man* can, according to context, mean "human" (as contrasted with "animal") or, on the other hand, "male" (as contrasted with "female"). But anybody who says "I saw a man enter just now" runs no risk of misunderstanding in ordinary circumstances, because common sense rules out the possibility that the speaker was contrasting the situation with that of an animal intruder. Since nearly all words have a multiplicity of associated senses, this kind of "uptake" or intelligent response by the hearer is essential if we are to make ourselves understood at all. Fortunately, we can usually count upon such response. Let us then consider the modified maxim that each word composing an utterance should have a unique meaning *in the context in which it is used.*

The most obvious ways of violating this maxim are the following: (1) The word in question may have no meaning, or no sufficiently clear meaning, in the context. I shall call this a case of *semantic anemia.* (2) The word may have two or more meanings, between which the hearer is unable to choose. I shall call this a case of *contextual ambiguity.*

SEMANTIC ANEMIA

It is an ancient complaint that speakers and writers are prone to use words to which they attach no clear meaning or to which no clear meaning *can* be attached. Where the thought fails, a word comes in handy, as Goethe once said. The words themselves may have no firm meanings attached to them: consider, for instance, the word "un-American"[13] or the troubles that judges and lawyers have with such expressions as "due process" or "present danger." It is easy to multiply examples. John Locke said: "One may observe, in all languages, certain words that, if they be examined, will be found, in their first original and their appropriated use, not to stand for any clear and distinct ideas" (*Essay,* bk. iii, ch.

---

[13]"Not American: not characteristic of or consistent with American customs, principles, or traditions"—*Webster's Third New International Dictionary.* It is interesting that the French, unlike the English, have no corresponding formation. And why does "un-Dutch" or "un-Spanish" sound so laughable to an Englishman? "Un-American" and "un-English" have somewhat disreputable functions in English, as those considerations confirm, but I am here neglecting "non-cognitive" aspects (see Chapter 5) for simplicity of discussion.

x, sec. 2). Locke was mistaken in thinking that such "insignificant terms," as he called them, have been introduced mainly by "the several sects of philosophy and religion." The everyday talk of our own times is disfigured by the same abuse—peppered with words lacking firm meanings, or with words having no assignable meaning in context.[14] Linklater's fictional account of a visit to the Senate is, alas, all too realistic:

> Juan wondered if words meant anything at all. Certainly they rarely meant as much as their users thought, and often they were meaningless as a bullfrogs' chorus. Nine-tenths of all words were parrot-noises, not weighed, savoured, and tested, but merely repeated; a token coinage, defaced by long usage; there were whole sentences that lay on the surface of public memory and were paid-out ten thousand times a day—flipped off the tongue, rebounding from the tympanum—without a thought to give them life; and to nine-tenths of this vain nine-tenths no one listened. So that it was doubly vain. A minute disturbance in the air (*Juan in America*, Jonathan Cape, Ltd., London, 1931, p. 280. Reprinted by permission of A. D. Peters & Co., London).

This description would fit current advertising as well as much contemporary political rhetoric. Indeed it would take an exceptionally complacent writer to suppose himself exempt from this vice.

Semantic anemia—the use of "insignificant terms"—is rarely open and unabashed: there is a general convention that talk, except upon such privileged occasions as cocktail parties, ought to mean something—or, at least, to *appear* to mean something. So the abuse is commonly disguised with the aid of tautology, cliché, and jargon. The first, exemplified in the legendary announcement of "the largest laundry of its size in the world" might be defined as the device of saying nothing, while seeming not to. It is most successful when the course of the tautological statement is long and winding—as in the many books where the author manages to wrap up platitudes

---

[14]Compare Locke's attack on those who "by an unpardonable negligence, . . . familiarly use words which the propriety of language *has* affixed to very important ideas, without any distinct meaning at all. *Wisdom, glory, grace, etc.,* are words frequent enough in every man's mouth; but if a great many of those who use them should be asked what they mean by them, they would be at a stand, and not know what to answer" (*Essay*, bk. iii, ch. x, sec. 3). A modern list of words regularly submitted to such abuse might include *relativity, Oedipus complex,* and *democracy.* Technical terms used in some popular sense and terms of high generality are especially subject to this kind of abuse.

in a hundred pages (*absit omen*). The use of clichés is a device for using shabby ready-made expressions to avoid the pain of original thought and expression; while jargon (or "gobbledygook," to use the more expressive term) refers to inappropriately learned or impressive language, used to cover nakedness of thought. Special disciplines are of course entitled to the use of technical terms, seemingly barbarous, but needed for fixing complex meanings. The objection is to the serious evil exemplified in such language as the following:

> In research centers, individual wishes for recognition are implemented by administrative imperatives, so that the intensity of competition and the large number of competitors multiply enormously the real and alleged contributions to the advancement of learning. That a strong emphasis upon scholarly productivity results in tremendous positive values from leading universities is generally known. That it also interferes with the performance of other functions and in marginal cases produces flamboyancy, exhibitionism, quantitativeness without regard for quality, and other results inimical to knowledge itself is not so generally known.[15]

I would be inclined to say that seldom were so many words used to say so little—but for the wide prevalence of such bullfrog chatter.

There seems little to do about these dismal swamps of linguistic abuse except to deplore them. Linklater's modest plea that words be "weighed, savoured, and tested" before use will be ignored as pedantic or condescending by those who most need to pay attention.

UNCERTAINTY OF COMMUNICATION: AMBIGUITY AND OTHER FAULTS

I have defined *contextual ambiguity* as the occurrence of words in two or more meanings, between which the hearer is unable to choose. This provisional formula is unsatisfactory in a number of respects: it uses the word "meaning," itself notoriously uncertain in meaning; and, consequently, it fails to distinguish between a number of distinct ways in which an utterance may, through no fault of the hearer, fail to convey a definite message.

We may, for a start, usefully distinguish between failure

[15]Logan Wilson, "The Functional Bases of Appraising Academic Performance," *American Association of University Professors Bulletin*, October, 1941, vol. 27, p. 449.

of *reference* and failure of *sense*. If I mention "Bonaparte," you may take me to be talking about the French Emperor, when all the time I had in mind Arthur Upfield's half-caste detective: that is a failure of reference. (And if the reader still cannot identify the fictitious character in question, that is another example of the same mishap.) But then I may go on to say that Bonaparte was feeble—and you may reasonably wonder whether I meant "feeble in action" or "feeble in health"—or something else again. "Ambiguity" is usually reserved for the latter kind of uncertainty,[16] confusion of reference, perhaps on account of its comparative rarity, having, so far as I know, no equally convenient label.

The main sources of ambiguity of senses in present-day languages are *homonymy* (from the Greek: literally, "same name") and *polysemy* (Greek again: *polys* "many" + *semeion* "sign"). It is hard to draw a sharp line between the two: homonymy occurs when one and the same word-sound has two quite distinct meanings[17] as, say, when *bore* means "tiresome person" and also "diameter of gunbarrel"; polysemy[18] occurs whenever a word has many senses regularly attached to it. The former is rather rare, the latter very common.

[16]However, the word is also unfortunately used to stand for other things. In William Empson's well-known and valuable book, *Seven Types of Ambiguity* (rev. ed., Chatto & Windus Ltd., London, 1947), for instance, he says, "I propose to use the word ['ambiguity'] in an extended sense, and shall think relevant to my subject any verbal nuance, however slight, which gives room for alternative reactions to the same piece of language" (p. 1). The *multiple meanings* that a word has in context need to be carefully distinguished from the defect that is here intended by "contextual ambiguity." Poets, as well as punsters, often get their best effects by meaning more than one thing at the same time (as some of Empson's examples illuminatingly show): these depend upon the schooled hearer or reader perceiving both meanings at once, not in order to hesitate between them, but rather in other to appreciate their relation and interplay.

[17]This may come about through gradual convergence in the sound of words originally unlike: as in the case of *meal* ("flour") from Old English *melo*, and *meal* ("repast") from Old English *mæl*. Another cause is the gradual divergence of senses originally so close as to seem attached to a single word: as in *pupil* ("scholar") and *pupil* ("apple of the eye"). Still another source is the influence of foreign borrowings. For all of these the reader may consult Stephen Ullmann's compact and interesting discussion of polysemy and homonymy in his *Semantics* (Basil Blackwell & Mott, Ltd., Oxford, 1962), especially pp. 176–180.

[18]This ugly word, invented by Bréal, is now, alas, firmly established in the lingo of linguists. Turning to Latin doesn't help, since "plurisignification" is just as ugly and more of a mouthful. "Multiple meaning" is needed for another purpose. The technical language of discussion about language is far from satisfactory and is unlikely to improve in the near future.

A casual glance at the *Oxford English Dictionary* will show any number of words listed with four or more senses, and words-of-all-work like *get*, *make*, *put*, and *do*, need many pages to do justice to the rich variety of meanings that cling to them.[19] While this makes lexical ambiguity possible, it is not itself a defect. As Ullmann says, "If it were not possible to attach several senses to one word, this would mean a crushing burden on our memory: we would have to possess separate terms for every conceivable subject we might wish to talk about. Polysemy is an invaluable factor of economy and flexibility in language; what is astonishing is not that the machine occasionally breaks down, but that it breaks down so rarely."[20] If anything, this understates the case. Within what is conventionally called "the same sense" closer examination will usually reveal variations of criteria and signification that invite conceptual confusion. The risk of more or less serious lexical ambiguity is therefore always present. We shall soon see that the serious disorder of thought labeled "verbal issue" has its roots in the multiple and shifting senses of key words.

Any adequate survey of the ways in which communication may be uncertain would have to include amphibology (from the Greek *amphi* "on both sides" and *ballein* "to throw")—in other words, uncertain grammatical construction. A more graceful label, also in common use, is "amphiboly." Books on English composition usually produce as examples such old chestnuts as the apocryphal advertisement, "Wanted, a piano by a gentleman with wooden legs" or the definition of anthropology as "The science of man, embracing woman." But more serious examples are not uncommon. Does the proverb "Feed a cold and starve a fever" mean that if you feed a cold you will have to cope with a fever—or merely that colds, by contrast with fevers, need an ample diet? Proverbs, and other maxims of conduct, are, like the Delphic oracles, typically ambiguous and amphibolous. Hence, their adaptability to a large class of situations and their compatibility with other saws at first sight in conflict. In this field, it has been said, "All truths are half-truths—including this

---

[19]This is one reason why projects, such as C. K. Ogden's Basic English, designed to construct a simplified form of a language, for ease in learning and in essential communication, are somewhat deceptive. The pupil needs to learn the separate senses separately, and the pattern of combinations of senses under a single label varies from one language to next. This is a constant source of solecism.

[20]Ullmann, *Semantics*, p. 168.

one!" When Dr. Johnson, on a famous occasion, said that "Patriotism is the last refuge of a scoundrel," was he making a derogatory remark about scoundrels—or about patriotism —or about both?[21]

An amphiboly in an uttered sentence leaves the hearer with a choice between alternative logical or grammatical relations. The cases most easily corrected are those of defective punctuation: just as the amphiboly in "4 + 5 × 2" (18 or 14?) can be removed by the insertion of brackets, so, in trivial linguistic instances, the insertion of commas, or the use of suitable pauses and stresses in speech, will usually resolve the uncertainty. The more troublesome cases are those in which the grammatical or logical uncertainty is masked by a shifting sense of a functional word, such as "and" or "or" (cf. the practice in commercial correspondence of using "and/or" and the logicians' use of distinct symbols to represent "disjunction" and "alternation").

Matters of life and death can turn upon such niceties:

> It is said that Sir Roger Casement was hanged on a comma in a statute of Edward III. And Professor Ifor Evans has adduced the strange case of Caleb Diplock who bequeathed half a million for "charitable or benevolent objects." Clear enough, one would have thought—though needlessly verbose. But the law regularly sacrifices brevity to make sure of clarity —and too often loses both. In this case legal lynxes discerned that "benevolent" objects are not necessarily "charitable." The suit was carried from the Court of First Instance to the Court of Appeal, from the Court of Appeal to the Lords; judges uttered seventy thousand words of collective wisdom; and poor Mr. Diplock's will was pronounced invalid. Much virtue in an "or." Well did the Chinese say that when a piece of paper blows into a law-court, it may take a yoke of oxen to drag it out again (Lucas, *Style*, p. 22).

It should not be too hastily assumed that uncertainty of meaning, as in the flagrant case cited by Lucas, is always an evil. A case can be made, in law, in diplomacy, and sometimes in everyday affairs, for leaving some discretion of interpretation to the immediate audience or to those who may subsequently need to rely upon the authority of the written

---

[21]The context seems to show that he was hitting especially at the "patriotism" of the Whigs (see Boswell's *Life* under 7 April, 1775). Boswell says he meant only "that pretended patriotism which so many, in all ages and countries, have made a cloak for self-interest." In the fourth edition of his *Dictionary*, Johnson defined one sense of *patriot* thus: "It is sometimes used for a factious disturber of the government."

word. And it is not too cynical to reflect that it is a function of language to conceal thought as well as to convey it.

> For the law is not to be confined in a nutshell. Fair, reasonable, equitable, proper, due, they are all familiar enough, and they are so empty nearly of any but emotional meaning that they express little more than an attitude. They are receptacles to be filled from some future context of circumstance. They are bourns to be achieved as well as believed. The bad draftsman squanders them. The good draftsman cherishes them, because they allow him to make his immediate meaning as scarce as he chooses. . . . Business could no more do without this cardinal verbal virtue of vagueness than businessmen could afford to lose their basic confidence in one another. If the meaning of legal documents were to be made as precise as lawyers have been brought up to believe it should be, our trade, our commerce, all our affairs, would have to choose between law and living. What we admire in legal draftsmanship is not precision. It is a precisely appropriate degree of imprecision (Charles P. Curtis, *It's Your Law*, Harvard University Press, Cambridge, Mass., 1954, pp. 75–76).

If this was intended seriously, it must rank as a curious defense, given its suggestion that "confidence" in business and legal affairs depends upon a judicious "scarcity of meaning." Would such confidence survive open acknowledgment of the deliberate use of key terms that are "nearly empty of any but emotional meaning"? The truth is that the learned jurist probably exaggerated the absence of specifiable meaning in the key legal terms he used for illustration. At any rate, he may be held faithful to his own precepts in so lightly using "vagueness" and "imprecision" as interchangeable synonyms.

This may be a good moment at which to make the somewhat obvious point that uncertainty of meaning and reference ("ambiguity," in any of the senses in which that overworked word is commonly in use) should be held distinct from *intended* indefiniteness of meaning. When I say that *somebody* has been tampering with my papers, I am not speaking at all imprecisely, even though I am in no position to specify further. Nor is there any uncertainty of reference, since I am not *failing* to identify the offender. The same applies in general: if I ask for a sheet of white paper, I may be indifferent to further specifying properties and it would therefore be absurd to accuse me of vagueness, imprecision, ambiguity, or some other fault of communication. The difference between a more definite and a less definite utterance can usefully be compared to the differences in focus between two photographs of the same scene. The choice of some definite focus, with corresponding variation in the relative definiteness of objects represented, is unavoidable and not to be deplored; double images, however, are nearly always a nuisance.

In order to be even reasonably adequate, any survey of "uncertainty of meaning" would need to take some account of the many ways in which the aspects of a speech act (other than "meaning" and "reference") can be equivocal. An utterance may be defective because it leaves the hearer uncertain about the speaker's attitude toward his subject, or to his audience; there may be uncertainty about the seriousness or "pregnancy" of the speaker's use and about his "tone" (*i.e.*, whether he is speaking playfully, ironically, and so on). All of these matters, which play so large a part in practical problems of understanding and interpretation, must, for all their importance, be left here with this bare mention.[22]

The Reduction of Misunderstanding

CORRECTION OF AMBIGUITY AND UNCERTAINTY OF MEANING

The chief strategies for correcting uncertainty of meaning (and reference, etc.) may be classified as (1) *distinction*, (2) *amplification,* and (3) *definition.* It will be found that the first and third of these can be treated as special cases of the second.

1. *Distinction of senses,* or the explicit separation of competing readings, can often be effectively used when a troublesome equivocation turns upon a single phrase or word. If a philosopher says, with whatever plausibility, that "Only the *desirable* can be properly treated as *a good*," he may reasonably be asked to make a distinction between *desirable* as "able to be desired" and *desirable* as "worthy of being desired." And he might, with no less reason, be asked to distinguish between *a good* as "something good in itself"—an *intrinsic* good—or, again, *a good* as "something held to be good." Similar demands for a more firmly anchored sense might be made for the expression *"properly treated,"* which occurs in the quotation I have used above. Such lurking ambi-

---

[22]They arise constantly in the work of translators, literary critics, and educators. The most perceptive and sustained discussions of such problems are to be found in I. A. Richards' works. The reader might, for instance, wish to consult his *How to Read a Page* (W. W. Norton & Co., Inc., New York, 1942) and then to proceed to his *Practical Criticism* (Routledge & Kegan Paul, Ltd., London, 1929).

guities in the philosopher's sentence are not necessarily a sign of poor expression; the difficulties of writing precisely, in non-technical language, about philosophical problems or topics of comparable abstraction are formidable. Serious efforts to overcome them, as in the exceptionally careful writings of G. E. Moore, who taught a whole generation of English and American philosophers the importance of clarity, are apt to defeat their object by generating intolerable prolixity.

The device considered may be regarded as consisting in marking differences of sense of an ambiguous word by attaching a supplementary label, which functions, at least in the context, as an approximate synonym. I have noticed that this device is commonly used in certain foreign languages, *e.g.,* in Japanese, in order to locate the sense of a technicality borrowed from another language. The pair consisting of the foreign word plus an appropriate synonym from the host language functions more effectively than any straightforward attempt at translation. Thus mathematicians find it convenient to distinguish between "convergence" and "uniform convergence"; logicians talk of "material implication," "strict implication," "formal implication," and so on.

The same device is used systematically in legal documents where strings of near synonyms, often with attached qualifications, serve to protect the intention of the drafter. Consider the following example:

You are the vice-president of a bank. You want your lawyer to put in a provision requiring the borrower to keep its working capital up to some fixed amount. You reject the phrase "working capital" as a bit too loose. You are not sure that it has enough technical meaning. Instead you ask him to put, "the excess of the total current assets over current liabilities," which has a firmer technical usage. And you make it the firmer by qualifying it, "determined in strict accordance with sound accounting practice." But then you remember that you are requiring annual audit reports by an accountant. So you tell him to add, "by the independent certified accountants responsible for the preparation of the audit report." Thus you adjust the scope and tether of the discretion you are delegating by adding qualifying words and phrases. For this is what they do. Every word you add modifies the future power of action of the person you address, here a prospective borrower. If you hadn't put in "independent," the borrower might have used his own accounting department. If you hadn't put in "certified," you could not have objected that he hadn't been certified (Curtis, *It's Your Law,* pp. 67–68).

Of course there is no end to this process of protecting the intended meaning against all conceivable misinterpretation and abuse. And Curtis, after the passage I have quoted, goes on to underline the importance of leaving some leeway to take account of unforeseen eventualities—as in the deliberate use of the adjective "sound" in the expression "sound accounting practice."

With this example, we have already crossed the boundary between the drawing of distinctions and more general procedures of elaboration and paraphrase.

2. *Elaboration of sense.* This is simply the common-sense procedure of using more words, in order to explain at greater length what was really intended. It may usefully be considered an attempt to answer in advance certain likely questions of interpretation. ("When you said 'coexistence,' did you mean to contrast it with 'war,' with 'economic competition,' with 'active cooperation'—or with all of these at once? Is 'coexistence' intended to imply any degree of active intercourse in economic, diplomatic, and cultural matters?" And so on.) The overriding advantage over the printed word of the lecture (American style) is that the audience has the chance to intervene with relevant questions of this sort. Elaboration and paraphrase are attempts to overcome, in some measure, the necessary limitations of a situation in which the writer addresses an unknown and necessarily passive audience.

There are fairly obvious limitations to the use of this procedure for protecting meaning. For one thing, the writer who uses many words will, given the impatience of the modern reader, be likely to remain unread. But even if the reader has the patience for a prolix discussion, the introduction of additional explanatory material is a further source of possible misunderstanding, since internal inconsistencies can thereby enter. The more you say, the more chance of being misunderstood. And, finally, there is the limiting factor of the absence in the speaker's or writer's mind of any meaning sufficiently definite to stand the sort of careful teasing out that is here in question. When one of the Beatles[23] gave great offense in 1966 by saying that "the Beatles are more popular than Jesus Christ," it is doubtful whether he knew any better than his audience what he really meant. (But

---

[23]For the benefit of future readers who may happily find this reference unintelligible, it may be recorded that the Beatles, at the time of writing, were a group of popular singers whose success with the young was sufficiently spectacular to provide England with an important source of invisible exports.

those who took offense were probably not far wrong in detecting a derogatory attitude toward Christianity. The disclaimers that invariably follow this kind of revealing utterance by a celebrity or notoriety can usually be discounted.) Now the same is true in graver contexts. The uncertainties in resolving Kant's intentions, that have kept generations of scholars busy with disputed interpretations, would almost certainly remain unresolved if the ghost of the philosopher could be consulted.[24] Which is of course no excuse.

3. *Definition.* Of all the current remedies for ambiguity, the most highly regarded is undoubtedly definition—which may, for present purposes, be itself defined as "explanation of the meaning of a word or expression."[25]

The merits of this procedure are too plain to need praise. However, the formal definitions assembled in dictionaries are likely to be disappointingly unhelpful in removing contextual ambiguity. Even the best dictionaries are disfigured by inaccuracies and all too often they shirk the difficult task of definition by relying upon relatively uninformative synonyms. And even at their best, dictionaries can roughly demarcate only standard senses, whereas what is important in serious cases of contextual ambiguity is uncertainty about the speaker's intentions in a particular case. But beyond all this, there is the disconcerting fact that definition—at least in its traditional sense of "bi-verbal definition"—replacing the term to be defined by another expression having exactly the same meaning—is only exceptionally feasible. Words that refer to immediately perceived qualities, like "scarlet" or "sweet," are refractory to such "bi-verbal definition"; and so, notoriously, are words standing for relations ("if-then," "cause," and many others). Unnecessary obstacles to the "explanation of the meanings of words" have been imposed by the ancient Aristotelian tradition that "correct" definitions ought to proceed by genus and differentiating condition (*per genus et differentiam,* in the old scholastic phrase). A more pragmatic approach to problems of definition, that concentrates upon removing possible misunderstanding or misidentification in the mind of a suitable hearer, will admit many other procedures as suitable for "definition" in the broader sense here rec-

[24]When G. E. Moore was once asked by a student what he meant by some passage in one of his essays, he replied "Did I say that? I wonder what on earth I could have meant!" Few philosophers are equally candid.

[25]The Oxford Dictionary has under "Definition" the entry: "A declaration or formal explanation of the signification of a word or phrase."

ommended: the exhibition of paradigmatic examples, the formulation of relevant, though not sufficient criteria, and much else.[26]

CREEPING AMBIGUITY AND VERBAL ISSUE

Out and out ambiguity (inability to choose between alternative readings of key terms) is less dangerous, because more obtrusive, than hidden shifts in the meanings of important words. This appears most insidiously when a number of speakers use such shifting words as "Democracy" or "Liberalism," "Justice" or "Morality," in substantially different ways. Agreement in word, though not in thought or intention, is a fertile source of eventual recrimination and accusations of bad faith. Still more striking than such comedies of misunderstanding and cross purposes is the spectacle of disputants locked in violent disagreement, for no better reason than unsuspected and conflicting uses of crucial words. Bertrand Russell told the story, once, of a theological student ending a night's bitter disputation by saying, "I see now: your God is my Devil; and my Devil is your God!" More troublesome cases of such talking at cross purposes arise when the shifts of meaning are sufficiently plausible and subtle to escape immediate inspection.

As a prime example of such *verbal issue* (a label that, as we shall presently see, is likely to mislead) we may as well adapt a famous discussion of the topic by William James.[27]

You enter a field, to find yourself faced by a bull; as you cautiously circle around him, prudently deciding to leave by the way you came, he constantly turns, so as always to face you. The question is: Did you or did you not *go around* the animal? (James's example is that of a man circling a tree while a squirrel, on the other side of the trunk, constantly facing in the opposite direction, circles so as to remain unseen throughout.) Well, says James, using a phrase congenial to philosophers, it "all depends upon what you mean"[28] by "going around." If you mean "walking around a closed loop,

[26]Richard Robinson's *Definition* (The Clarendon Press, Oxford, 1950) is the only modern book on this important subject. Robinson's treatment is comprehensive, but somewhat idiosyncratic. His terminology has found little acceptance.

[27]In his book *Pragmatism* (Longmans, Green & Co., Ltd., New York, 1943), p. 43.

[28]James says it depends "on what you *practically mean*" (*Pragmatism*, p. 44, italics in original). His aim is to "interpret each notion by tracing its practical consequences" (p. 45).

containing the bull in its interior throughout," then you *did* go around him; but if you mean "gradually changing your relative orientation, so that you were first in front of him, then to one side, then behind him and finally in front again," then you did *not*. The crucial point is that the answer does not turn upon any questions of fact but upon the preferred manner of *description* of those facts. (If the reader considers the example excessively trivial, let him ask the parallel question about the relative motion of the earth and the moon, or about either of them and the sun—and let him reflect upon the centuries of intellectual effort needed to disentangle a clear idea of the idea of *relative* motion.) If two men were to waste their time arguing whether the man did *really* go around the bull—or, what is substantially the same issue, the question whether the earth really does revolve around the sun—their dispute, it seems, could rapidly be brought to an end by an agreement to provide definitions. What may have looked like an authentic disagreement is unmasked as a mere misunderstanding: there are really at issue two distinct propositions, expressed by the same word, and once this has been noticed, the "dispute" evaporates. To continue argument once the "verbal" character of the dispute has been revealed would be as unreasonable as to suppose that there is a genuine difference of opinion between two men who say "I like bananas" and "I don't like bananas" (though here, of course, there is a shift of reference, not of sense).

It follows that the expression "verbal issue," in its accepted uses, is somewhat analogous in underlying logical structure to "imaginary man" or "fictitious beast." It is intended to apply to something that is not a genuine dispute—appearances notwithstanding—arising through unnoticed differences in the meanings of crucial words or expressions. It must, of course, not be confused with a dispute *about* words, which may be plainly "factual" and not verbal in the relevant sense. (Whether "almost" and "nearly" are strict synonyms in English is a question of fact, however hard it may be to know the right answer; it is not a "verbal issue.")

For more complex and more interesting examples of verbal issues, we might consider almost any current dispute about free will and determinism. We can imagine the argument to take the form of the following dialogue:

A. Imagine a talented composer of music. His mind buzzing with the themes of some sonata, he sits down to write out the score. Everything goes smoothly: he has the satisfaction of doing just what he wants to do and knowing that it is good. Such a man is free in every sense of the word. You see, therefore, that cases of freedom do occur—however rarely.

But then comes an attempted refutation:

B. I disagree. All human actions are determined by sufficient causes. There is every reason, therefore, to suppose that your happy composer is doing only what must necessarily follow from the initial state of his body, its surroundings, and so on. However complex his behaviour, he is in principle no freer than a planet revolving immutably in its orbit.

This case is obviously far more complicated than our trivial first example of the man and the bull. For one thing, we can hardly say here that there is complete agreement between the parties about the relevant facts, which we took to be one of the hallmarks of a simple verbal issue. Our hypothetical arguer, *A,* might well dispute the deterministic assumptions of his antagonist, relying perhaps upon the well-known, but in this context irrelevant, indeterminism of modern quantum physics. Yet the unresolved question of whether human actions do in fact have sufficient causes, a question much more complicated than this brief reference to it might suggest, is in a certain sense irrelevant. From the arguments used by the two disputants, a useful clue to the senses in which they are using the key terms, it is plain to see that they are in fact relying upon different—and perhaps conflicting—criteria. For *A* a man is free, we may guess, if he is under no external restraint, and able to do what he most wants to do and approves of doing. For *B,* on the other hand, it seems that an action is free only if it is *uncaused.* These criteria seem so widely separated that it might seem hardly better than a pun to use the same word for both senses.

It is doubtful, however, whether this divergence of meaning could be resolved by a simple agreement upon alternative definitions of the word "freedom." For one thing, the highly complex and unstable notion of "freedom"[29] has a number of features that go far to justify *B*'s assumed definition of the term. That is to say, if *A* offered the definition I have sug-

---

[29]In Part iii of his book *Freedom and Civilization* (George Allen & Unwin Ltd., London, 1947), Bronislaw Malinowski speaks of "a complete chaos in the domain semantically covered by the words freedom and liberty" (p. 43). He ends with an elaborate analysis in which the key sense "absolute absence of all restraint" is flanked by eight subsidiary and related senses (p. 54).

gested, *B* might be able to talk him out of it, by arguing, more or less plausibly or correctly, that a man whose actions really were the inevitable consequences of the state of his body and its surroundings could not really be held to be free.[30]

Writers impressed by the dangers of entanglement in verbal issues have been prone to take the somewhat simpleminded view that they can be readily dispelled by definitions of the equivocal terms. Barbara Wootton, for instance, choosing the question whether Russia is a socialistic country as an example of a "sterile verbal issue"[31] writes that this question "is a matter of linguistic convenience *which should be settled in a moment by an agreed convention:* and inasmuch as the word 'socialism' has no precise technical meaning . . . *it is a matter of indifference which way the matter is decided.*"[32]

This is wholly to overlook the strong valuations that have, in many parts of the world, attached themselves to the term "socialism," as a consequence of its history. (Of course, in such combinations as "socialized medicine" the word has an opposite polarity.) To speak, as Wootton does, about the "strong emotional associations" of the disputed labels is to do less than justice to the issues at stake.

Professor W. B. Gallie sees more profoundly into the problems when he writes:

Different uses of the term "work of art" or "democracy" or "Christian doctrine" subserve different though of course not altogether unrelated functions for different schools or movements of artists and critics, for different political groups and parties, for different religious communities and sects. Now once this *variety* of functions is disclosed we might expect that the disputes in which the above-mentioned concepts figure would at once come to an end. But in fact this does not happen. Each party continues to maintain that the special functions which the term "work of art" or "democracy" or "Christian doctrine" fulfils on *its* behalf or on *its* interpretation, is the correct or proper or primary, or the only im-

[30]This, in its turn, would almost certainly involve debatable shifts in the senses of the words "necessity" and "cause." Part of the trouble in this exceptionally difficult case is that the analyst is faced with a network of concepts, rather than with one that can be treated in isolation.

[31]Not all verbal issues are sterile. They may reveal strains in our conceptual frameworks and lead to useful revision of our basic notions.

[32]Barbara Wootton, *Testament for Social Science*, George Allen & Unwin Ltd., London, 1950, p. 53. Italics added.

portant, function which the term in question can be said to fulfil. Moreover, each party continues to defend its case with what it claims to be convincing arguments, evidence and other forms of justification.[33]

Socialism is in fact an "essentially contested concept," to use Gallie's useful label. The absence of agreed definitions of "socialism" is a symptom of deep and unsettled controversies about the desirable and most efficient forms of human society. To suppose that the label, with all its rich historical associations,[34] will be willingly relinquished in order to resolve the intellectual confusions we have called "verbal issues," is to take altogether too naïve a view of the relations between words, thoughts, and actions.

VAGUENESS AND "LOOSE CONCEPTS"

Some very ancient puzzles, which still raise problems of contemporary importance, turn upon the difficulty of knowing when and how to "draw a line":

> No faculty of knowing absolute limits has been bestowed upon us by the nature of things to enable us to fix exactly how far to go in any matter; and this is so not only in the case of a heap of wheat from which the name is derived,[35] but in any matter whatsoever—if we are asked by gradual stages, is such and such a person a rich man or a poor man, famous or undistinguished, are yonder objects many or few, great or small, long or short, broad or narrow, we do not know at what point in the addition or subtraction to give a definite answer (Cicero *Academica*, 93, tr. H. Rackham, *Loeb Library*, 1951, p. 585).

It seems absurd to say that the loss of a single penny can convert a rich man into a poor one, or the loss of a single hair change a hirsute man into a bald one. Yet if this is unacceptable, so is the alternative of denying any objective difference between wealth and poverty—or between a well-

[33]*Philosophy and the Historical Understanding*, Chatto & Windus Ltd., London, Schocken Books, New York, 1964, p. 157. The chapter entitled "Essentially Contested Concepts" (pp. 157–191) is highly relevant to the topics discussed here.

[34]Cf. the trick used by the Nazis in choosing the title "National Socialism"—a fiendishly clever combination of two profoundly evocative words.

[35]The puzzle has been traditionally known as "the heap" (*sorites*) or "the bald man" (*falakros*). Each grain of corn makes no sound when dropped, but a *heap* of them does: plucking one hair from a man's head doesn't make him bald, but continuing the process long enough turns him *bald*.

thatched man and a bald one. It might be thought that the
difficulty is tied to words like "bald," "rich," "many," and
"few," which would commonly be regarded as exceptionally
"vague" in lacking fixed boundaries of application. These
words, certainly, leave unusual discretion to their users, but
the same difficulty is found in connection with words like
"chair," which seem relatively precise in their application.

> Think of armchairs and reading-chairs and dining-room
> chairs, and kitchen chairs, chairs that pass into benches,
> chairs that cross the boundary and become settees, dentist's
> chairs, thrones, opera stalls, seats of all sorts, those miraculous
> fungoid growths that cumber the floor of the Arts and Crafts
> exhibitions, and you will perceive what a lax bundle in fact
> is this simple straightforward term. In co-operation with an
> intelligent joiner I would undertake to defeat any definition
> of chair or chairishness that you gave me (H. G. Wells,
> *First and Last Things*, Constable & Co., Ltd., London, 1908,
> p. 16).

Wells is here conflating two distinct features of the meaning of *chair*. The first, its *variety of application* to such
things as dentist's chairs, thrones, and opera stalls, might be
met, where the context demanded it, by further specification.
The second, which here engages our interest, is less easily
removable: specify as you please, by heaping up adjectives
or switching to specialized words, the term you obtain will
still admit of possible *borderline cases*, with respect to which
it will be impossible in principle to decide whether or not the
term applies. The existence of such recalcitrant borderline
cases—comprising in their entirety what is sometimes called
a *penumbra of meaning*, a No Man's Land, in which there
are no firm principles of application—may be taken as indicating the looseness of concepts[36] or the looseness of the language expressing the concept.

"Looseness" of concepts is more than an occasional nuisance: its presence seems unavoidable whenever we use language to apply to the real world. In an artificial system, we
can legislate against the existence of borderline cases—
in bridge, for instance, we tolerate no intermediate cases
between, say, spades and hearts—but as soon as we try to fit
the system to nature, we run the risk of encountering anom-

[36]The more usual term is "vagueness," which has the defect, however,
of being easily confused with the sense in which *bald* is, but *chair* is
not, vague. For full discussion of the questions involved, see M. Black,
"Vagueness," in *Language and Philosophy* (Cornell University Press,
Ithaca, N.Y., 1949), pp. 25–58; and the same author's "Reasoning with
Loose Concepts," *Dialogue* (Montreal), vol. 1 (1963–64), pp. 1–12.

alies—*e.g.*, cards so worn that it is impossible to determine their suit.[37]

Nature everywhere presents us with continuous gradations: colours and species, powers and capacities, habits and institutions, shade off into one another by imperceptible steps. The lines we draw across such continua, in the interest of manageably simple classifications, may therefore seem arbitrary—yet we can hardly do otherwise. To draw a sharp distinction in the three-dimensional continuum of colours between *red* and *yellow*, or between *yellow* and *green*, may seem crude enough, from a certain standpoint, but to deprive ourselves of the benefit of these convenient terms would be perverse. It might be possible, in some cases at least, to replace prevailing "loose" terms by others having narrower "penumbras" but it by no means follows that we should gain in clarity and precision. Consider, for instance, the effects of rigidly defining "wealthy" in terms of some arbitrarily chosen criterion of size of income. By becoming more tight, the word would lose much of its present usefulness, which depends upon our freedom to introduce further restrictive defining conditions at will. In any case, the same phenomenon of "looseness" or "vagueness" would reappear in connection with the newly delineated concepts: we can counteract "looseness" by suitable *ad hoc* devices, when it becomes a nuisance, but the project of eliminating it entirely, even from the language of science and mathematics,[38] is chimerical.

[37] The common sense retort is: "Discard the cards, then, and play with a fresh pack!" But who is to decide when the cards are *sufficiently* worn? That looseness of concepts is usually no practical hindrance to their use is, of course, not the point.

[38] Mathematicians rightly pride themselves upon the precision and sharpness of application of their key concepts. But even in mathematics, where we are not faced with the problem of accommodating our thought to the unforeseeable vagaries of external reality, and the rules of definition seem wholly under human control, the same phenomenon of "looseness" emerges at the fringes of the subject. The history of mathematics repeatedly shows that such fundamental concepts as those of *number, function,* and *proof* come to grief upon uncertainties of application that need to be resolved by adaptation and redefinition of terms that to an earlier generation seemed altogether "clear and distinct." In the light of the fundamental discoveries of Gödel, it appears that, even in mathematics and logic, there are absolute limitations upon the process of recording rules for the application of a concept in the form of explicit instructions. In the very act of "formalizing" (reducing to explicit rule) the conditions of application of the concept, or the term expressing it, we necessarily create conditions for the defeat of those instructions. Thus the intelligent use of mathematical language inevitably requires the use of unformalized insight and tact. And this is, of course, true in far greater measure of the languages of empirical service and everyday life.

THE REDUCTION OF "LOOSENESS" OF CONCEPTS

To reconcile oneself to the inevitable looseness of language is to submit to two inconveniences. The first, of a mainly theoretical order, threatens to render the application of logic impossible. For it is a cardinal logical principle (the so-called Principle of Excluded Middle) that a "proposition" (or, if one prefers, a "statement") is either true or false—in other words, has a determinate truth value. Now if a particular man falls within the "penumbra" of the term *rich,* so that it is impossible to say with certainty that he is rich, and equally impossible to say that he is not, it seems that this Principle is violated and that logic falters. For this reason, a logician as eminent as Gottlob Frege did not scruple to say that "a concept that is not sharply defined is wrongly termed a concept."[39] But to take this admonition seriously would be tantamount to exempting ordinary language and the language of all the sciences and the specialist disciplines from the controls of right reasoning—a price too high to pay for the preservation of an immaculate conception of the nature of logic. Nor would it really help to adopt the desperate expedient recommended by some writers, of jettisoning traditional logic in favour of some "three-valued" logic in which "uncertainty" would be recognized as a third alternative on a par with truth and falsity.[40] A more plausible answer to the problem of the application of logic to reasoning with loose concepts is to argue that such application *presupposes* a sufficiently sharp demarcation between truth and falsity (or, alternatively, between positive and negative instances of a concept) in the cases on hand. Whether the case considered is one in which the requisite demarcation is "sufficiently" sharp, *i.e.,* whether the instances considered are or are not to be treated as "borderline" is not within the province of logic itself to determine, but must be left to the insight and discretion of those who wish to apply logical standards of appraisal and criticism. Similarly a knife does not incorporate instructions for deciding whether it is sufficiently sharp to be used for a particular purpose, this being left to the intelligence of its users. But that a knife is unsuited for a

[39]P. Geach and M. Black, eds., *Translations from the Philosophical Writings of Gottlob Frege,* Basil Blackwell & Mott, Ltd., Oxford, 1952, p. 159.

[40]The reasons are too complex for discussion here. The interested reader may consult the article "Reasoning with Loose Concepts," cited earlier.

particular purpose, whether because it is too sharp or because it is too blunt, is no reflection upon its sharpness. And the same may be said about logic. Logic is an incomparably sharp instrument for making distinctions and developing their consequences; this does not limit its usefulness but does imply a non-formal obligation upon its user to determine when its use is appropriate.

This element of necessary discretion in the use of logic in connection with loose concepts appears again, in another form, in the chief practical inconvenience arising from such concepts—the occasional necessity to adjudicate doubtful cases. The difficulty is felt acutely in legal actions, where much will turn upon the place at which the "line" is "drawn":

> In law we make sharp consequences hang upon these words of gradation. The question whether a man is left in freedom or detained in a mental institution depends on whether he is judicially classified as sane or insane, as also does the question whether his dispositions of property are upheld or not. Whether a man is punished or acquitted may turn simply and solely upon whether an attempt to commit a crime was sufficiently "proximate," or upon whether a statement that he falsely swore was "material" to a judicial proceeding; and in a murder case it may be literally a question of life or death whether the accused intended to hurt by means of an act "intrinsically likely to kill." . . . In tort we have one rule for reservoirs, another for duck-ponds; and the Court somehow has to draw the line between the two. A libel is in "permanent" form and a slander in "transient" form; but permanency is a matter of degree. In the law of negligence and nuisance the defendant pays full damages or nothing according as the Court puts his conduct at the "reasonable" or "unreasonable" end of what is in fact a continuous gradation. So also with remoteness of damage (Glanville Williams, "Language and the Law," *Law Quarterly Review*, vol. 61, Stevens & Sons, Ltd., London, 1945, p. 183).

If these are cases where a decision as to the application of the crucial notion cannot be avoided, they at least have the advantage that no appeal to general principle need be employed: it is sufficient to *decide* the case on hand by whatever insight or standards of "reasonableness" are available to the Judge. And because there can, in general, be no absolute principles for drawing the line, resentment at the decision can hardly have any reasonable basis. The arbitrariness of such decisions may be disturbing, but is inescapable.

Judges refuse to be frightened by these difficulties. They are not intimidated from saying that the case is on one side or the other of the line merely because they discover that the line is difficult to draw. Thus in one of the cases working out the limits of the rule against remoteness, where a limitation was upheld as not infringing the rule, Lord Nottingham said: "It hath been urged at the bar, where will you stop if you do not stop at *Child and Bayly's Case?* I answer, I will stop everywhere when any inconvenience appears, no where before." . . . "Courts of Justice," said Chitty J., "ought not to be puzzled by such old scholastic questions as to where a horse's tail begins and where it ceases. You are obliged to say, 'This is a horse's tail,' at some time" (Glanville Williams, cited above).[41]

Philosophical Obsession with Language

A striking feature of some of the most influential movements of Western philosophy in the 20th century has been preoccupation with problems of language and especially with problems of meaning. Philosophers have in the past repeatedly struggled with the difficulties of communicating abstract thoughts in an adequate terminology. But such linguistic problems, for all their importance, have traditionally been regarded as mere preliminaries to the substantive problems of forming adequate conceptions about the nature of the universe, about the nature of man, the foundations of ethics, and so on. Even if ordinary language, invented for quite other purposes than philosophical argument, could be converted into a satisfactory vehicle for metaphysical thought, the work of philosophy would all remain to be done. It has been left to the contemporary philosophers who represent what is, often contemptuously, labeled "linguistic philosophy" to maintain the provocative thesis that, in a sense to be explained below, the philosophical task consists entirely of a radical examination of language. For better or worse, this kind of attitude has introduced a distinctively new style into philosophical investigation. To some of its many critics, this movement has seemed like a betrayal of the two-

[41]But in the same article Williams concedes that ". . . it is to the interest of legal certainty that, other things being equal, the rules of law should be as clear of application as possible. Some words have a wider fringe of uncertainty than others, and for legal purposes those with the narrowest fringes are generally the best." He proceeds to give some interesting examples of how the "uncertainty" in such legal terms has in fact been gradually reduced, *e.g.,* by the laying down of definite times instead of using the excessively loose term "ancient."

thousand-year-old tradition of wrestling with fundamental metaphysical problems.[42] Yet perhaps the verdict of a writer with broad sympathies is a fair verdict upon the potentialities, if not always of the actual achievements, of the "new turn" in philosophical method:

> In the fundamental notion of symbolization . . . we have the keynote of all humanistic problems. . . . If it is indeed a generative idea, it will beget tangible methods of its own, to free the deadlocked paradoxes of mind and body, reason and impulse, autonomy and law, and will overcome the checkmated arguments of an earlier age by discarding their very idiom and shaping their equivalents in more significant phrase. The philosophical study of symbols . . . has arisen in the fields that the great advance of learning has left fallow. Perhaps it holds the seed of a new intellectual harvest, to be reaped in the next season of the human understanding.[43]

It would be quite impossible here to give an adequate account of the many and varied ways in which interest in "the fundamental notion of symbolization" has affected the work of philosophers in the 20th century. I shall confine myself to tracing in outline some of the issues raised by a stream of ideas that can be traced back, through Ludwig Wittgenstein, G. E. Moore, and Bertrand Russell, to earlier Positivism and the Empiricism of the 18th and 19th centuries. The value of such a survey arises in part from the prominence with which it reveals certain recurring and fundamental questions about the nature of meaning and the nature of language.

THE SEARCH FOR A CRITERION OF MEANING

Philosophy has always borne the burden of self-distrust. If all that is uncritically accepted by the man in the street— the reality of the external world, the existence of other

---

[42]"Since human behaviour includes verbal behaviour, we are led still further to the deification of the Facts of Language. Appeal to the logical and moral authority of these Facts (or alleged Facts) is, it would seem, the ultimate wisdom of philosophy in our time." (Karl R. Popper, *Conjectures and Refutations*, Routledge & Kegan Paul, Ltd., London, 1963, p. 346.)

[43]Susanne K. Langer, *Philosophy in a New Key*, Harvard University Press, Cambridge, Mass., 1942, p. 25. Professor Langer's notable book was strongly influenced by the work of Ernst Cassirer and by the idealist tradition of which he was a distinguished representative. Her interests are therefore considerably broader than those of most of the writers to be discussed in this section.

minds, the validity of logical argument, and much else—is made to seem problematic and hence in need of clarification and justification, it is too much to expect that the practice of philosophy itself should be exempted from self-criticism. And so, while wrestling with the intractable problems of his craft, the philosopher has constantly heard in the background the mocking voice that asks "How is it *possible* for you to answer such questions as these?" and "What sort of defensible method are you proposing to use?" and, still more disturbingly, "Perhaps, after all, you are transgressing the bounds of human knowledge?" The force of such potentially skeptical questions about philosophical method has, since the 16th century, been much intensified by the striking contrast between the inconclusiveness of philosophical debate, on the one hand, and the progressively demonstrated success of scientific method, on the other. The suggestion constantly recurs that philosophers should learn from the triumphs of science that the only method of acquiring knowledge that history has shown to be fruitful, progressive, and self-correcting is that of appeal to experience. Philosophers are repeatedly admonished to desert their armchairs, to get out into the world and to "look about them" like a scientist. In schematic histories of philosophy, the short name for this attitude has been *empiricism,* the doctrine that all knowledge must be derived from sensory experience or from its elaboration by logical and mathematical calculation.[44]

It has long been recognized that the adoption of such an empiricist criterion of knowledge would severely restrict philosophical inquiry, given its traditional pretensions to raise questions transcending experience. But if the authors of such famous discussions of philosophical method as Hume's *Treatise,* Locke's *Essay,* or Kant's *Critique* clearly saw that exclusive reliance upon experience, modeled upon the practice of the empirical sciences, was bound to restrict the possibility of *known* answers to philosophical problems, they only rarely faced the disturbing possibility that such imitation of scientific method might bring into question the very *meaningfulness* of distinctively philosophical discourse.

A hint of what was to come may be found in the famous concluding section of Hume's *Enquiry:*

> When we run over libraries, persuaded of these principles [*i.e.*, those of empiricism, as Hume analyzed them], what

---

[44] How the existence of the a priori disciplines of logic and mathematics is to be explained has been a tremendous stumbling block for would-be consistent empiricists.

havoc must we make? If we take in our hand any volume; of divinity or school metaphysics, for instance; let us ask, *Does it contain any abstract reasoning concerning quantity or number?* No. *Does it contain any experimental reasoning concerning matters of fact and existence?* No. Commit it then to the flames: for it can contain nothing but sophistry and illusion.

Hume prudently abstained from asking if his own book would pass the test.

It is hard to know when and why philosophical preoccupation with the limitations of knowledge became transmuted into preoccupation with questions about the limitations upon the meaning of statements purporting to express knowledge. Toward the end of the 19th century, however, the older questions, "How is knowledge possible?" and "What kinds of knowledge are humanly attainable?" had increasingly come to be replaced by the questions "How is it possible to speak meaningfully?" and "What kind of meaning can human discourse have?" The quest for a criterion of knowledge was displaced in favour of a search for criteria of intelligibility.

I shall here confine myself to three of the most influential attempts made in modern times to supply such criteria of meaning: those associated with "Pragmatism," with "Operationalism," and with "Logical Positivism" (or the "Vienna Circle").

PEIRCE AND THE PRAGMATIC MAXIM

In 1878 the great American philosopher Charles Sanders Peirce published a famous article, "How to Make Our Ideas Clear,"[45] that marked a decisive stage in the movement that came to be known as "Pragmatism."

The title of Peirce's essay alludes to Descartes' ancient doctrine of "clear and distinct" ideas—a famous outcome of that earlier scrutiny of philosophical method to which I have already referred. In Peirce's version, an idea is "clear," in the

---

[45]First published in *Popular Science Monthly*, vol. 12, and often reprinted in collections of Peirce's essays and elsewhere. Peirce was a highly original but eccentric thinker, whose important ideas were made known to the public in his lifetime mainly through the somewhat refractory medium of his great friend and admirer William James. Only with the posthumous publication of Peirce's *Collected Papers* (Harvard University Press, Cambridge, Mass., 8 vols., 1931–58) has his towering stature come to be adequately appreciated. An excellent introduction to Peirce's richly diversified thought is W. B. Gallie's *Peirce and Pragmatism* (Pelican Books, London, 1952; rev. ed., 1966).

Cartesian sense, if it is recognized whenever met and is never mistaken for another; and an idea is "distinct" when it contains no unclear components—that is to say, Peirce comments, "when we can give a precise definition of it, in abstract terms."[46] To the doctrine that we ought to seek clear and distinct ideas, whether in the form of the doctrine stated by Descartes, or in its elaboration by Leibniz, Peirce objects, in effect, that it fails to provide any way of distinguishing between ideas that *seem* clear and those that are really so. The Cartesian test for clarity comes to little more than a demand that the ideas shall be *familiar;* and the requirement for explicit definition ("distinctness"), while useful, does not go far enough.

In seeking what he calls "the higher perspicuity of thought," Peirce relies upon the principle "that the whole function of thought is to produce habits of action"—from which in turn he derives the precept, later known as "The Pragmatic Maxim": "Consider what effects, that might conceivably have practical bearings, we conceive the object of our conception to have. Then, our conception of these effects is the whole of our conception of the object." This maxim itself, in its use of the less than pellucid phrase "practical bearings," might be said not to attain even to that degree of Cartesian clarity that Peirce wished to surpass. For we can hardly be confident that we shall be able to identify an instance of "practical bearing" whenever we encounter it. Still, Peirce's illustrations of the meanings of *hard* and *heavy* more or less adequately explain what he had in mind.

In calling a thing hard we are taken to mean "that it will not be scratched by many other substances" and "To say that a body is heavy means simply that, in the absence of opposing force, it will fall." So, in general, one may assume that what Peirce's maxim comes to is this: "Let W be a word whose meaning is to be determined. Let S be a sentence stating the conditions that would establish that W is correctly applied to an arbitrary instance. Then S is a full and complete expression of the meaning of W." More briefly, a statement of the necessary and sufficient conditions for the proper application of the word in question is an adequate expression of its meaning. (It needs to be understood that "condition for application" stands for some *publicly observable* process such as seeing that a stone is not scratched by other bodies—or

---

[46] Whether Peirce does full justice to Descartes is not in point here.

that a body falls when unsupported.)[47] Upon this interpretation, the maxim is a notable early anticipation, however imperfectly expressed, of the later attempt to link meaning with verification, which I shall be discussing in connection with the Principle of Verifiability below. [48]

OPERATIONALISM

It is a long step from Peirce's essay of 1878 to the appearance of Percy W. Bridgman's[49] *The Logic of Modern Physics* (The Macmillan Co., New York) in 1927. Yet Bridgman's analysis of a concept sounds at first hearing very much in the spirit of Peirce's pragmatism: "In general, we mean by any concept nothing more than a set of operations; *the concept is synonymous with the corresponding set of operations.*"[50]

[47]This, however, fails to take account of Peirce's emphasis upon *conduct* as involved in "practical bearing." One of the predictable ironies of philosophical theories about meaning is the amount of room they invariably leave for misunderstanding and misinterpretation of the very doctrine itself. Sufficient evidence for this in the present case is the ample disagreement concerning the meaning of Peirce's maxim exhibited by the four distinguished philosophers who comment on his essay in *Studies in the Philosophy of Charles Sanders Peirce* (edited for the Peirce Society by P. P. Wiener and F. H. Young, Harvard University Press, Cambridge, Mass., 1952). Peirce himself, in later life, was a severe critic of his early essay.

[48]I must pass over Peirce's notable attempt to apply the Maxim to the notion of Truth. An adequate discussion of the history of the movement known as Pragmatism would need to pay attention to the particular twist that William James gave to his own version of the Maxim. When James wrote that "the serious meaning of a concept lies . . . in the concrete difference to someone which its being true will make" (Perry, vol. 2, p. 408), he was a long way from the interpretation here given to the Maxim. Although James, with characteristic generosity, hailed Peirce as the father of pragmatism, the leading ideas of that movement have a much older lineage (cf. Perry, vol. 2, p. 407). Ralph Barton Perry (*The Thought and Character of William James*, Little, Brown and Company, Boston, 1935) says that "the modern movement known as pragmatism is largely the result of James's misunderstanding of Peirce" (vol. 2, p. 409).

[49]Bridgman (1882–1961) was a Harvard physicist who earned the Nobel prize for work on materials at high pressures. His many papers and books on the philosophy of science exerted a strong influence on his many readers. Operationalism may rank with Freudianism as one of the major intellectual forces in the Western world between the first two World Wars.

[50]Bridgman, *Logic*, p. 5. Bridgman claims to derive this idea from Einstein, whose "greatest contribution" he takes it to be. The "operations" intended may be either "physical," as in the measurement of a physical magnitude, or "mental," as in the application of mathematical concepts such as continuity.

This notion is perhaps no clearer than Peirce's and has in the long run proved even less viable, for all its attraction to hard-headed scientists. Its fundamental weakness resides in an oversimplified conception of the role of theoretical terms in a scientific system. That any term such as *length* or *weight, electron* or *gene, intelligence* or *libido,* should be so used as to have observable consequences is a reasonable demand, thoroughly consonant with the fact-seeking pretensions of empirical science. But it is going much farther than this to insist, as Bridgman did, that such theoretical terms should be wholly definable in terms of the procedures by which they are applied to concrete cases. Such a conception of scientific theory proves untenable, even as an account of the actual practice of the empirical sciences. It is still less defensible when offered as a general analysis of the meaning of terms. However, such criticisms as these can be left for further elaboration in connection with the Principle of Verifiability, to which I shall now turn.[51]

THE VIENNA CIRCLE AND LOGICAL POSITIVISM

Empiricists, pragmatists, and operationists alike have all been strongly inspired by the ambition to extend the sway of scientific method. These movements were all instances of *scientism,* which may be given the weak sense of "an attitude of admiration for the natural sciences and the wish to extend their virtues to other disciplines,"[52] or the strong sense of "the thesis that knowledge can be obtained only by the application of scientific method." The culmination of scientism in this strong sense was reached in the movement, known by its members as "The Vienna Circle," but more commonly by the outside world as "Logical Positivism." Its special interest

[51]A thorough and judicious criticism of operationalism will be found in A. Cornelius Benjamin, *Operationism* (Charles C. Thomas, Springfield, Ill., 1955). Benjamin's conclusion is worth reproducing: "If the operationist insists on *perfect* clarity his language is reduced to a series of such words as 'this' and 'that' and his activity to a series of gestures of pointing. But if he is willing to grant that knowing is more than mere discerning and involves anticipating what nature will later disclose, he can permit himself a more extended language and a more varied series of cognitive acts, but he is then committed to an element of vagueness and uncertainty. . . . If we are content with what we already know—facts—we can be both very clear and very certain, but if we wish to know something else—hypotheses—we must sacrifice to a degree both clarity and certainty" (Benjamin, pp. 141–142).

[52]W. M. Simon, *European Positivism in the Nineteenth Century,* Cornell University Press, Ithaca, N.Y., 1963, p. 3.

for us is the original linguistic twist it gave to earlier positivistic doctrines.

The Vienna Circle was at first a loose association of philosophers, scientists, and mathematicians, that met under the leadership of Moritz Schlick after World War I. By 1929, it had become a self-consciously radical movement, waging war upon the "nonsense" of traditional metaphysics and actively propagandizing on behalf of a "scientific philosophy."[53] The Circle's doctrines were introduced to the English-speaking world in a greatly influential book, A. J. Ayer's *Language, Truth and Logic*,[54] which immediately achieved a *succès de scandale* and has ever since remained a favourite target of those who see in "Logical Positivism"[55] (a term often pejoratively extended to any thinkers who believe in appeal to experience and systematic argument) a root of atheistic evil.

These interesting and, to many people, alarming or positively shocking implications of the doctrines persuasively presented in Ayer's book rest almost entirely upon the principle now to be examined.

THE PRINCIPLE OF VERIFIABILITY

"The meaning of a proposition is its method of verification." This is the classical form in which Friedrich Waismann, himself a member of the Vienna Circle, expressed in 1930 what came to be known as "The Principle of Verifiability." The intended meaning of the principle can be spelled out as follows. Let there be a sentence before us, say, "Smith is angry." Consider the sentences expressing the observations

[53]For a good brief history of the Circle and the relations between its doctrines and related movements in England and elsewhere, see the "Editor's Introduction" to A. J. Ayer's anthology, *Logical Positivism* (The Free Press, Glencoe, Ill., 1959). There is a fuller account in Viktor Kraft, *The Vienna Circle* (Philosophical Library, New York, 1953).

[54]The first edition appeared in London in 1936 (Victor Gollancz). The second revised edition of 1946 contained important modifications, notably in the form of a long new section on "The Principle of Verification."

[55]"Positivism" is intended to suggest a kinship with the 19th-century doctrines of Auguste Comte, who preached among other things the importance of replacing the "metaphysical" stage of thought by a "positive" (*i.e.*, a factual) study of human nature and human societies. The adjective "Logical" marks the interest of the members of the Circle in the use of logical and mathematical methods and their adherence to a novel view of the character of these a priori disciplines—roughly speaking, that logical and mathematical truth express or arise from linguistic conventions.

that would show that first sentence to be true—say, "Smith is pale," "Smith is clenching his fists," "Smith is uttering such and such obscenities," and so on. Call these the "verifying sentences." Then the meaning of the sentence about Smith's anger is the same as the meaning of all those observation sentences by which its truth could be tested. (More precisely: to say that Smith is angry is to mean either that he is pale, etc., *or* that he is clenching his fists *or . . . .*)

It follows that sentences to which no class of verifying sentences can be associated in this way must be regarded as "meaningless" or "nonsensical."[56] It it this negative consequence that has provoked most alarm and offense. That metaphysics, traditionally aiming at truth about "ultimate reality," should fail to pass the test of meaningfulness and come to be stigmatized as "nonsense" by the standard of the verifiability principle might well leave clerics and educators unmoved. (Metaphysics has been under a cloud ever since its inception.) The case is otherwise when religious assertions are rejected as "pseudo-assertions" or, not to put a fine edge on the accusation, "nonsense."[57] And even agnostics and atheists may well suffer from mixed anxiety and resentment when the same accusation of meaninglessness is lodged against the "pseudo-propositions" of ethics and aesthetics.[58]

In the palmy days of the Vienna Circle, its adherents were prepared to take such consequences in stride. It might be disconcerting to realize that all discourse outside the natural sciences and logic (considered as embracing mathematics) must shed its pretensions to express knowledge or to aim at truth; but sufficient ingenuity, it was felt, could invest even the "venting of feeling" and the "expression of attitudes"

[56]A special exception is made for what used to be called, following Wittgenstein, the "tautologies" of logic and mathematics.

[57]Cf. such remarks as these: ". . . our view that all utterances about the nature of God are nonsensical" and ". . . the religious utterances of the theist are not genuine propositions at all . . ." (Ayer, *Language, Truth and Logic*).

[58]Ethical judgments are mere expressions of feeling" (Ayer, *Logical Positivism*, p. 112). "It appears, then, that ethics, as a branch of knowledge, is nothing more than a department of psychology and sociology" (p. 112). "Aesthetic terms are used in exactly the same way as ethical terms. Such aesthetic words as 'beautiful' and 'hideous' are employed, as ethical words are employed, not to make statements of fact, but simply to express certain feelings and evoke a certain response" (p. 113).
It should be added that subsequent "emotive theories" of ethics have achieved a much greater degree of sophistication and a correspondingly higher plausibility. See, for instance, the well-known work of C. L. Stevenson, *Ethics and Language;* also Avrum Stroll, *The Emotive Theory of Ethics* (both cited in Chapter 5).

with at least a semblance of rationality, and thus preserve aesthetic, ethical, and political discussion from the babel of total arbitrariness.[59] As for philosophy itself, its re-interpretation as a kind of handmaiden to the sciences, seeking to analyze and to make sense of the difficult idioms of the various special disciplines, might reserve for it a respectable, if somewhat modest, function.

Quite unexpected, however—although easily predictable— were the destructive implications of the verifiability principle for science itself. The principle proved, indeed, to be a kind of sorcerer's apprentice. By insisting that the meaning of any significant assertion must be wholly analyzable in terms of logical functions of statements about the directly observable,[60] it seemed to reduce statements about persons to statements about their behaviour (or rather to complex conditional statements about what their behaviour would be if certain test situations were instituted); it seemed to convert statements about the past to statements about the future (conditional statements again about what, for instance, would result from the examination of documents and other "traces" of what we, perhaps naïvely, think of as the past); and in general, the cash value of all statements except the most trivial registrations of immediate experience would seem to lie in terms of as yet unfulfilled outcomes of testing procedures. Meaning, it began to seem, would always have to be construed as lurking in the "bye and bye."

Pretty soon, it began to be seen, beyond question, that this

[59] See, for instance, Moritz Schlick's *Problems of Ethics* (Prentice-Hall, Inc., Englewood Cliffs, N. J., 1939), in which he manages to reconcile a tough-minded positivistic analysis of ethical discourse with an authentic and warm-hearted liberalism. Most adherents of an "emotive theory of ethics" have in fact been highminded, somewhat in the tradition of earlier utilitarianism.

[60] The precise form of such experiental statements—the so-called protocol-sentences—provided endless problems in earlier stages of the movement. In trying to reduce them to assertions about experience, entirely free from interpretation or inference, one seemed to end with no better than what Schlick called *Konstatierungen*, bare linguistic gestures of recognition, incommunicable to others and unfit to serve as the basis for any kind of logical inference or elaboration. If, on the other hand, the protocol-sentences were viewed, more realistically, as the kind of reports that might be found in the notebooks of a practising scientific observer, it seemed that these in turn had further verifiable implications for subsequent experience and could, therefore, not constitute a final terminus for analysis. The full story of this fascinating debate and of its influence upon the gradual development of the doctrines of Logical Positivism is too lengthy, and involves issues too technical, for discussion here.

type of conception of meaning, and the proposed analyses or "explications" that it fostered, must withhold the accolade of "sense" from *all* general statements. For the meanings of even such superficial general statements as "All swans are white" can never be exhausted by any finite logical functions of statements about the directly observable,[61] and the same is true in even higher degree of the more recondite theoretical statements of science, such as Newton's laws of motion. It became necessary, accordingly, to weaken the verifiability principle by substituting "confirmation" for "verification" and by admitting that "significant statements" need only have verifiable *consequences*.[62] Step by step, the original high pretensions of the verifiability test of meaning have had to be qualified and hedged around with protective clauses. What originally looked like a universal touchstone for meaning now functions chiefly as a technical criterion for determining the operative efficacy of theoretical terms within given scientific systems.[63] In becoming progressively more defensible, the verifiability principle has also become progressively less interesting for all but specialists in the philosophy of science.

Seen in retrospect, the most vulnerable point in the program of Logical Positivism was the dogmatic character of the verifiability principle upon which the movement leaned so heavily. What justification is there, one might ask, for identifying meaning with verifiability, leaving aside the technical difficulties in making that test viable? It seems that it could have only the status of a definition, or, as some mod-

[61] No finite set of statements of the form *If you do such and such you will see such and such* can capture the full force of *All swans are white*. The generalization's scope extends beyond any finite set of its instances.

[62] The technical ingenuity needed to salvage the verifiability principle, even in its so-called weak later forms, is well illustrated by the discussion of this matter in the second edition of Ayer's *Language, Truth and Logic*. He distinguishes between directly and indirectly verifiable statements, the latter being understood as "logical bridges," one might say, whose function it is, in conjunction with directly observable, primitively experiential, statements, to yield further experiential statements. But every such amendment of the original radical form of the principle has proved vulnerable to equally ingenious counter-examples. There seems, now, little prospect of patching up the principle to make it safe against such attack—nor does the game seem worth the candle.

[63] The current state of this problem can be exhaustively studied in Professor C. G. Hempel's *Aspects of Scientific Explanation* (The Free Press, New York, 1965). I must not leave the reader with the impression that the sustained work of Logical Positivism and its critics has yielded no lasting gains. It is fair to say that current thought concerning the nature of theoretical entities, the nature of explanation, and allied topics, is vastly more sophisticated than it would have been, but for the development that I have been sketching.

erate members of the Vienna Circle liked to say, a "proposal." But then one might expect some justification for a proposal so inhospitable to types of discourse that look intelligible to common sense. No such justification was ever forthcoming —nor, by the nature of the case, could it really be expected. Why the principle should have seemed plausible to the point of apparent self-evidence is clear enough: the zeal of the early Logical Positivists arose from optimistic confidence in the power of scientific method to resolve intellectual problems, and a profound contempt for the meddling pretensions of metaphysicians who claimed to teach science its place by preaching a "higher" and "deeper" truth about the world. These motives were respectable enough, but they encouraged too narrow a view of science itself and too simplified a conception of the nature of meaning in general. As Gilbert Ryle has well said:

> The needle's eye of the generalised Verification Principle was so narrow that it excluded not only a few Teutonic camels, but nearly all domestic animals as well. But we must not be ungrateful to it. The question "What sort of evidence or reasons, if any, would establish or refute an assertion of this or that sort?" has proved to be a philosophically fertile question—fertile, not because it has done what was intended, namely segregated one class of legitimate statements from a huge congeries of illegitimate statements; but because it has done what was not intended, namely brought out a great variety of differences between lots of classes of legitimate utterances. What was bought as a lens has worked as a prism. It has helped to reveal the important fact that we talk sense in lots of different ways, and we can talk nonsense in lots of different ways.[64]

Logical Positivism has seen its best days[65] but it has seemed worthwhile to recall its history, as a prime illustration of the havoc that can be wreaked by excessively narrow conceptions of meaning.

LINGUISTIC PHILOSOPHY

I shall end this chapter by drawing the reader's attention

[64]Gilbert Ryle, "The Verification Principle," *Revue internationale de Philosophie*, vol. 5, 1951, p. 250.

[65]Its ablest exponents were exiled from Europe, with the onset of fascism and Nazism. The influence, especially in the United States, of such distinguished scholars as Carnap and Reichenbach has shown itself in the undogmatic form of reliance upon certain methods of philosophical investigation rather than in adherence to any specifiable doctrines.

to a vigorous contemporary movement, variously known as "Analytical Philosophy," "Ordinary Language Philosophy," and "Oxford Philosophy." A better label than any of these might be "Linguistic Empiricism," which would serve as a reminder of the formative influence of the "classical" empiricist doctrines of Berkeley, Locke, and Hume.

Like the Logical Positivists, "Ordinary Language Philosophers" (who usually dislike that description, but have nothing better to offer) agree that close attention to language can be highly valuable in the investigation of philosophical problems. They agree also that the most important tasks of contemporary philosophy are to analyze concepts, rather than to attempt the bold speculative syntheses of the great metaphysicians of past ages, and in this way to contribute to clarity rather than to synoptic vision. Logical Positivists, however, have typically taken a cool and even distrustful view of the "ordinary language" that laymen use, and have expected to find it disfigured by vagueness, imprecision, and even inconsistency. Remembering the crucial role played in the advance of science by the invention of appropriate technical dialects, they have steadily advocated the reform of "ordinary language," and, if necessary, its replacement by artificial sub-languages free from its defects. Ordinary language philosophers, on the other hand, have had a higher respect for the ways in which all of us speak about such fundamental matters as freedom, reason, motive, cause, and much else of profound philosophical interest. In the words of one of their ablest members, Professor J. L. Austin, they tend to think that

> . . . our common stock of words embodies all the distinctions men have found worth drawing, and the connexions they have found worth marking, in the lifetimes of many generations: these surely are likely to be more numerous, more sound, since they have stood up to the long test of the survival of the fittest, and more subtle, at least in all ordinary and reasonably practical matters, than any that you or I are likely to think up in our armchairs of an afternoon—the most favoured alternative method.[66]

They think also that the most promising way to become clear about what our basic concepts are is to determine as accurately as possible the rules of use for the words that express that concept. The program, in Austin's brief but suggestive formula, is to discover, or perhaps to remind ourselves,

[66]*Philosophical Papers*, The Clarendon Press, Oxford, 1961, p. 130.

"what we should say when, and so why and what we should mean. . . ."[67] The way to achieve clarity about "the nature of causation," as philosophers of an earlier generation would say, is, if this program is adopted, to consider carefully the rules of use for "cause" and the words related to it in meaning. The investigations needed to achieve this go far beyond conventional lexicography: it is necessary, for instance, to determine whether there are absolutely clear or so-called paradigm situations, in which refusal to apply the word "cause" would be a sign merely of linguistic ignorance or ineptitude. That the task is indeed much harder than would be anticipated is shown by the disputes in the ranks of ordinary language philosophers about the correct outcomes of such linguistic investigations.

The program of ordinary language philosophy has provoked attacks of an altogether surprising fury. Some of the accusations of the most envenomed critics—for instance, that the movement is intellectually conservative, indefensibly attached to the modes of speech of special coteries, and in any case willfully blind to "the nature of things"—can rather easily be met. A more serious question is whether this sustained attempt to apply linguistic methods to philosophical problems can yield sufficient results to justify the immense labour that it requires. The verdict can reasonably be based only upon the specific contributions that adherents of the movement have made to outstanding philosophical problems.[68]

---

[67]*Philosophical Papers*, p. 129.

[68]The following brief introductions can be recommended to the general reader: J. O. Urmson, *Philosophical Analysis* (The Clarendon Press, Oxford, 1956) and Gilbert Ryle, ed., *The Revolution in Philosophy* (Macmillan & Co., Ltd., London, 1956). There is a sympathetic, but not uncritical, account of linguistic philosophy in John A. Passmore, *A Hundred Years of Philosophy* (Duckworth & Co., Ltd., London, 1957).

CHAPTER 7

THE MEANINGS OF MEANING

> "We need more light to find your meaning out" (Love's Labour's Lost, Act V, scene 2, line 21)

> "Pending a satisfactory explanation of the notion meaning, linguists . . . are in the situation of not knowing what they are talking about." (Quine[1])

STATING THE PROBLEM

QUESTIONS ABOUT MEANING often arise in ordinary life and when they do they are apt to be important. Much may turn upon the meaning of a will, a law, a treaty, or a love-letter. We typically ask about meanings when we fail to understand what has been said—or wish to understand better. And since the need to understand is at the very centre of human relations, the importance of sound mastery of the techniques of explaining meaning can hardly be overestimated.

Linguists, philosophers of language, and other theorists interested in general questions about language are also constantly compelled to face questions about meaning, in more radical and searching ways than the man in the street. For communication and expression of meaning, whatever we mean by that phrase, is of the very essence of language. To the extent that we are unclear about what meaning is, we are, in Quine's phrase, in the position of "not knowing what (we)

[1]W. V. Quine, *From a Logical Point of View*, Harvard University Press, Cambridge, Mass., 1953, p. 47.

are talking about." Since this essay has been devoted to exploring, in a number of different ways, what we "are talking about" when we talk about language, a critical survey of what has been said about the analysis of the concept of meaning will serve as a fitting conclusion. It will also have the merit of illustrating, in application to a particularly important example, some of the points already stressed concerning useful ways of revealing and clarifying meaning.

We may begin by noticing that, *pace* Quine, there is a sense in which all of us do know what we are talking about when we talk about meaning. Questions of the form, "What did he mean by that?" "What does that word mean?" and "What does that sudden drop of temperature mean?" are readily intelligible in ordinary contexts; and, unless we are unlucky, we may expect to receive equally intelligible answers to such questions. We are, in short, usually able to use the word "meaning" or related words without serious trouble. But we readily become perplexed when we ask "What is a meaning?" or "What kinds of things are meanings?"

No plausible answer immediately comes to mind, and when we turn to the writings of linguists or philosophers we find an extraordinary variety of conflicting views. This situation is not unusual. Compare the simplicity and clarity of simple questions about numbers with the extreme difficulty in the philosophy of mathematics of saying what a number is or what kinds of things numbers are. After considering some of the most popular answers to the general questions about the nature of meanings, I shall suggest some reasons for the remarkable lack of agreement on this topic, and will end with some suggestions for a more fruitful approach to the problem.

MEANING AS THE THING-INTENDED

One of the oldest theories of meaning, and in some ways the most plausible, runs somewhat as follows: The word "Paris" stands for a certain city, the capital of France, and it means that city; the word "red" stands for a certain colour, the colour of blood, and it means that colour; the word "courage" stands for a certain virtue, and it means that virtue; and so, in general, any word having meaning does so because it stands for a certain "thing," and its meaning is that thing. Here, a "thing" is supposed to be something *non-linguistic* (a city, a person, a property, a structure, and so on) actually found in the "real world." One attraction about this approach is that it seems to explain why language should have any importance; just because words are, so it is claimed, linked with real "things," what a man says is "linked" with reality and is therefore true or false. Conversely, if words were not, by convention, linked with things, speech would be an idle play of sounds, "signifying nothing." This view is sometimes called the "bearer-theory" of meaning, because it conceives of a "thing" as bearing its name like an arbitrary label.

An argument in favour of the bearer theory is that we do sometimes use the verb *to mean* in a way which the theory seems to fit. We may ask "Which city did you mean when you said 'Paris'?" and receive the answer "The capital of France," where the city in question, a place in which people live, something nonverbal, is indeed identified as the "thing" that the speaker meant. And similarly in other cases. Now the question "Which city did you mean?" is readily paraphrased as "To which city you *intend to refer?*" Hence the theory may be described as one identifying meaning with *intended reference* (or, as I shall say for short, the *thing-intended*).

Objections immediately leap to mind. First, there seems something distinctly bizarre about literally *identifying* the meaning of a word with the thing-intended. The population of Paris is constantly increasing: are we then required to say that the population of a *meaning* is constantly increasing—or, in other connections, that meanings die, give birth, join political parties, and the like?[2] And if the "thing" is destroyed, shall we say that the meaning of the word perishes? Did the expression "The Titanic" lose its meaning after the ship had sunk? These oddities may seem sufficient to show that something is wrong with the theory.

In the next place, we seem to be able to use words meaningfully to which no "real things" are uniquely attached: we talk about centaurs, or Mr. Pickwick, or the perpetual motion machine, even though we know that no such things are to be found in the world. Those who reply that we are then talking about "ideas" are turning to the type of theory to be discussed in the next section.

But the most telling objection to the theory concerns the use of the word "thing" in its formulation. To call cities, persons, virtues, colours, all "real things" makes a kind of

[2] A firm believer in the bearer theory might reply, Yes! And he might add that these consequences sound odd merely because we are not usually interested in thinking of persons, say, *as* meanings.

rough sense. For some of these can be perceived, measured, described, or independently identified, and all of them, it seems, have properties that can be discovered independently of the labels by which they are introduced into discourse. But what are we to say about words like "every," "no," or "with" or the terminal "*-es*" that indicates plural number?[3] Shall we insist that these too stand for "things"? If so, we risk reducing the theory to vacuity by taking "thing" to mean nothing in particular.

On the whole, the bearer theory may be condemned for confusing meaning with reference or intended reference. One of the things we do when we speak is, sometimes, to refer to things; and so it might be held that the theory in question does succeed in reminding us of one function of language, as indeed do the theories yet to be examined. But it fails as a *comprehensive* account of meaning or significance.

MEANINGS AS IDEAS

A serious weakness of all theories of meaning, such as those considered in the last section, that locate meaning in "the world" (something objective, independent of both hearer and speaker), is their neglect of the *indirectness* of the meaning relations. It is obvious enough, but worth repeating, that persons and things do not come into existence bearing appropriate linguistic labels: if "Napoleon" stands for a certain historical personage, or *"Drosophila"* means a certain kind of fruit fly, that can only be in virtue of the mediation of human intentions and purposes. A case might even be made for regarding the use of "mean" in contexts such as "I mean to . . ." with the sense of "intend," as primary and basic. When God had created all the animals, he still had to find names for them.

Hence many writers on language, however widely they disagree about the nature of meaning, have united in insisting on the *triadic* character of the meaning relation. The basic situation is taken to have the structure: *S means such-and-such to P,* where *S* is a sign, symbol, word, or expression, and *P* is either a single person, or some group of persons (*e.g.,* a speech-community).

Ogden and Richards say: "Between the symbol and the referent there is no relevant relation other than the indirect

---

[3]These are examples of the so-called syncategorematic words, that are not suitable for use in the context "An *X* is a kind of *Y*." We can say "Paris is a kind of city," but not *"No* is a kind of . . ."

one, which consists in its being used by someone to stand for a referent."[4] And they add,

> It may appear unnecessary to insist that there is no direct connection between say "dog," the word, and certain common objects in our streets, and that the only connection which holds is that which consists in our using the word when we refer to the animal. We shall find, however, that the kind of simplification typified by this once universal theory of direct meaning relations between words and things is the source of almost all the difficulties which thought encounters.[5]

Having started in this way, by recognizing the essential role of the speaker in grounding the indirect and plainly conventional relation between word and thing-intended, it is exceedingly plausible to take the further step of locating the meaning of the word in question *in the speaker.* If, in the last instance, the meaning of "dog," as I use the word, is *my* meaning and if it is, in any case, *my* meaning that ought to concern the hearer, then it seems there ought to be something *in me* that supplies the meaning.[6] Thus we pass, in a very plausible transition, from a relational theory to what might be called a "personal" one.

What could there be in an individual speaker or thinker that established the bond between word and thing—that, as it were, supplied the word with semantic vitality and efficacy? The most natural answer has seemed, for some two thousand years: something *mental.*[7] And so we come at last to the theory that meaning consists of "ideas"—or, sometimes, "concepts"—at any rate, something occurring in the *mind.*

In one form or another, such a "mentalistic" approach has seemed correct—even obviously correct—to a vast number of writers who have otherwise differed radically in their

---

[4]Ogden and Richards, *Meaning,* 3rd ed., p. 11.

[5]In *Meaning,* p. 12. This emphasis on the indirectness of the meaning relation is expressed in Ogden and Richards' famous "triangle of reference" in which a bent line running along two sides of the triangle connects the "symbol," first with the "thought or reference" and only then with the "referent." A dotted line, running along the base of the triangle, from symbol to reference, is said to represent a merely "imputed," or "unreal," relation (*Meaning,* pp. 11–12).

[6]It is easily seen that this line of reasoning, however plausible, is fallacious. A house may be *my* house, yet there is nothing "in me" that makes it mine. Possession of something (house, meaning, or whatever) does not logically imply the presence of that something—or anything corresponding to that something—in the possessor.

[7]Ogden and Richards resist this last move—and so do most 20th-century psychologists, as we shall see in the next section.

analyses of speech and language. The following quotations may serve as sufficient samples of what has been said:

> In order to separate from the whole of speech the part that belongs to language, we must examine the individual act from which the speaking circuit can be reconstructed. . . . A given concept unlocks a corresponding sound-image in the brain; this purely *psychological* phenomenon is followed in turn by a *physiological* process: the brain transmits an impulse corresponding to the image to the organs used in producing speech (Ferdinand de Saussure, *Course in General Linguistics,* Philosophical Library, New York, 1959, pp. 11–12).[8]
>
> The linguistic sign unites, not a thing and a name, but a concept and a sound image (De Saussure, p. 66).
>
> Symbols are not proxy for their objects, but are *vehicles for the conception of objects.* . . . In talking *about* things we have conceptions of them, not the things themselves, and *it is the conceptions, not the things, that symbols directly "mean"* (Langer, *Philosophy in a New Key,* pp. 60–61, italics in original).

To these might be added, for instance, the quotations from John Locke used in my earlier discussion of the relation between thought and language (see above, pp. 145, 154).[9]

This is a convenient point at which to mention that *any* appeal to such "mental entities" as images, ideas, thoughts, concepts, or conceptions, would be vigorously condemned by many psychologists and by some philosophers as "unscientific" or even "nonsensical." Since the days of J. B. Watson, it has been widely held that talk about "what goes on in the mind" is in principle unverifiable and hence unfit to appear in any discourse that aims at precision, intelligibility, and truth. A tolerant "methodological behaviourist," who recognizes that statements about alleged mental contents are meaningful, but insists on their uselessness for science, will probably agree with Charles Morris' temperate statement of the case against "mentalism":

[8]In tracing the "speech circuit" further, De Saussure speaks of "the psychological association of the *image* with the corresponding *concept*" (p. 12, italics added) in the hearer's mind. De Saussure's account is unusual in its stress upon the occurrence of a "sound-image" of the word. His book (first French edition, 1915) has been immensely influential.

[9]That previous discussion is relevant to the present topic and might be consulted by the reader.

Suppose, for instance, the mentalist should argue—as he often does—that for something to be a sign to some interpreter it must give rise to an "idea" in his mind, must cause him to "think" of something else. . . . Unless the mentalist furnishes a criterion such that other persons may employ it to test whether [the sign-user] has or has not an idea there is no way to determine the precision, interpersonality, or unambiguity of the term. Hence there is no way to control by observation statements made about the signs of the [sign-user]; and this means that no science of signs is possible. . . . But if this is so, the only scientifically relevant part of the claim that the buzzer is a sign to the dog [or to any other sign-user] is the part couched in biological terms (*Signs, Language, and Behavior,* Prentice-Hall, Inc., Englewood Cliffs, N. J., 1946, pp. 28–29).[10]

A more radical believer in the Principle of Verifiability[11] will take the further step of denying any *significance* to statements about ideas.

I have given reasons, earlier in this essay, for rejecting the unbridled claims once made on behalf of the Principle of Verifiability. And it is no longer as plain as it once seemed to psychologists aiming at scientific standards of concept-formation for their discipline that "mentalistic terms" such as "idea" and "image" must be necessarily placed upon the Index. More sophisticated ideas about the nature of scientific theory would permit such notions to occur as "intervening variables" or as theoretical terms whose meanings are, roughly speaking, definable in terms of their uses within theoretical systems having complex and indirect correlations with observations. Yet the qualms of Morris, and those who think with him, point to a serious difficulty that requires the attention of any defender of a "mentalistic" theory of meaning.

Suppose, for the sake of argument at least, that the meaning of a word can be correctly described as an "idea" or some other mental factor: how is the occurrence of the *right* idea in a hearer to be determined? It is part of the "mentalistic" conception to assume that the "idea" is something "private" to its possessor, something of which only he can be directly aware. But if so, how am I to *convey* my "idea" to you—or to be sure that the idea that you have corresponds sufficiently closely to my own?

[10]Morris' own theory of language belongs to the "behavioural" type, considered in the next section.

[11]See the discussion of this principle, above, pp. 181–185.

The difficulty raised here is not, as might first appear, of how we can *get at* another person's "ideas": it is not comparable to the difficulty that a surgeon might have in penetrating to some exceptionally inaccessible part of the human body. The difficulty is rather that of understanding what is *meant* by the "idea" which is supposed to accompany the utterance of a word and to invest that word with meaning.

A relatively specific meaning of "idea," though somewhat odd to the contemporary ear, is that of *image*. There seems no good reason, *pace* the "methodological behaviourists," to deny that images do occur on pronouncing or hearing *some* words. Yet people who are markedly deficient in imagery have no trouble in *understanding* what is said to them; and even those whose imagery is profuse and vivid will report their images as containing much that is irrelevant to their meaning function. When I hear the word "three" I may "see" three white spots arranged as a triangle on a green background (perhaps through association with green blackboards seen in school) but I know that the arrangement of the spots and their colour "does not count," is irrelevant. But this means that the image itself, even if it does occur, *must be interpreted.* Images are perhaps not as "inaccessible" as those who insist upon the privacy of consciousness believe: I might paint my "picture" of the number *three* so skilfully that the figure looked very like what I actually "image" and then you, or anybody else, by looking at that figure, might have a pretty fair notion of what I "imagine." But then there would still remain the question of what that picture or image *means* when it occurs in my mind. (The sound "three" might conceivably evoke the image of a pentagon, and the name of a colour might evoke the image of a *complementary* colour.) Thus recourse to images, even when they do occur, accomplishes nothing of importance in the search for an entity to serve as the meaning of a given word. The image itself *stands for* something, *has* meaning, and we have merely pushed the search for meaning one stage further.

But at best the identification of meaning with images will work only for a limited class of words (words used in *slow speech* and standing typically for colours, scents, and other sensory qualities). When we come to abstract notions, like freedom, and to logical or grammatical notions, the conception that a word must be escorted by a characteristic image loses attraction. A defender of a "mentalistic" view must, in such cases, turn to a more abstract conception of an "idea"—

and then it is by no means clear what he really means. It begins to look as if the invocation of supporting "ideas" to back all meaningful words or word-elements only shows a determination to locate meaning at all costs in the realm of the mental. It is like the maneuver of some philosopher who, insisting that the universe is full of matter, deals with a vacuum by postulating the existence of invisible and undetectable "matter" in the shape of an "ether." Metaphysical prejudices about what the world *must* be like invariably lead to the invention of useless fictions.

On the whole, then, the prospects of "mentalistic" theories look distinctly unpromising. That they draw attention to something important, the involvement of the word-user in assigning meaning to words and the consequent indirect character of the meaning relation, is undeniable. But it is a long step from this to the model of a point-by-point connection between words and their supposedly concomitant "ideas." The "ideas" invoked are no better than idle ghosts.

CAUSAL THEORIES OF MEANING

An alternative title for this section might have been "psychological theories of meaning," because the views to be considered have been mainly elaborated by behaviouristically oriented psychologists, interested in exploring the causal mechanisms by which stimuli come to be "significant"—come to mean something to an organism. The main ideas have all emerged from experimental work upon learning behaviour in lower organisms, especially in the white rat, the favourite "experimental animal"; extensions to the human uses of *verbal* symbols are almost entirely based upon analogy and speculation.

Let us recall the famous experiments of Pavlov.[12] The main points of interest are the following. A hungry dog will (by a "reflex action") salivate when shown food: suppose now that the sight of food is constantly accompanied in the laboratory by the sound of a buzzer; in the course of time, the sound of the buzzer by itself will be found to induce salivation.[13] A few simple technical terms will be convenient.

[12]These are summarized in most modern texts of experimental psychology.

[13]This crude summary omits nearly everything of technical interest in Pavlov's work. That stimuli can become "associated" has been matter of common knowledge for centuries. The scientific interest of Pavlov's researches and the hundreds of similar experiments it has inspired lies in the specific laws of "reinforcement," "extinction," etc., that have been discovered.

The sight of the food is called a *stimulus,* the salivation of the dog when affected by that stimulus, its *response*. When the dog has been trained to respond to the new stimulus of the heard buzzer by salivating, this response is said to have become *conditioned*. Let us call the sight of the food (the original stimulus) S, and the sound of the buzzer T. We can also call the (original, unconditioned) response to S, R_1 and the (modified, conditioned) response to T, R_2.

Faced with the facts that have been reported, it is very natural for the layman (and the scientist too) to say that T *has become a sign of* S for the dog: or, in anthropomorphic language, that the sound of the buzzer "means" to the dog something like "Food coming!" The evidence on which this contention rests is that the dog responds to T by salivating (roughly speaking) *as if* S were present. To be sure, he does not respond to T precisely as he would to S (*e.g.,* by insanely trying to eat the buzzer) and even the salivation induced by the buzzer (R_2) differs from the salivation induced by sight of food (R_1) in quantity and in other ways. Yet the dog does respond to T approximately in the same way as he did to S: the one has replaced the other. If we are willing to speak about the dog as we would about humans, we might say that the buzzer's sound has caused him, as a result of the process of conditioning, to "expect" or to "prepare for" the imminent arrival of food: the conditioned response can plausibly be regarded as an anticipatory response to the food-to-come. The dog is ready for something that has not yet happened. It might also be said that the sound of the buzzer (T) has come to serve as a substitute for the original sight of food (S): just as S would normally cause the animal to salivate, reach toward the food source, etc., so, as a result of training, conditioning, or, if one pleases, "learning," T causes the dog to salivate, to get set to move toward the food source, and so on.

Similar behaviour can often be observed in nature. To take a single illustration: a herd of grazing deer may post a "sentinel" who, on seeing an approaching lion or other predator, will produce a characteristic cry of "warning." The deer respond to the cry "as if" they could see the lion— take flight as if they could look over the ridge into the valley beyond. Here, as before, it is plausible to say that the sentinel's cry "means" something like "Enemy coming!" and serves as a substitute for the actual sight of danger. Presumably this has come about by a process of "natural conditioning" in the wild.

The next step is to identify the meaning of the "sign" (the buzzer, the warning cry) with some aspect of the *reaction* of the responding animal. I use "reaction" here, more broadly and more loosely than "response," to stand for whatever it is about the animal at the instant of receiving the sign that makes that sign bear its definite signification or meaning. We must not assume that the "reaction" will be identical with the "conditioned response."

Causal theories, like the "mentalistic" theories considered in the last section, insist upon the importance of the "mediational process" induced by perceiving the sign. The sign has meaning or signification only because, when perceived, *something happens in the receiving organism* (let us call it the "interpretation"): hence it is plausible to identify the meaning of the sign—or, more cautiously, an essential aspect or component of that meaning, with such "interpretation."[14] Where causal or "behaviouristic" theories of meaning differ from "mentalistic" theories is in their conception of the "interpretation." They reject as "unscientific" any identification of the interpretation as a "thought" or an "idea" and hope to locate it in some, theoretically observable, feature of the organism's brain, body, or behaviour. This might be called the search for a *tangible* "interpretation."

I shall now report upon some of the attempts to treat the organism's "interpretation" (whatever it is about him that makes a stimulus meaningful to him) as "tangible."

The crudest theory of this sort would simply identify the "interpretation" with the animal's conditioned response. In the case of Pavlov's dog, this would amount to saying that the meaning to *him* of the heard buzzer is the salivation it induces; and, in the case of the deer, that the meaning of the sentinel's "warning cry" is their headlong flight. This theory, however, is too fanciful to be attractive. If it were adopted, we should have to say that a "sign" meant different things to each of the animals that respond to it—and even different things to a single animal upon various occasions of its reception. It seems impossible to raise any satisfactory theory of sign-using behaviour upon such a rickety foundation.

A somewhat more complex theory was proposed by Ogden and Richards.[15] Consider the example in which the sight of a match being struck leads us to "expect" a flame. It is sup-

---

[14]Thus Charles Stevenson says that what he calls "meaning in the psychological sense" must "be defined in terms of the psychological reactions of those who use the sign" (*Ethics and Language*, p. 42).

[15]Ogden and Richards, *Meaning*, 3rd ed., p. 53.

posed that repeated observation of struck-match-plus-ensuing-flame causes in the brain an "engram" (something like a memory trace, perhaps): when the match is now seen by itself, the engram is activated and *causes* a "modified cerebral event" that is "similar" to the original response to struck-match-plus-flame. Ogden and Richards call this modified response to the sight of a struck match the "reference" (the same as what I have been calling the "interpretation").

This view differs from the simple identification of interpretation with response mainly in postulating an "engram," a hypothetical structure in the brain. It is vulnerable to the objections I have already urged—and, indeed, to many others.[16]

A serious weakness of attempts of this sort may be put in common sense language as follows: We may understand a sign (or a sentence) without being moved to any action. Even a "lower organism," such as a dog or a rat, will not react to a simple stimulus (sight of food, sight of a predator) *invariably:* the dog needs to be hungry, the deer may be paralyzed with fear. When we think of "higher organisms" such as human beings, with their greater flexibility of response, the point is still more obvious. I may perfectly understand and believe the remark "It has begun to rain," but whether I look for a raincoat, shrug my shoulders, swear, or do nothing at all, will depend upon my state of mind, my intentions, and so on.

In order to cope with this difficulty, writers who think that some form of a causal theory of meaning must be right are apt at this point to invoke the notion of a *disposition to respond*. Thus Charles Stevenson says that the meaning of a sign is "a dispositional property of the sign, where the response, varying with attendant varying circumstances, consists of psychological processes in a hearer, and where the stimulus is his hearing the sign."[17] Roughly speaking, the sign is supposed to induce a *tendency to respond* in some definite way, which may or may not be activated, according to the condition of the sign-receiver: if somebody says in a warning tone, "Hot!" when I am about to touch something, I shall have a tendency (or be disposed) to draw back—whether I in fact do so or not. But such a tendency or "dispositional property" seems less "tangible" than might have been hoped. Since there seems no independent way of observ-

[16]For a detailed criticism of Ogden and Richards' theory the reader may consult Chapter 8 of M. Black, *Language and Philosophy*.
[17]Stevenson, *Ethics and Language*, p. 54.

ing its presence, it begins to look suspiciously like something that is postulated, without evidence, as necessarily being present. Introspection will reveal no such "disposition"—nor would the report of introspection be given any weight by the kind of theory here under discussion. In order to be sure that there is any such alleged "disposition to respond," we must first establish in some other way that the supposed "sign" really does have a meaning for the organism concerned. Thus among its other weaknesses, this type of theory is useless as an aid to the practical *art* of interpretation. If I want to know whether a given verbal or non-verbal event "means anything"—and, if so, what its meaning is—reference to some hypothetical disposition in the mind or brain of myself or other sign-users will be quite useless. "Dispositions," even if they exist, are at least as "inaccessible" to observation as the "ideas" of the despised "mentalists."

However unsatisfactory these first attempts at a causal theory of meaning may be, psychologists will continue to pursue a legitimate interest in unraveling the causal mechanisms by which "signs" come to have meaning. But even if such attempts should ultimately be successful, there seems to be a serious difficulty of principle in using this type of approach to explain how *words* are understood.

I have already pointed out that "one-word sentences" such as *Fire!*, *Hot!*, *Delightful!*, *Engaged!*, evoke no discoverable response or disposition to respond on the part of those who understand them. (What action is *Engaged!* supposed to induce in me? Is it assumed that I believe what I hear? And even so, what is it that I am supposed to do—or to be inclined to do?) But the point is still more obvious when we come to consider words, whether occurring in isolation or as parts of sentences. The word *green,* for instance, cannot plausibly be said to induce any congruent response. It is not even the case that it ought to lead the hearer to expect something green, since it may well occur in a negative sentence which *denies* that something is green. Nor can it be said, plausibly, to act as a substitute for the sight of something green, since such an experience induces in human beings nothing as regular as salivation in the presence of food.

It seems, in short, as if any psychological theory of sign-using behaviour is bound to be hopelessly inadequate—without the kind of supplementation that cannot begin to be imagined at present—as an account of the vastly more complex pattern of behaviour involved in understanding speech. The very use of "behaviour" in this connection is misleading, if it is intended to recall the response to stimuli by experimental animals in laboratories. In a certain sense, even such animals are not free to *behave*. They surely have little freedom to *act* in any meaningful fashion.

A PITFALL FOR THEORIES OF MEANING

In formulating theories of meaning—that is to say, in trying to get clearer about "the nature of meaning"—there is great danger of committing a subtle but important logical fallacy.

Consider the apparently straightforward sentence, *The meaning of "jaune" is yellow*. Here the meaning of the French word, *jaune*, seems to have been *identified* (a word that deserves to be emphasized) as a certain colour. It is also correct to say that *Yellow is a colour*. Hence we seem entitled to conclude that *The meaning of "jaune" is a (certain) colour*, and also, by parity of reasoning, that *The meaning of "yellow" is a (certain) colour*. Now colours are familiar "things," which we are able to recognize and to distinguish from one another. So it seems as if in this simple case we can, after all, easily pick out or identify *what* the meaning of a given word is: the meaning is just as "tangible" as what we see when looking at a dandelion. If this line of thought seems correct, we shall want to say that the sentence *"Jaune" means yellow* has pretty much the same form as *Mary loves Mopser*: the subject *stands for* a certain word in the French language (as "Mary" stands for a certain person) and the grammatical object ("yellow") *stands for* a certain colour (as "Mopser" stands for a certain cat). There will, of course, remain a problem about the character of the relation between the word and the colour, expressed by the verb, "means"—and perhaps the most natural thing to say about this is that it is the relation established when a convention arises for using the one as a *name* for the other.

"Jaune" means yellow, yellow is a colour: therefore, "jaune" means a colour. The form of this plausible argument is as follows: *X has the relation Y to Z; Z is a W; therefore, X has the relation Y to a W*. It is, however, easily seen that an argument of this form can sometimes lead to a wrong conclusion. Consider, for instance, the following argument: *I am looking for the man who stole my purse; the man who stole my purse is a Mormon; therefore, I am looking for a Mormon*. Here, the premises may be true, while the conclusion is false. I might not know that the thief was a Mor-

mon, so I could not be *looking for* a Mormon—though I might be looking for a thief who *happened to be* a Mormon. Or, to take a somewhat different example, consider the absurdity of arguing as follows: *Robinson despises the average man; the average man is a husband; therefore, Robinson despises a husband.*

The moral of such examples is plain enough: a word, or a description of the form "the such-and-such," may *seem* to designate something[18]—may seem to stand for some "thing," while closer examination will show this to be a mistake. Neither "the man I am looking for," nor "the average man" *designates* anything.

It will be useful to consider one more example. In the sentence, *The price of this book is five dollars,* it is tempting to treat the subject-expression as "designating something." For, after all, it is possible to say "I have the price of this book in my pocket," or even, with a certain oddity, "I have lost the price of this book." In short, to speak roughly, the expression "The price of this book" has a tendency to be transferable as a unit into other contexts. This comes to treating the original sentence as an identity: The price of this book *is the very same thing* as five dollars (*i.e.,* a certain sum of money). But this temptation, to take the sentence about the price of the book as an identity, is removed (or ought to be!) as soon as we realize that the sentence can be paraphrased in some such way as: *If anybody wants to buy this book he will have to pay five dollars.* We now see that the original expression *The price of this book is* . . . means the same as *If anybody wants to buy this book he will have to pay* . . . . It is obviously absurd to regard *this* as "designating something."

Let us now apply this analysis to sentences about meaning. In *"Jaune" means yellow,* shall we regard *"yellow"* as "designating something"? If we do, we shall have to say that we can see some meanings with our eyes, that a house can be painted a certain meaning, and so on. And in other cases we shall have to say that meanings can be eaten, handed from one person to another—and such like absurdities. But there is no need to accept these paradoxes—any more than it is

---

[18]Here, I am using "designate" as shorthand for the following: In a sentence of the form *X has the relation Y to Z,* the expression in the place occupied by *"Z" designates something* when and only when it follows from *Z is a W* that *X has the relation Y to W.* (Philosophers could easily pick holes in this explanation, but it will serve for the present.)

necessary to think it possible to shake the average man by the hand. We may hope to show (as I shall try to do in the next section) that there are ways of paraphrasing sentences of the form *The meaning of X is Y* which will remove the illusion that they have the form of identities. We shall find that it is quite feasible to assign comprehensible meanings to the whole of such sentences without supposing that the expressions occurring in the subject-positions "designate something." In short, we shall find that there are intelligible *uses* for expressions of the form "The meaning of X" which do not commit us to treating them as designative.

The point I have been trying to make in the preceding paragraphs might be put more crudely and inexactly as follows: There is a temptation, perhaps partly due to certain peculiarities of Indo-European languages,[19] to suppose that nouns and noun-like expressions (*e.g.*, expressions of the form "the such-and-such") must stand for *things*. This is what writers sometimes have in mind when they deplore the "reification" or "hypostatization" of entities. A special case of this is the search, on the part of a number of the theorists previously considered, for "tangible" things to be recognized as the meanings of words or other verbal units. For "mentalists" and "anti-mentalists" alike seem to agree that the right answer to the question "What are meanings?" ought to be of the form "the meaning of *W* is such-and-such," where the subject-expression occurs designatively. But this is a pitfall that can be avoided. The lack of success of the theories previously criticized may indeed be due to their failure to recognize this.

THE MANY MEANINGS OF "MEANING"

An obvious, but still a most striking, thing about language is the extent to which a single word comes to be used in a variety of related but different ways. Thought constantly outruns facile expression: when we need to say something for which there is no ready-made expression, we stretch old words to fit new cases, relying upon the imagination and "uptake" of our hearer to get our drift. Things related in fairly obvious ways whether as part to whole, by similarity

[19] I mean the ease with which "nominalizations" can be formed. Almost any part of speech can be converted into a related noun-clause, whose presence then encourages what is perhaps a deeper tendency to think that some "thing" must answer to the expression. If we pass from the word "no" to the noun "negation," it becomes easier to think "that there must be such a thing as" negation in the universe.

of function, or in virtue of some temporal relation come to have the same name: factory-workers are "hands," a cover for an automobile engine is a "hood" or "bonnet"; a "board" means "table used for meals" and changes to "food served at table" (cf. "board and lodging"). In less obvious cases, a resourceful speaker falls back on simile and metaphor: a cardinal bird is like the church dignitary in having a red "robe"; we talk of "spiking" a drink. And so on.[20] So many of these individual shifts and variations come to be accepted as useful extensions of the standard vocabulary that an unabridged dictionary will need several pages to list the various but related senses of a versatile word.

A little reflection will show "meaning" and its cognates to be one of the most overworked words in the language: it is a very Casanova of a word in its appetite for association. Any "theory of meaning," any attempt to do reasonable justice to the ways in which "meaning" is actually used, will need to take account of this extraordinary shiftiness of the word. And any monolithic, "single-factor," analysis of meaning is so implausible as to deserve little respect.

Consider, for instance, some typical occurrences of the verb "to mean."

(a) I mean to read this book.
(b) You see that peculiar formation of clouds? That means that a cold front is approaching.
(c) What did he mean by wrinkling his nose?
(d) ". . . he, I mean the Bishop, did require a respite" (Henry VIII, Act II, scene 4, line 176).
(e) "All the clerks, I mean the learned ones, in Christian kingdoms" (Henry VIII, Act II, scene 2, line 93).
(f) "Equanimity" means evenness of mind or temper.
(g) $m = 2n$. That means that m is even.

A sensitive reader will probably have the immediate impression that shifts of sense are occurring from one of these examples to the next. That this is indeed the case can be readily shown by the techniques of "logical grammar."[21]

For instance, it is obvious that "intend" is an approximate synonym of "mean" in (a). But the corresponding insertion in (b), (f), or (g) produces nonsense. The cases of (c), (d),

[20]A reasonably adequate account of the nature of such meaning-changes and their causes is bound to be very complicated. See, for instance, the numerous examples and intricate classifications in Gustaf Stern, *Meaning and Change of Meaning* (Indiana University Press, Bloomington, Ind., 1931).

[21]See discussion above, Chapter 4, pp. 105–112.

and (e) are not *clearly* discriminated by this test, however. Similarly, "signifies" may plausibly replace "means" in (b), but this will not do at all for contexts (d) and (e). In (g), we may substitute "shows" for "means"; but the corresponding substitution produces nonsense in all cases except (b). In (d) and (e), "mean" has the force of "refer to," but not in any other case with the possible exceptional of (f).[22]

These preliminary results would be confirmed if we tried to paraphrase the whole sentences in which the verb "to mean" occurs in our examples. Thus a crude rewriting of (a) might yield "I shall read this book, unless I change my mind," while obviously nothing parallel will emerge from the other examples. In the case of (b), we might rephrase the second remark as "hence we can *infer* that a cold front is approaching." This tactic will also serve for (g), but not at all for the other cases, with the possible exception of (c).

Another way of exploring the differences of sense would be to notice the variety of things that are, in the above examples, said to "mean": the subjects may be, it seems, persons [as in (a), (c), (d), and (e)], or a fact [in (b)], a word [in (f)], or even an algebraic equation (g). However, this is clearly not the place to pursue further what must necessarily be a somewhat intricate and even tiresomely detailed examination of the sense-differences exemplified.

A natural way to control some of the most regular ways in which "meaning" and its associates shift in meaning is to attach convenient labels to some of the most common senses of the word.

For instance, we can usefully distinguish one common use of "meaning" by preferring to talk about *referring*. In this sense, a remark of the form, "I mean so-and-so" is an answer to the question, "To whom are you referring?" or, more simply, "Whom are you talking about?" This sense is exemplified by the illustration (d) above, possibly also by (e), but not by the other examples. That there is a clear difference between referring to somebody and meaning something (in another sense of "meaning") can easily be seen by the following argument. The expression "My next-door neighbour" means the same (in a certain sense of "means") whenever it is used; yet, just as plainly, it will refer to different persons on the different occasions of its use: *who* my next-door neighbour is will depend upon a question of fact, and not merely upon the meaning of the expression used in

---

[22]The qualified outcomes of this synonymity test are a sign of the complexity of the relations between the various senses exemplified.

order to single him out. One important weakness of some of the theories of meaning previously considered is their failure to make this elementary distinction.[23]

Quite another way of distinguishing senses of the verb "to mean" relies upon differences in the type of subject that can be attached to the verb. As I have already remarked, a sign can often be regarded as a certain fact (or, if the reader prefers, a certain event): the fact that the temperature has suddenly fallen is a sign that (or signifies, indicates, means) that there will be snow; the fact that the patient has a red rash is a sign (or: a symptom) that he has measles; and so on. These might be called cases of *factual meaning*. But situations in which we wonder what a speaker or somebody else means do not fit this pattern: if somebody has said "I am sleepy," the fact that he said what he said may (factually) mean that he is sleepy, or is trying to persuade us that he is, and so on. But the question, "What did *he* mean by 'sleepy'?" will obviously not be answered by adducing any of these facts. Here we might perhaps speak of *personal meaning*. Finally, there is the case which arises when we wish to know *the* meaning of a word or expression. The question, "What does 'irenic' mean?" is not an inquiry about the (personal) meaning attached to the word by any identifiable user of it—even though the best way of finding out might be to ask an expert what he would mean if he used the word. Here we might speak of *standard meaning*. The interplay between factual, personal, and standard meaning in any given utterance offers tantalizing vistas for further research.

The multi-faceted concept we call "meaning" can also be viewed from quite another perspective. In an earlier chapter, I have urged the importance of distinguishing different dimensions or functions of language.[24] When we have a well-designed and generally acceptable analysis of these functions, we shall have a firm basis for distinguishing between, say, "cognitive," "expressive," and "dynamic" meaning. Meanwhile, we neglect even crude distinctions of this sort at our peril. To ignore, for instance, the "emotive meaning" of a

[23]The importance of distinguishing between "reference" (*Bedeutung*) and "sense" (*Sinn*) was made abundantly clear by the work of the great German philosopher and logician, Gottlob Frege, whose theories may be conveniently consulted in *Translations from the Philosophical Writings of Gottlob Frege*, edited by Peter Geach and Max Black. This distinction is close to the better-known contrast drawn by John Stuart Mill between "denotation" and "connotation." In spite of intensive discussion, the topic of reference remains somewhat obscure.

[24]See above, Chapter 5, pp. 117–118.

word (whatever we really mean by that expression) may well be in certain cases to overlook the real point of using it.

Again, we may often have occasion to distinguish between *explicit* and *implicit* meaning—between what lies near to the surface and what needs to be teased out by reference to the speaker's unspoken intentions, the grammatical and logical rules of the language, and so on.[25]

This preliminary exploration of the "many meanings of 'meaning'" might be continued—but perhaps the reader has already had more than enough. The crude distinctions sketched in the preceding paragraphs allow for something like $2 \times 3 \times 3 \times 2$ or 36 different senses of "meaning"—and this may prove to be only a beginning.[26] Let the reader not dismiss this as mere pedantry and scholarly folly. The more he penetrates into the thickets of problems that obstruct problems of meaning, the more he is likely to agree that distinctions in the language in which we speak about meaning are essential. The neglect of such essential distinctions is one of the main causes of obscurity in this important but confused subject.

EXPLANATIONS OF MEANING

What happens if we abandon, once and for all, the idea that the meaning of a word must be some "tangible," independently observable, entity? Does this mean that we must treat meaning as a mystery beyond the scope of rational discussion? Not at all. There remains the resource of investigating *how words are used:* in becoming clear about this, we may, perhaps, hope to become sufficiently clear about their "meaning." This program is all the more plausible because it clearly yields results in the case of non-verbal instruments. An engineering tool presumably has no meaning; but a layman may first be puzzled about its use and then, if all goes well, may learn *how* it is used. Perhaps, then, we might hope for explanations of the uses of words that resemble explanations

[25]See the earlier discussion of implication at Chapter 5 in this article.
[26]It would be natural to ask what binds these various senses together. For it is at least plausible that the use of the same word in all the different cases is not a case of willful equivocation. One clue to the answer to this difficult question might be found in the connections between meaning and both *inference* and *understanding.* To know the meaning of something (in whatever sense) is often to be able to infer what otherwise would remain unknown—or again to understand what was previously mysterious or perplexing. Meaning might be said to provide a link between the seen and the unseen (or, more often, the heard and the unheard). But an epigram is, of course, no substitute for the hard work of analysis.

of the uses of non-verbal tools or instruments. Words and sentences are instruments for certain human purposes (communication, expression, and so on); it seems reasonable to expect, therefore, that a detailed statement of the uses of these verbal instruments may contribute something important to the theory of meaning.

Words are primarily used in the context of a full sentence. Our program of considering the typical uses of the verb "to mean" will therefore call for the examination of the uses of simple sentences in which that verb occurs.

I shall confine myself to one or two simple examples. While I am playing in my first game of Australian football, a member of my team yells "Now!" When I ask, "What does he mean by 'Now!'?" the answer is "He means 'Kick!' " I shall call a remark of the form "So-and-so means such-and-such (by a certain utterance or gesture)" a *meaning formula*. (In terms of our discussion in the previous section, we are dealing in such cases with explicit [imperative] *personal* meaning.)

Again, while driving in England, I notice a motorist ahead of me put his hand outside his car to make a circling motion. To the question, "What does he mean by that?" my English companion replies "He means 'Pass,' " or "He means 'All right to pass,' " or "He means: clear road ahead" (the variability in response is typical: it would be futile to argue whether the signal *really* meant one thing or the other).

How are such meaning formulas to be analyzed? I have already given reasons in the previous sections against thinking that the grammatical object of a meaning formula (the expression replacing the "such-and-such" in the formula of the preceding paragraph) *stands for* anything.[27] (Cf. such a sentence as "By *entweder* he means 'whether,' " in which a conjunction, "whether," seems typically to function as a noun. This is already a good indication that the grammatical object is not functioning as a straightforwardly designating expression.) I suggest, instead, that in the meaning formula, "He meant 'Kick!' " the word "Kick" is occurring in a special way in order to exemplify and to illustrate the use of the expression being explained. It is as if the explainer said: " 'Kick!'— you know how *that* would be used in this situation (what would be demanded of you); well, 'Now!' was being used in just *that* way." Similarly, one might explain the use of some

---

[27]The reader wishing to pursue this point further will find detailed arguments in Chapter 2, "Explanations of Meaning," M. Black, *Models and Metaphors*.

unfamiliar engineering tool by pretending to use some more familiar instrument, and then adding: "That's the way the other thing is used." In such cases, the instrument used in the explanation is not being used in its primary way—to drive nails home, or whatever—but rather in order to *show its own use*. Similarly, the man who explains to me "That means 'Kick'" is not using the imperative "Kick!" in order to get me to kick the ball, but rather in order to bring to my attention the way that the imperative expression is primarily used. (We have then an important example of the "self-reflexive" capacity of language, to which reference has already been made.[28])

When a word or other symbol qualitatively resembles what it signifies, as in the case of a roadside sign in which a painted cross stands for the intersection of two roads, it has become customary to follow Peirce in speaking of an *iconic* symbol. We might therefore say that in the meaning formula "He meant 'Kick!'" the word "kick" is occurring iconically. We are, as it were, miming the intended use of the word—just as we might mime the use by pretending actually to kick the ball.

Obviously a great deal more would have to be done before this kind of approach could be regarded as satisfactory. Without much more discussion and analysis, the term "use," which has occurred so often in this section, might itself prove just as obfuscating as "meaning," and for somewhat similar reasons. But perhaps enough has been said to suggest the possibility of new ways out of some of the impasses of earlier theories of meaning. If a label is needed for the approach to meaning here recommended, the adjective "functional" might serve. For the main underlying idea is that the meanings of words (when suitable distinctions have been made, in the manner explained in the last section) turn out to be matters of coordinated and interrelated functions of words. Meaning, one might perhaps say, will prove to be more like a handclasp than like a crystal.

ENVOY

This labyrinth of language, in which we have wandered together, has no Ariadne's thread. One moral I have tried to suggest throughout is that any simple theory about language must be over-simple. But this is no reason for lachrymose

[28]See Chapter 4, pp. 102–103.

complaints about the sophistry of language: the fault is not in our words but in ourselves. If our ancestors had the wit to make this incomparable instrument, it should be within our power to master its proper uses. I hope to have provided some glimpses of the profusion and variety of resources already available for this important task.

BIBLIOGRAPHY

AUDEN, W. H. "Squares and Oblongs," in *Poets at Work*. New York: Harcourt, Brace, 1948.

AUSTIN, J. L. *How to Do Things with Words*. Oxford: The Clarendon Press; Cambridge, Mass.: Harvard University Press, 1962.

———. *Philosophical Papers*. Oxford and New York: The Clarendon Press, 1961.

———. *The Province of Jurisprudence Determined*. Ed. H. L. A. Hart. London: George Weidenfeld & Nicolson, 1954.

AYER, A. J. *Language, Truth and Logic*. New York: Dover Publications, 1946.

———. *Logical Positivism*. Glencoe, Ill.: The Free Press, 1959.

BEARDSLEY, MONROE C. *Aesthetics*. New York: Harcourt, Brace & Co., 1958.

BENJAMIN, A. CORNELIUS. *Operationism*. Springfield, Ill.: Charles C. Thomas, 1955.

BENTHAM, JEREMY. *Handbook of Political Fallacies*. Ed. H. S. Larrabee. Baltimore: Johns Hopkins Press, 1952.

BLACK, MAX. *Language and Philosophy*. Ithaca, N.Y.: Cornell University Press, 1949.

———. *Models and Metaphors*. Ithaca, N.Y.: Cornell University Press, 1962.

———. *Problems of Analysis*. Ithaca, N.Y.: Cornell University Press, 1954.

———. "Reasoning with Loose Concepts," *Dialogue*, Vol. 1 (1963–64), pp. 1–12.

BLOCH, BERNARD, and TRAGER, GEORGE L. *Outline of Linguistic Analysis*. Baltimore: Waverly Press, 1942.

BLOCH, MARC. *The Historian's Craft*. New York: Alfred A. Knopf, 1953.

BLOOMFIELD, LEONARD. *Language*. New York: Holt, Rinehart and Winston, 1933.

BLOOMFIELD, MORTON W., and NEWMARK, LEONARD. *A Linguistic Introduction to the History of English*. New York: Alfred A. Knopf, 1963.

BOCHENSKI, I. M. *A History of Formal Logic*. Notre Dame, Ind.: University of Notre Dame Press, 1961.

BRIDGMAN, PERCY W. *The Logic of Modern Physics*. New York: The Macmillan Co., 1927.

BROWN, ROGER W., and LENNEBERG, ERIC H. "A Study of Language and Cognition," in Sol Saporta (ed.). *Psycholinguistics*. New York: Holt, Rinehart and Winston, 1961.

BÜHLER, KARL. *Sprachtheorie*. Jena: Gustav Fischer, 1934.

BURGESS, ANTHONY. *Language Made Plain*. London: English Universities Press, 1964; New York: Crowell Collier, 1965.

CARROLL, JOHN B. *The Study of Language*. Cambridge, Mass.: Harvard University Press, 1953.

CHOMSKY, NOAM. *Cartesian Linguistics*. New York: Harper & Row, 1966.

———. "Current Issues in Linguistic Theory," in J. A. Fodor and J. J. Katz (eds.). *The Structure of Language*. Englewood Cliffs, N.J.: Prentice-Hall, 1964.

CRYSTAL, DAVID. *Linguistics, Language and Religion*. London: Burns & Oates, 1965; New York: Hawthorn Books.

CURTIS, CHARLES P. *It's Your Law*. Cambridge, Mass.: Harvard University Press, 1954.

DE GROOT, ADRIANUS D. *Thought and Choice in Chess*. The Hague: Mouton, 1965; New York: Basic Books, 1966.

DE SAUSSURE, FERDINAND. *Course in General Linguistics*. New York: Philosophical Library, 1959.

EMPSON, WILLIAM. *Seven Types of Ambiguity*. Rev. ed. London: Chatto & Windus, 1947; New York: New Directions.

ENTWISTLE, WILLIAM J. *Aspects of Language*. London: Faber & Faber, 1953.

FREGE, GOTTLOB. *Translations from the Philosophical Writings of Gottlob Frege*. Ed. Peter Geach and Max Black. Oxford: Basil Blackwell & Mott, 1952.

FRIES, CHARLES C. "The Bloomfield School," in Christine Mohrmann (ed.). *Trends in European and American Linguistics.* Utrecht: Spectrum, 1961.

GALLIE, W. B. *Peirce and Pragmatism.* Rev. ed. London: Pelican Books, 1952; New York: Dover.

————. *Philosophy and the Historical Understanding.* London: Chatto & Windus; New York: Schocken Books, 1964.

GEACH, P. T. *Reference and Generality.* Ithaca, N.Y.: Cornell University Press, 1962.

GLEASON, H. A. *An Introduction to Descriptive Linguistics.* New York: Holt, Rinehart and Winston, 1955.

GREENBERG, JOSEPH H. (ed.). *Universals of Language.* Cambridge, Mass.: The MIT Press, 1963.

HALL, R. A. *Linguistics and Your Language.* Garden City, N.Y.: Doubleday & Co., 1960.

HARE, R. M. *The Language of Morals.* Oxford and New York: The Clarendon Press, 1952.

HAYAKAWA, S. I. (ed.). *Language, Meaning and Maturity.* New York: Harper & Row, 1954.

HEMPEL, C. G. *Aspects of Scientific Explanation.* New York: The Free Press, 1965.

HEVESI, J. L. (ed.). *Essays on Language and Literature.* London: Allan Wingate; Port Washington, N.Y.: Kennikat Press, 1947.

HOCKETT, CHARLES F. *A Course in Modern Linguistics.* New York: The Macmillan Co., 1958.

HOIJER, HARRY. *Language in Culture.* Chicago: University of Chicago Press, 1954.

JAMES, WILLIAM. *Pragmatism.* New York: Longmans, Green & Co., 1943.

JESPERSEN, OTTO. *Language.* London: George Allen & Unwin, 1922; New York: W. W. Norton & Co.

————. *The Philosophy of Grammar.* London: George Allen & Unwin, 1924; New York: W. W. Norton & Co.

KLUCKHOHN, CLYDE, and LEIGHTON, DOROTHEA. *The Navaho.* Cambridge, Mass.: Harvard University Press, 1946.

KRAFT, VIKTOR. *The Vienna Circle.* New York: Philosophical Library, 1953.

LANGER, SUZANNE K. *Philosophy in a New Key.* Cambridge, Mass.: Harvard University Press, 1942.

LEE, DOROTHY. "Linguistic Reflection of Wintu Thought," in *Freedom and Culture*. Englewood Cliffs, N.J.: Prentice-Hall, 1959.

LEWIS, C. I. *An Analysis of Knowledge and Valuation*. La Salle, Ill.: Open Court, 1946.

LUCAS, F. L. *Style*. London: Cassell & Co., 1955; New York: Collier.

MALINOWSKI, BRONISLAW. *Coral Gardens and Their Magic*. London: George Allen & Unwin, 1935; Bloomington, Ind.: Indiana University Press, 1965.

———. *Freedom and Civilization*. London: George Allen & Unwin, 1947; Bloomington, Ind.: Indiana University Press, 1960.

———. "The Problem of Meaning in Primitive Languages," in C. K. Ogden and I. A. Richards. *The Meaning of Meaning*. 3rd ed. London: Routledge & Kegan Paul, 1930; New York: Harcourt, Brace & World.

MEGGED, AHARON. "Reflections on Two Languages," *Midstream*, Vol. 12, No. 8 (October, 1966).

MORRIS, CHARLES. *Signs, Language, and Behavior*. Englewood Cliffs, N.J.: Prentice-Hall, 1946.

MYERSON, ABRAHAM. *Speaking of Man*. New York: Alfred A. Knopf, 1950.

OGDEN, C. K. (ed.). *Bentham's Theory of Fictions*. London: Routledge & Kegan Paul, 1932; New York: Humanities Press.

———, and RICHARDS, I. A. *The Meaning of Meaning*. 3rd ed. London: Routledge & Kegan Paul, 1930; New York: Harcourt, Brace & World.

PASSMORE, JOHN A. *A Hundred Years of Philosophy*. London: Duckworth & Co., 1957; New York: Basic Books, 1966.

PEIRCE, CHARLES SANDERS. *Collected Papers*. 8 vols. Cambridge, Mass.: Harvard University Press, 1931–58.

———. "How to Make Our Ideas Clear," *Popular Science Monthly*, Vol. 12 (1878).

PERRY, RALPH BARTON. *The Thought and Character of William James*. Boston: Little, Brown & Co., 1935.

POPPER, KARL R. *Conjectures and Refutations*. London: Routledge & Kegan Paul; New York: Basic Books, 1963.

QUINE, W. V. *From a Logical Point of View*. Cambridge, Mass.: Harvard University Press, 1953.

RICHARDS, I. A. *How to Read a Page*. New York: W. W. Norton & Co., 1942.

————. *Practical Criticism*. London: Routledge & Kegan Paul, 1929; New York: Harcourt, Brace & World.

————. *Principles of Literary Criticism*. London: Routledge & Kegan Paul, 1925; New York: Harcourt, Brace & World.

ROBINS, R. H. *Ancient and Mediaeval Grammatical Theory in Europe*. London: Bell & Sons, 1951.

ROBINSON, RICHARD. *Definition*. Oxford and New York: The Clarendon Press, 1950.

ROSS, A. S. C. *Etymology*. London: André Deutsch; New York: Oxford University Press, 1958.

RUSSELL, BERTRAND. *The Principles of Mathematics*. Cambridge: Cambridge University Press, 1903; New York: W. W. Norton & Co., 1938.

RYLE, GILBERT (ed.). *The Revolution in Philosophy*. London: Macmillan & Co., 1956.

————. "The Verification Principle," *Revue internationale de Philosophie*, Vol. 5 (1951).

SANDMANN, MANFRED. *Subject and Predicate*. Edinburgh: Edinburgh University Press, 1954.

SAPIR, EDWARD. *Language*. New York: Harvest Books, 1955.

SCHLICK, MORITZ. *Problems of Ethics*. Englewood Cliffs, N.J.: Prentice-Hall, 1939.

SHANNON, CLAUDE E., and WEAVER, W. *The Mathematical Theory of Communication*. Urbana, Ill.: University of Illinois Press, 1949.

SIMON, W. M. *European Positivism in the Nineteenth Century*, Ithaca, N.Y.: Cornell University Press, 1963.

SMITH, LOGAN PEARSALL. *All Trivia*. New York: Harcourt, Brace & Co., 1934.

STERN, GUSTAF. *Meaning and Change of Meaning*. Bloomington, Ind.: Indiana University Press, 1931.

STEVENSON, CHARLES. *Ethics and Language*. New Haven, Conn.: Yale University Press, 1944.

STOKOE, WILLIAM C. *et al. A Dictionary of American Sign Language on Linguistic Principles*. Washington, D.C.: Gallaudet College Press, 1965.

STROLL, AVRUM. *The Emotive Theory of Ethics*. Berkeley, Calif.: University of California Press, 1954.

TWADELL, W. FREEMAN. "On Defining the Phoneme," in Martin Joos (ed.). *Readings in Linguistics.* 3rd ed. New York: American Council of Learned Societies, 1963.

ULLMANN, STEPHEN. *Semantics.* Oxford: Basil Blackwell & Mott; New York: Barnes & Noble, 1962.

URMSON, J. O. *Philosophical Analysis.* Oxford and New York: The Clarendon Press, 1956.

VENDRYES, J. *Language.* London: Routledge & Kegan Paul; New York: Barnes & Noble, 1925.

VOSSLER, KARL. *The Spirit of Language in Civilization.* London: Routledge & Kegan Paul, 1932.

WELLS, H. G. *First and Last Things.* London: Constable & Co., 1908.

WHITEHEAD, ALFRED NORTH. *Adventure of Ideas.* New York: The Macmillan Co., 1933.

WHORF, BENJAMIN LEE. *Language, Thought and Reality: Selected Writings of Benjamin Lee Whorf.* Ed. John B. Carroll. Cambridge, Mass.: The MIT Press, 1956.

WIENER, P. P., and YOUNG, F. H. (eds.). *Studies in the Philosophy of Charles Sanders Peirce.* Ed. for the Peirce Society. Cambridge, Mass.: Harvard University Press, 1952.

WILLIAMS, GLANVILLE. "Language and the Law," *Law Quarterly Review,* Vol. 61 (1945).

WILSON, LOGAN. "The Functional Bases of Appraising Academic Performance," *Bulletin* (American Association of University Professors), Vol. 27 (October, 1941).

WIMSATT, W. K., JR. *The Verbal Icon.* New York: Noonday Press, 1958.

WITTGENSTEIN, LUDWIG. *Philosophical Investigations.* Oxford: Basil Blackwell & Mott, 1953.

————. *Tractatus Logico-Philosophicus.* London: Routledge & Kegan Paul, 1922; New York: Humanities Press.

WOOTTON, BARBARA. *Testament for Social Science.* London: George Allen & Unwin, 1950.

INDEX